EU FOOD LAW AND POLICY

EU Food Law and Policy

by

DEBRA HOLLAND

and

HELEN POPE

KLUWER LAW INTERNATIONAL
THE HAGUE / LONDON / NEW YORK

Library of Congress Cataloging-in-Publication Data

Holland, Debra.
EU food law/by Debra Holland & Helen Pope.
p.cm.
Includes index.
ISBN 90-411-2124-2 (HB: alk. paper)
1. Food law and legislation—European Union countries. I. Pope, Helen. II. Title.

KJE6778.H65 2003
344.404′232–dc22 2003060647

ISBN 90-411-2124-2

Published by:
Kluwer Law International,
P.O. Box 85889, 2508 CN The Hague, The Netherlands
sales@kluwerlaw.com
http://www.kluwerlaw.com

Sold and distributed in North, Central and South America by:
Aspen Publishers, Inc.
7201 McKinney Circle, Frederick, MD 21704, USA

Sold and distributed in all other countries by:
Turpin Distribution Services Limited
Blackhorse Road, Letchworth, Herts.,
SG6 1HN, United Kingdom

Printed on acid-free paper

Printed in the Netherlands

Table of Contents

Preface

In recent years, the whole question of food safety has become ever more important in the minds of consumers. Food scares such as the BSE crises, the outbreak of foot and mouth disease, *E. coli* poisoning and dioxin contamination have dealt a huge blow to consumer confidence in the food industry. The advent of biotechnological processes has heightened consumer concerns in relation to the food products they purchase.

On 12 January 2000 the European Commission issued its White Paper on Food Safety. In this the Commission has underlined its commitment to restoring consumer confidence by putting into effect the most up-to-date and effective food safety regime in the world.

The White Paper sets out the overall aim of the Commission as putting into place the necessary legislation and structures that will guarantee the highest possible level of protection for consumers in the consumption of food. Indeed the White Paper outlines a comprehensive range of actions (over 80 measures) that are aimed at achieving a comprehensive and integrated approach at all levels of the food chain; 'from farm to fork'.

On 21 February 2002 the cornerstone Regulation, which sets out the general principles of food law and establishes the European Food Safety Authority, came into force. This Regulation, foreseen in the White Paper, for the first time establishes food law as an autonomous branch of EU law and will underpin all future food and feed legislation. Moreover the Regulation also established an independent European Food Safety Authority with particular responsibilities for both risk assessment and communication of food safety issues.

A significant phase of the reform of EU food law as foreseen in the White Paper has been completed and provides us with a timely moment to take stock of the reforms so far and the emergence of this dynamic and emotive branch of law.

It seemed to us that there was a need for a book devoted solely to EU food policy and legislation. It is with this in mind that we have written this book with the aim of providing a timely and practical overview of the history and development of this fast-moving area of EU policy and legislation. This work is for food business operators, legal practitioners, policy makers and those who are generally interested in this sector.

We would like to thank members of the Lovells' regulatory department, in particular Andrew Skipper, without whose support this book would not have been possible.

To the best of our information, belief and understanding the law is stated as it was on 1 November 2003.

Debra Holland **Helen Pope**

Biographical Notes

Debra Holland was called as an English Barrister in 1996 and joined the Brussels office of Lovells in 2001. She specialises in EU food law and policy and has a wide range of experience of general EU matters for a variety of multinational companies. On a daily basis Debra deals with regulatory issues advising a number of companies active in the agra-food, pharmaceutical and consumer good sectors in respect of processing, compositional and labelling obligations under EU law. Other issues with which she deals include claims, promotions and placing products on the market. In addition she advises companies on product liability and product safety issues. Debra has helped clients to address queries and potential challenges received from national authorities, the EU institutions and has represented companies before the European Courts. Debra is also a door tenant at the Chambers of Roger Henderson QC in London.

Helen Pope is a solicitor with the international law firm Lovells, based in their Brussels office. She advises and represents clients on matters of EU law and policy specialising in food and consumer issues. Helen has written numerous articles on the subject.

Table of Treaties

Table of European Community Secondary Legislation

Directives

2001/13/EC: OJ L 075, 15/03/2001 P. 26–28 … 111
2001/15/EC: OJ L 052, 22/02/2001 P. 19–25 … 83–84
2001/15/EC: OJ L 055, 24/02/2001 P. 59–61
2001/18/EC: OJ L 106, 17/04/2001 P. 01–39 … 113, 117
2001/22/EC: OJ L 077, 16/03/2001 P. 14–21 … 145
2001/30/EC: OJ L 146, 31/05/2001 P. 01–23 … 56
2001/35/EC: OJ L 136, 18/05/2001 P. 42–48 … 153
2001/39/EC: OJ L 148, 01/06/2001 P. 70–77 … 153
2001/46/EC: OJ L 234, 01/09/2001 P. 55–59 … 148
2001/48/EC: O J L 180, 03/07/2001 P. 26–33 … 148, 153
2001/50/EC: OJ L 190, 12/07/2001 P. 14–17
2001/52/EC: OJ L 190, 12/07/2001 P. 18–20 … 56
2001/57/EC: OJ L 208, 01/08/2001 P. 36–43 … 148, 153
2001/61/EC: OJ L 215, 09/08/2001 P. 26–29 … 141
2001/62/EC: OJ L 221, 17/08/2001 P. 18–36 … 138
2001/82/EC: OJ L 311, 28/11/2001 P. 01–66 … 151
2001/110/EC: OJ L 010, 12/01/2002 P. 47–52 … 99
2001/111/EC: OJ L 010, 12/01/2002 P. 53–57 … 105
2001/112/EC: OJ L 010, 12/01/2002 P. 58–66 … 106
2001/113/EC: OJ L 010, 12/01/2002 P. 67–72 … 108
2002/05/EC: OJ L 034, 05/02/2002 P. 07–12 … 153
2002/17/EC: OJ L 058, 28/02/2002 P. 19–24 … 138
2002/23/EC: OJ L 064, 07/03/2002 P. 13–19 … 153
2002/26/EC: OJ L 075, 16/03/2002 P. 38–43 … 145
2002/27/EC: OJ L 075, 16/03/2002 P. 44–45 … 145
2002/42/EC: OJ L 134, 22/05/2002 P. 29–36 … 153
2002/46/EC: OJ L 183, 12/07/2002 P. 51–57
2002/66/EC: OJ L 192, 20/07/2002 P. 47–53 … 153
2002/67/EC: OJ L 026, 30/01/2002 P. 17–17 … 66
2002/69/EC: OJ L 209, 06/08/2002 P. 05–14 … 145
2002/71/EC: OJ L 225, 22/08/2002 P. 21–28 … 153
2002/76/EC: OJ L 240, 07/09/2002 P. 45–50 … 153
2002/78/EC OJ L 031, 01/02/2002 P. 01–24
2002/79/EC: OJ L 291, 28/10/2002 P. 01–19 … 153
2002/82/EC: OJ L 292, 28/10/2002 P. 01–28 … 56
2002/97/EC: OJ L 343, 18/12/2002 P. 23–30 … 153
2002/100/EC: OJ L 002, 07/01/2003 P. 33–38 … 153
2002/113/EC OJ L 049, 20/02/2002 P. 01–160
2003/14/EC: OJ L 041, 14/02/2003 P. 37–40 … 85

Decisions

90/424/EEC: OJ L 224, 18/08/1990 P. 19–28 … 198
91/516/EEC: OJ L 281, 09/10/1991 P. 23–24 … 197

Regulations

Table of Cases

Cases 51–54/71 *International Fruit Company NV and others* v. *Produkschap voor Gruenten en Fruit Joint* [1971] ECR 1107 … 10
C-2/73 *Geddo* v. *Entr Nazionale Risi* [1973] ECR 865 where the court ruled that the suspension of imports of pork by the Italian authorities from other Member States was contrary to Article 28 … 6
C-8/74 Procureur du Rov Dassonville [1974] ECR 837 … 6
C-120/78 *Rewe-Zentral AG* v. *Bundesmonopolverwaltung für Branntwein* [1979] ECR 649 … 5
C-788/79 Herbert Gilli and Paul Andres [1980] ECR 2071 … 8
C-27/80 *Anton Adriaan Fietje* v. *Arrondissementsrechtbank Assen* – Netherlands [1980] ECR 3839 … 7
C-130/80 *Criminal proceedings Fabriek* v. *Hoogwaardige Voedingsprodukter Kelderman BU* [1981] ECR 517 … 8
C-53/80 *Offices van Justitie* v. *Koninklijke Kas Fabrek Eyssen BV* [1981] ECR 409 … 8
C-261/81 *Walter Rau Lebensmittelwerk* v. *De Smedt PvbA* [1982] ECR 3961 … 8–9
C-178/84 *Commission* v. *Federal Republic of Germany* [1987] ECR 1227 … 9
C-407/853 *Glocken GmbH and Gertraud Kritzinger* v. *USL Centro-Sud and Provincia autonoma di Bolzano* [1988] ECR 4233 … 9–10
C-298/87 Proceedings for compulsory reconstruction against Smanor SA [1988] ECR 4489 … 10
C-205/89 *Commission* v. *Hellenic Republic* [1991] ECR 1361 … 10
Joint Cases C - 267–268/91 Bernard Keck and Daniel Mithouard [1993] ECR I-6097 … 11, 12
C-298/96 *Oelmühle Hamburg AG and Jb. Schmidt Söhne GmbH and Co. KG* v. *Bundesanstalt für Landwirtschaft und Ernährung* [1998] ECR I-4767 … 126
C-293/96 *Kingdom of Denmark, Federal Republic of Germany and French Republic* v. *Commission of the European Communities* [1999] ECR I-01541 … 126
C-299/96 *Kingdom of Denmark, Federal Republic of Germany and French Republic* v. *Commission of the European Communities* [1999] ECR I-01541 … 126
C-405/98 *Konsumentombudsmannen (KO)* v. *Gourmet International Products AB* (GIP) [2001] … 12–13
ECR I-1795.
Case C-248/99 *French Republic* v. *Monsanto Company and Commission of the European Communities* [2002] ECR I-00001 … 147
C-12/00 *Commission of the European Communities* v. *Kingdom of Spain* [2003] ECR … 102
C-14/00 *Commission of the European Communities* v. *Italian Republic* [2003] ECR … 102

Chapter 1

Introduction

The Importance of the Agro-food Sector

The production and consumption of food is central to any society. It has economic, social and environmental consequences. All these elements play an important role in food law and policy. In its White Paper on Food Safety 2000 the European Commission acknowledged the significant role the EU Agro-Food sector plays in the European economy as a whole. The food and drink industry is a leading industrial sector in the European Union and has an annual production worth almost €600 billion (CIAA, Confederation of the food and drink industries of the European Union). This amounts to about 15 per cent of total manufacturing output in the European Union. At the international level, the European Union is the worlds' largest producer of food and drink products. The food and drink industry employs 2.6 million people in the European Union, of which about a third are in small and medium enterprises. The agriculture sector has an annual production of about €220 billion and provides about 7.5 million full time jobs.

The Elevated Profile of Food Safety in Recent Years

Consumers must be able to buy food without risk. Recently, in European and other westernised countries, various food scares have raised questions over the safety of food. The BSE crisis, foot-and-mouth disease, *E. coli* poisoning and dioxin contamination have affected the European food chain once again highlighting the vulnerability of consumers in the very normal activity of purchasing food. Consequently, the whole question of food safety has been elevated in importance in the minds of European consumers. Consumer and trading partner confidence in the industry has been badly shaken and now it needs to be rebuilt.

The advent of biotechnological processes, in particular genetic modification, has heightened consumer fears in relation to the food they purchase. At present there is a vigorous debate waging (in very general terms) between those in the biotechnology industry, particularly in the United States, who believe that food products created using these processes are good, wholesome to eat, bring with them global benefits of productivity, and more certain supply, and those consumer associations/interests groups, in particular in the European Union, who are, for example, fearful of the long-term health and environmental effects of eating genetically modified foods.

Moreover, eating habits and diet form part of the European culture and tradition. The diversity and variety of foods available throughout the European Union adds to the richness of European culture. Whilst aiming for a high level of health and consumer protection, care must be taken not to stifle this creative expression or to destroy the heritage of the European citizens.

Meeting the Needs of Consumers

According to consumer associations now, more than ever before, European consumers are concerned with quality, taste, appearance, nutritional properties and ethical values with regard to food. They want food to be produced and processed with respect for the environment and for the welfare of the food producing animals. People are increasingly aware of the environmental 'footprint' the agro-food industry leaves and are demanding that sustainable methods of food production are promoted. For example, the recent foot-and-mouth disease crisis highlighted the large-scale transport of animals and consumers have begun questioning if it is necessary and more generally if the intensive farming practices used today are necessary. However, consumers are also concerned that the price they pay for food does not increase. It is unclear how these demands for cheap food can be balanced with the cost implications if qualitative standards are to be improved.

Consumers, according to the European Commission, want to receive more and clear information about the food they buy. They expect complete and accurate information to appear on labelling. However, this information must be understandable and not overly complex. They want relevant, comprehensive and meaningful information presented in a clear and unambiguous way. This information should relate to the composition, nutritional value and processing of the foodstuffs in order that they can make informed choices.

Summary of Some Recent History in EU Food Law and Policy

On 12 January 2000 the Commission issued its White Paper on Food Safety. In this the Commission has underlined its commitment to restoring consumer and trading partner confidence by putting into effect the most up-to-date and effective food safety regime in the world. Commissioner Byrne, the European Commissioner for Health and Consumer Protection, has acknowledged that the 'shopping trolley is one of the most potent weapons on the face of this earth'. The Commission has generally recognised that the existence (or not) of consumer confidence in the food industry can have huge repercussions on farmers, producers and the industry in general.

The White Paper sets out the overall aim of the Commission as putting into place the necessary legislation and structures that will guarantee the highest possible level of protection for consumers in the consumption of food. Indeed the White Paper outlines a comprehensive range of actions (over 80 measures) that are aimed at achieving this. They aim towards an holistic and integrated approach at all levels of the food chain, 'from farm to fork'.

On 21 February 2002 the cornerstone Regulation,[1] which sets out the general principles of food law and establishes the European Food Safety Authority (EFSA), came into force. This Regulation, foreseen in the White Paper, for the first time establishes food law as an autonomous branch of EU law and will underpin all future food and feed legislation. Historically, food law and policy has emerged gradually. Originally, it was based on the rules of the free movement of goods contained in the Treaty of Rome, but, over time, a large body of food specific EU legislation has been adopted with the aim of completing the internal market and protecting consumers. In addition, there has been a substantial amount of case law produced by the European Courts. The adoption of an overarching Regulation is of fundamental importance because the principles it sets out will appear in all EU Food Legislation in the foreseeable future.

The European Food Safety Authority has particular responsibilities for both risk assessment and communication of food safety issues. The EFSA is intended to be independent, based on best science, transparent and should have a high level of accountability to the European institutions. Following the Laeken summit in 2002, Brussels has been identified as a temporary seat for the EFSA.

The adoption of this key piece of legislation was only possible due to political agreement reached in record time between the Member States in the Council and all political groups in the European Parliament. This is a clear demonstration of the sheer political determination to achieve a major overhaul of the EU Food Safety system and the way scientific advice feeds into policy making.

The adoption of this Regulation is a significant phase of the reform of EU food law as foreseen in the White Paper and provides a timely moment to take stock of the reforms so far and the emergence of this dynamic and emotive area of law and policy.

This book begins by setting the historical and social context against which this new branch of law is emerging. Before evaluating the achievements to date, it examines the aims and policies identified by the European Commission in the White Paper and considers how the goals have shifted by looking at various aspects of food law. Some of the continuing underlying debates are considered: the purpose of food labelling, appropriate hygiene standards, the authorisation and labelling of GMOs to name a few. Finally, the book considers the way forward for the wide ranging reform and the future operation of the new EFSA.

This book is not comprehensive and certain sectors, notably meat and beef, are not considered in any detail. Neither is it a substitute for detailed legal advice in specific cases.

---

[1] Regulation 178/2002 – OJ L 031, 01/02/2002 P. 01-24.

Chapter 2

Free Movement of Goods

Introduction

Article 3 of the EC Treaty sets out the following fundamental goal for the European Community: 'an internal market characterised by the abolition, as between Member States, of obstacles to the free movement of goods'.

The most obvious example of a barrier to the free movement of goods is a customs duty. However, Member States have also tried to protect domestic industry from imported competition in a number of ways, in particular, by quantitative restrictions. Such quantitative restriction could involve, for example, limiting the quantity of good that may be imported (in other words a quota). Alternatively, Member States have used measures having an equivalent effect to quantitative restrictions, for example, an administrative practice that effectively hinders the import of a particular good. In light of this Article 28 EC provides: 'quantitative restrictions on imports and all measure which have equivalent effect shall be prohibited between Member States'. Article 29 EC provides: 'quantitative restrictions on exports and all measures having equivalent effect, shall be prohibited between Member States'.

The principle of free movement of goods is one of the fundamental freedoms laid down in the EC Treaty and it has direct effect, in other words individuals can enforce rights under this freedom before national courts.

However, the Treaty does provide exemptions and derogations from the basic rule of free movement of goods where there is justification for doing so in Article 30:

> 'the provisions of Articles 28 and 29 shall not preclude prohibitions or restrictions on imports, exports or goods in transit justified on grounds of public morality, public policy, or public security; protection of health and life of humans, animals or plants; the protection of national treasures possessing artistic, historical or archaeological value; or the protection of industrial or commercial property. Such prohibitions shall not, however, constitute a means of arbitrary discrimination or a disguised restriction on trade between Member States.'

The Development of Food Law through the Rules on the Free Movement of Goods

The original Treaty of Rome made no explicit mention of consumer protection and public health as fundamental aims. These references were added after amendments by the Single European Act and the Maastricht Treaty. Thus EU food law began developing within a purely economic framework and in a rather piecemeal fashion. Both the Commission and the European Court of Justice (ECJ) concentrated on the free movement of foodstuffs throughout the Common Market. The ECJ handed down a number of landmark judgments relating to food products which shaped the development of the body of free movement of goods case law, for example, Cassis de Dijon[2] (see below). It is worth noting that at the same time, in parallel, the Commission began to adopt a number of single market legislative measures and policy initiatives, for example, the first directive on food colours in 1962, a communication in 1985 entitled 'The Completion of the Internal Market: Community Legislation on Foodstuffs' and in 1989 a communication entitled 'The Free Movement of Foodstuffs within the Community'. So in effect food law began to develop on two parallel paths with both the ECJ and the Commission relying on the single market rules.

Mutual recognition

Under the principle of mutual recognition, Member States cannot prohibit the sale within their own territory of products that are lawfully produced or marketed in another Member State. This principle applies even if the product was produced according to different standards to those required under the national legislation of the Member State. Member States are only permitted to prevent the sale of such products under very strict conditions to protect public health, consumers or the environment, this is known as justification. If a Member State justifies a prohibition of the sale of a product under one of these headings, the Member State would also have to prove that the prohibition was proportionate and could not be achieved by a less restrictive method.

The principle of mutual recognition applies where full harmonisation of legislation does not exist at EU level. If legislation has been adopted at EU level, then Member States may still be allowed to apply stricter rules where expressly permitted to do so. In such circumstances the principle of mutual recognition still applies.

The Commission recently estimated that the economic value of trade, within the Community, of products covered by the principle of mutual recognition is approximately 430 billion euro. In 1999, the Commission published a Communication[3] on mutual recognition. The Commission was concerned that the principle of mutual recognition was not operating satisfactorily partly because economic operators and Member States lacked knowledge of how to apply the principle. The Commission set out in its Communication some proposed actions for improving the application of mutual recognition one of which was for the Commission to prepare a guide to be

---

[2] Case 120/78 Ruwe Zentral v Buntesmonopolberwaltung Für Branntwein [1979] ECR 649.

[3] Communication on mutual recognition in the context of the follow-up of the action plan for the single market COM (1999) 0299.

published by 2000. At the time of writing, the Commission had not published the guide.

The Commission has published regular reports on the 'Application of the Principle of Mutual Recognition in the Single Market'. The most recent report, at the time of writing, was published in July 2002.[4] The Commission concluded in this report that the principle of mutual recognition is operating satisfactorily for products which pose few safety problems, such as bicycles. However, for more technically complex products or products which can pose safety or health problems, the Commission found that the principle is not operating satisfactorily because as acknowledged in its previous report, companies and national administrations are not sufficiently familiar with the principle.

Long awaited guidelines, which the Commission intends to publish, could help to overcome these difficulties by explaining the rights and obligations of parties where the principle of mutual recognition should be applied. However, this will not remedy the situation where a Member State or economic operator deliberately does not apply the principle for their own reasons.

The development of the case law on food law

Below is a summary of some of the important judgements relating to free movement of goods and food law.

Dassonville. The notion of a quantitative restriction is well understood and clearly defined: 'the prohibition on the quantitative restrictions covers measures which amount to a total or partial restraint of, according to the circumstances, imports, exports or goods in transit'.[5] However, the definition of the phrase 'measures having equivalent effect' is more difficult.

It was not until the cornerstone case of Dassonville[6] in 1974 that a general definition of measures having equivalent effect to quantitative restriction on imports was set down. The phrase was defined as 'all trading laws enacted by Member States which are capable of hindering, directly or indirectly, actually or potentially, intra-community trade'. The case concerned the importation of Scotch whisky into Belgium via France being purchased from French distributors. Belgium legislation required that goods be accompanied by a certificate of origin which must be made out in the name of the Belgian importer. The Scottish whisky in question did not have the required certificates. The case was before the national courts and was referred to the Court of Justice for preliminary ruling. The ECJ ruled that the Belgian legislation in fact was a hindrance to trade between Member States.

---

[4] The second report on mutual recognition adopted in July 2002 COM (2002) 419.

[5] Geddo v Entr Nazionale Risi C-2/73 [1973] ECR 865 where the court ruled that the suspension of imports of pork by the Italian authorities from other Member States was contrary to Article 28.

[6] Procureur du Rov Dassonville C-8/74 [1974] ECR 837.

Cassis de Dijon. The case of Cassis de Dijon[7] concerned the importation of an alcoholic drink 'Cassis de Dijon' into Germany. German legislation prohibited the marketing of liqueurs of an alcoholic strength of less than 25 per cent. In fact 'Cassis de Dijon' contained between 15 and 20 per cent. A German national court referred the question to the Court of Justice as to whether the national legislation was consistent with Article 28 EC. The Court found that the national rules had a restrictive effect (which meant there was no need for the element of discrimination to be found) and therefore the national rules were in violation of Article 28 EC. In practice French liqueurs contained a lower level of alcohol than German liqueurs. Therefore the practical effect of these principles was to prohibit the marketing of French liqueurs on the German market. The ECJ stated:

> the requirements relating to the minimum content of alcoholic beverages do not serve a purpose which is in the general interest such as to take precedence over the requirements of free movement of goods, which constitutes one of the fundamental rules of the Community.

The Court decided that provided the product had been lawfully produced and marketed in one Member State it should be free to move throughout the European Commission. This is the first case that recognised the concept of 'mutual recognition'. If the case had been decided in a different way, this could have meant that French liqueurs would have been excluded from the German market, while typical German liqueurs, which would have generally complied with French laws, would have enjoyed access to the French market. In other words, traders in highly regulated markets would have enjoyed advantages over traders situated in less regulated markets.

The Court also gave some insight as to the scope of the derogations permitted under Article 30 EC. The German Government had argued that the legal provisions were designed to protect the consumer against the adverse effects of alcohol to their health. The Court decided that, although there could be some merit to the arguments, it was not sufficient to allow a derogation from Article 28 EC.

Fietje. In the Netherlands, the 'Decree on Liqueurs' requires that alcoholic products of a strength at least 22 per cent by volume be described as 'likeur'. The Fietje[8] case concerned criminal proceedings against a dealer in beverages who is charged with having supplied a beverage, imported from Germany, that was 25 per cent volume and did not bear the indication 'likeur'. In their defence the accused argued that this labelling rule was incompatible with the Article 28 EC, and a reference was made to the ECJ for a preliminary ruling. The ECJ ruled that a provision which prohibits the sale of certain alcoholic beverages under a description other than one prescribed by national law to beverages imported from other Member States, making it necessary

[7] C-120/78 Ruwe Zentral v Buntesmonopolberwaltung Für Branntwein [1979] ECR 649.

[8] Case 27/80 [1980] ECR 3839.

to change the label under which the imported beverage is lawfully marketed in the exporting Member State, is a restriction and prohibited under Article 28, provided that the details given on the original label supply the consumer with information on the nature of the product in question which is equivalent to that in the description prescribed by the national law. The ECJ left it to the national court to decide if there was equivalence in the information.

Gilli and Andres. This case again concerned criminal proceedings, this time in Italy.[9] The case of fraud was brought against two traders for marketing apple vinegar made in Germany containing acetic acid not derived from acetic fermentation. The Italian law in question prohibited the marketing of vinegar containing acetic acid not derived from the acetic fermentation of wine. The defendants challenged the compatibility of an Italian law in relation to Article 28 EC. The ECJ found that this rule was 'a measure having an equivalent effect' to the quantitative restriction on imports where the product involved is vinegar lawfully produced and marketed in another Member State.

Eyssen. Criminal charges were brought against a Dutch producer of cheese for holding quantities of processed cheese intended for sale and consumption which contained an additive not authorised under Dutch law.[10] Nisin, the additive in question, is generally used for its preserving characteristics. At the time of judgement there was no harmonising legislation on preservatives at an EC level (this situation has now changed see Chapter 6). The Court concluded that, in accordance with Article 28 EC a Member State was not precluded from having national measures prohibiting the addition of nisin to home-produced or imported processed cheese, even if they limit such a prohibition only to products intended for sale on the domestic market. However please note that such a national requirement would no longer be compatible with EC law.

Kelderman. An importer of 'brioches' from France to the Netherlands faced criminal charges because the amount of dried matter contained in the 'brioches' fell outside permitted limits set down in the Dutch Bread Act.[11] The Dutch court asked the ECJ whether the prohibition on marketing of products not containing a dry matter content within the parameters set down by the Bread Act was a 'measure having an effect equivalent to quantitative restrictions on imports' in Article 28 EC. The ECJ answered that where the national rules applied to the importation of bread lawfully produced and marketed in another Member State they were restrictive and incompatible with Article 28 EC.

---

9 Case 788/79 [1980] ECR 2071.

10 Offices van Justitie v Koninklijke Kas Fabrek Eyssen BV Case 53/80 [1981] ECR 409.

11 Fabriek v Hoogwaardige Voedingsprodukter Kelderman BU Case 130/80 [1981] ECR 517.

Rau. This case concerned the issue of whether a requirement under Belgium legislation that the packaging of margarine, sold by retail, be cube-shaped was compatible with EC law.[12] The question arose in a contractual dispute between a German seller and a Belgium buyer. The margarine that was supplied was packed in plastic tubs with a cone shape. The ECJ was asked to rule on the compatability of the Belgian rule with EC law following a preliminarily reference from the German court dealing with the contractual dispute. The Belgian Government intervened and made two key arguments:

(a) the packaging requirement cannot be a real barrier to trade because it was possible to adapt the presentation for retail sale or sell the product wholesale,
(b) the requirement of the cubic form is necessary for the protection of the consumer, to prevent butter and margarine being confused in the mind of the consumer.

To the first of these points the ECJ said that the packaging requirement rendered the marketing of margarine from other Member States more difficult and more expensive by either barring it from certain channels of distribution or owing to the additional costs brought about by the need to package the margarine in special packs. The Court noted that there was practically no margarine of foreign origin on the Belgian market.

As to the consumer protection argument, the Court found that the requirement for margarine to be packaged in cubes was disproportionate to the objective. Applying the principle of proportionality the Court said that less restrictive measures, such as clear labelling, would achieve the same aim of informing the consumer of the nature of the product. Therefore, the requirement that margarine was packaged in cubes is a restriction having an effect equivalent to a quantitative restriction and not compatible with EC law.

Commission v Germany. The Commission challenged Germany's requirement that 'beer' should not be marketed unless it fell with certain specifications laid down in German law and in particular placing a general ban on the use of additives in beer.[13] The Court found that the prohibition on the use of additives in beer was contrary the principle of proportionality and therefore Germany had failed to fulfil its obligations under Article 28 EC. Moreover the Court ruled that by prohibiting the marketing of beers lawfully manufactured and marketed in another Member State where they did not meet the requirements the German law, breached Article 28 EC.

Drei Glocken. This case concerned the question whether national provisions, in Italy, prohibiting the sale of pasta products made from common wheat or a mixture of

---

12 Walter Rau Lebensmittelwerk v De Smedt PvbA Case C-261/81 [1982] ECR 3961.

13 *Commission* v. *Federal Republic of Germany Case* C-178/84 [1987] ECR 1227.

common wheat and durum wheat are compatible with Community law.[14] The Court found that a prohibition on the sale of such pasta products is an obstacle to the importation of pasta products lawfully manufactured in other Member States. The Court went on to find that such a measure could not be justified on the grounds of the protection of public health and was disproportionate. It was therefore contrary to the EC rules on free movement.

Smanor. Smanor SA is a French company that specialises in the production and wholesale of deep-frozen products, in particular yoghurts which it deep-freezes.[15] On several occasions the French authorities have tried to ban 'deep-frozen yoghurt' on the basis of national rules prohibiting the marketing of such products under the name yoghurt and requiring it to sell them under the name 'deep-frozen fermented milk'. Despite the question arising in relation to the application of French law to a French company it could equally apply to imported products. Although the national rule requiring the product to be sold under a different name does not completely prelude the importation into France of products originating in other Member States or its free circulation, it would make marketing more difficult. It was therefore considered to impede trade (indirectly) between Member States and so falls within Article 28 EC. The justifications of the protection of health and consumers were pleaded. The ECJ ruled that it was for the national court to decide whether the deep-frozen yoghurt differs from the requirements of national rules relating to fresh yoghurt sufficiently to justify a different name in order to protect the consumer.

International Fruit Company. In this case the ECJ was asked whether the requirement of a licence for import and export was a 'quantitative restriction' or 'a measure having equivalent effect' when in fact the licence was always granted when the import/export was from/to another Member State.[16] The ECJ clearly states the requirement of an import licence is precluded under the EC rules on free movement of goods, even purely as a formality.

Commission v Greece. The case questioned whether the requirement of a veterinary certificate for imported pasteurised butter amounted to a quantitative restriction or a measure having equivalent effect.[17] The Court ruled that it was and therefore Greece had failed to comply with Article 28 EC.

---

[14] Case 407/85 [1988] ECR 4233.

[15] Proceedings for compulsory reconstruction against Smanor SA Case 298/87 [1988] ECR 4489.

[16] International Fruit Company NV and others v Produkschap voor Gruenten en Fruit Joint Cases 51 to 54/71 [1971] ECR 1107.

[17] Commission v Hellenic Republic Cases C-205/89 [1991] ECR 1361.

The Application of Article 28 to Sales Promotions and Advertising

The above examples relate to foodstuffs themselves (i.e. their composition, packaging or labelling) and do not refer to methods of selling, sales promotion or advertising (collectively referred to as selling arrangements). There is a series of case law examining the application of these rules to the methods of selling. Not all of cases below concern foodstuffs but the principles they set out apply equally to food.

The Keck judgement. The culmination of many years of case law concerning Article 28 seemed to be in the case of Keck and Mithouart.[18] Mr Keck and Mr Mithouart were prosecuted for reselling products in an unaltered state at a price lower than their actual purchase price which was contrary to French legislation. As a defence they argued that the prohibition on resale at a loss was incompatible with Article 28 EC and the national Court made a reference to the ECJ.

For many years the ECJ had applied Articles 28 and 30 to Member State laws concerning all types of selling arrangements. However, in this judgement, the ECJ decided that Article 28:

- applies to national legislation which lays down rules specifically concerning goods, for example, requiring a product to be labelled in a particular way or to have a certain composition;
- does not apply to national provisions restricting or prohibiting selling arrangements generally (e.g. prohibiting resale at a loss) provided that the rules apply indiscriminately to all traders operating in the territory concerned and affect both domestic and imported products in the same manner.

Therefore following this judgement it was widely assumed that:

- national restrictions concerning on-pack advertising are subject to the rules of free movement of goods; but
- national restrictions on advertising which are of general application (e.g. restrictions on advertising to children and advertising of alcohol) will usually fall outside the scope of the free rules on free movement of goods because they apply indiscriminately. They could, however, infringe the rules on free movement of services.

De Agostini. In the case of De Agostini,[19] the ECJ considered an outright ban on advertising aimed at children less than 12 years of age and of misleading advertising.

---

[18] Joint Cases C-267-268/91 [1993] ECR I6097.

[19] De Agostini (svenska) förlagat [1997] ECR 1-3843.

The court noted that the national measures at issue applied to relevant traders operating within the national territory and therefore ruled that such a ban was not within the scope of Article 28. However the Court did note that it is possible for such a ban to affect products from another Member State with a greater impact and that could be caught by Article 28. If that was in fact the case then it would be necessary to consider justification under Article 30.

The Gourmet judgement. In March 2001 the ECJ delivered judgment in a case of Konsumentombudsmannen (KO) v Gourmet International Products AD (GIP).[20] It is possible that this judgment may make it easier to challenge certain national restrictions on advertising consumer goods in the future.

The Gourmet case concerned a Swedish law from the 1970s concerning the marketing of alcoholic drinks which prohibited the advertising in Sweden of alcoholic drinks on radio or television and provided that advertising may not be used to market spirits, wines or strong beers in magazines other than trade press. GIP is a publisher of a magazine entitled 'Gourmet' which carried a number of adverts for alcoholic drinks. The Konsumentombudsmannen applied for an injunction against GIP to stop it from publishing the advertisements and requested that the company be fined under the Swedish legislation. GIP pleaded in its defense that the Swedish legislation was contrary to the European Community law and therefore the case was referred by the Swedish National Court to the ECJ for guidance on whether a prohibition on advertising such as that contained in the Swedish law is in breach of the EC rules on free movement of goods and free movement of services.

As noted above it was generally considered, that following the case of Keck, Article 28 did not apply to national provisions restricting or prohibiting selling arrangements to (e.g. prohibiting re-sales at a loss) provided the rules apply indiscriminately to all traders operating within the territory concerned and affected both domestic and imported products in the same manner. Therefore, following Keck it could have been assumed that the national restrictions on advertising of general applications such as this restriction on advertising of alcohol would have fallen outside the scope of the free movement of goods.

However in the Gourmet case the ECJ found that the general restrictions on advertising imposed by Member States will still be subject to the rules on free movement of goods if they prevent access to the market even if they are non-discriminatory. The ECJ stated:

> 'if National provisions restricting or prohibiting certain selling arrangements are to avoid being caught by Article 28 of the Treaty, they must not be of such a kind

[20] C-405/98.

> *as to prevent access to the market by products from another Member State* or to impede access any more than they impede the access of domestic products.' (emphasis added)

This could represent a significant shift in the ECJ's attitude since Keck although it does not necessarily contradict the De Agostini Case (see above). Although the ECJ was given the opportunity to adopt such a test in that case and failed to do so, it did note that if access to imported products was impeded more severally than domestic products it will be necessary to justify the restriction. However following the Gourmet Case the ECJ contemplates that generally applicable rules that actually prevent access to the market may fall within Article 28.

In the Gourmet Case, the ECJ decided that the prohibition of all spirits advertising directed at consumers in the form of advertisements in the press, radio, television and direct mail was likely to impede access to the market by products of other Member States more than it impeded access by domestic products. However it did decide that the prohibition could still be justified on public health grounds as long and it was proportionate to the objective sort to be achieved. The ECJ left it for the national court to decide whether the protection of public health against harmful effects of alcohol can be assured by less restrictive measures than a total prohibition of advertising.

The Gourmet Case illustrates the possible willingness of the ECJ to apply a market access test and this may mean a challenge to national advertising rules could be more possible under the free movement of goods rules. It will be a question of fact whether the access to the market has in fact been prevented. Once an advertising restriction has fallen within the scope of Article 28 it will still be possible for Member States to justify the restriction of trade on grounds of public policy under Article 30.

The free movement of services is outside the scope of this book, however, it is noted that this judgement does not establish any new principles of law regarding the free movement of services. The ECJ did find that the Swedish prohibition on alcohol advertising would affect the cross border supply of advertising space and therefore did restrict free movement of services and breached Article 49. It was therefore necessary for the Member State to justify this restriction on public health grounds and that decision was left to the national courts.

Conclusion

In conclusion foodstuffs have been the subject of many important cases before the European Courts concerning the free movement of goods. It is clear that Article 28 EC applies to national legislation concerning the foodstuff itself, for example, its composition or labelling. It now appears that Article 28 EC could also be a useful tool in challenging national restrictions on selling arrangements, advertising or sales promotions. However, in the 2 years since this judgement no such challenge has been brought. In practice this clarification of the application of Article 28 EC to these selling arrangements may not be of limited or historical interest as there is currently a proposal to harmonise sale promotions and a further proposal on consumer protection is expected to address advertising and methods of trading.

Chapter 3

New Approach – Green Paper and White Paper

In April 1997, the Commission published its Green Paper 'The General Principles of Food Law in the European Union'.[21] The messages in this consultation document are largely of historical interest but it is worth comparing them to the ideals expressed in the White Paper in the development of food policy. It began by noting that food law is a matter of great public concern. Effective control and security is necessary in order to ensure food safety. Food law and policy should also ensure the supply of wholesome food and effective protection of all the interests of consumers. The Green Paper had four aims:

- to examine the extent to which legislation is meeting the needs and expectations of consumers, producers, manufacturers and traders;
- to consider how the measures, to reinforce the independence and objectivity, equivalence and effectiveness of the official control and inspections systems, are meeting their basic objectives to ensure a safe and wholesome food supply, and the protection of all the interests of consumers;
- to launch a public debate on our food legislation; and thereby,
- to enable the Commission to propose appropriate measures for the future development of Community food law, where necessary.

It sets out six goals which were stated to be necessary for Community food law:

- to ensure a high level of protection of public health, safety and the consumer;
- to ensure the free movement of goods within the internal market;
- to ensure that the legislation is primarily based on scientific evidence and risk assessment;
- to ensure the competitiveness of European industry and enhance its export prospects;
- to place the primary responsibility for safe food on industry, producers and suppliers, using hazard analysis and critical control points (HACCP) type systems, which must be backed up by effective official controls and enforcement;
- to ensure that legislation is coherent, rational and user-friendly.

The Green Paper set out the desirable objectives of the simplification and rationalisation of Community legislation. However, it clearly stated that this could not

---

[21] Green Paper – COM(1997) 176.

result in a lowering of the level of protection of public health or consumer protection. It was (and still is) important to strike a balance between general provisions setting principles and detailed prescriptive legislation, as well as between the use of binding legislation and other voluntary instruments such as self-regulation.

The Green Paper identified the need for a review of the existing legislation. In order to do so, it required extensive consultation with the Social Partners in order to ensure that any proposed legislation would meet its stated goal. The Social Partners were to be encouraged to participate more actively in the evaluation of the costs and benefits of new legislation. The Green Paper put forward the argument that the increased use of regulations, as the preferred legislative instrument, rather than directives would increase transparency. This would also avoid discrepancies and difficulties arising from delay or inconsistency in transposition. Directives are a good instrument for framework legislation. In particular the field of hygiene was considered overly complicated with eleven vertical hygiene directives co-existing with a general directive on hygiene of foodstuffs. Priority was to be given to ensuring that there is a coherent and consistent body of Community hygiene rules.

Even as far back as 1997, the field of labelling was identified as a problem and the Green Paper notes that it is necessary to strike a balance to ensure that consumers receive 'all useful information, whilst avoiding unnecessary detail provisions'.

The Green Paper acknowledges that the Treaty requires the Community to contribute to the maintenance of the high level of protection of public health, the environment and consumers. It suggests a full risk assessment, to be applied before a measure is taken and when this is not possible the application of the precautionary principle. The importance of independence and objectiveness in scientific advice is emphasised. Scientific advice is considered in the Green Paper as having primary, although not exclusive, importance. It also notes that other factors, in particular consumer needs and concerns, must be taken into account. It talks about the extension of product liability directives to cover primary agricultural production in order to improve the level of protection to consumers. It also notes, however, that this extension should not be considered as an alternative to appropriate product safety rules and effective official control systems. This was in direct reaction to the BSE crisis. It considers the importance of the labelling of beef.

The Green Paper emphasises the importance of ensuring effective implementation of the internal market rules. Timing and correct implementation of the Community legislation is crucial to the effectiveness of the internal market. The Community was not in a position to replace the Member States in the field of control but it was felt that the Community should verify that the necessary controls were being carried out in an effective and equivalent manner throughout the Member States.

In the Green Paper, the Commission took into account that the Community is a major importer and exporter of foods, and that Community food legislation must be seen in the wider context of the international market. It must be ensured that imported food meets the same standards as food produced within the Community. In addition, the Community must be able to assure governments and consumers in third countries that food produced within the Community is as safe as food produced in their country. All legislation should also be compatible with international obligations, particularly those arising under the WTO.

White Paper

Following extensive consultation, the Commission issued a White Paper on food safety on 12 January 2000[22] which sets a radical new approach to food law and policy. The approach is integrated and comprehensive. A successful food safety policy has to recognise the interlinked nature of food production; from 'stable to table' or 'farm to fork'.

The White Paper foresees the EU's food policy being founded upon the very highest food safety standards to both protect the consumer and promote health. Given the central role of food in society the White Paper highlights many different policy areas upon which it impacts, for example economic, social and environmental.

The Commission notes that the European Union should not be exclusively responsible for all aspects of food safety. Although all aspects need to be addressed at EU level in order to effectively run the intended EU market, enforcement should remain a national, regional and local responsibility. The White Paper identifies three areas in which the European Union needs to re-establish the confidence of consumers and trading partners:

- food science,
- food law,
- food controls.

The White Paper sets out a comprehensive range of actions which the Commission believes are essential to complement and modernise the existing EU legislation.

A European Food Authority

Central to the new approach outlined in the White Paper is the establishment of an independent European Food Authority. The White Paper envisaged the authority having particular responsibility for risk assessment and risk communication on food safety issues. The authority, as foreseen in the White Paper, would be entrusted with a number of key tasks: independent scientific advice on all aspects of food safety; the operation of a Rapid Alert System (see below); communication and dialogue with consumers on food safety in health issues, as well as, networking with national agencies and scientific bodies.

The role of an authority needed to be defined in the context of risk analysis which comprises of risk assessment, risk management and risk communication. The Commission generally accepted that it needed to separate the functionality of risk assessment and risk management. The main objective of risk assessment is the provision of scientific advice. Risk management comprises of legislation and control. The passing of legislation implies a political decision and involves judgement calls based on other legitimate factors, and not science alone. Risk communication is crucial. It ensures consumers are adequately informed with accessible and understandable

[22] White Paper – COM(1999) 719.

information. The Commission as guardian of the EC Treaty is responsible for ensuring that Member States properly transpose, implement and enforce Community legislation.

The control function is primarily carried out by the Commission's Food and Veterinary Office (FVO). In light of these issues, among others,[23] the Commission in the White Paper recommended that the authority take a risk assessment role, with the risk management competencies remaining with the Commission. Risk communication was foreseen as a key role for the authority.

The authority needs to meet the fundamental principles of independence, excellence and transparency in order to fully realise its goals of contributing to a high level of consumer health protection in the area of food safety, through which consumer confidence could be restored and maintained.

The White Paper highlights that the authority must be:

- guided by best science;
- independent of industrial and political interests;
- open to vigorous public scrutiny;
- scientifically authoritative;
- work closely with national scientific bodies.

In the White Paper, the Commission aimed to have a European Food Authority in place by 2002.

The principles

The guiding principle throughout the White Paper is a comprehensive and integrated approach. This includes all food sectors, all Member States, at the EU external border and between Member States. The Commission states that the roles and responsibilities of all the stakeholders must be clearly defined. The stakeholders identified are feed manufacturers, farmers, food manufacturers/operators, the competent authorities in Member States and third countries, the Commission and consumers. Feed manufacturers, farmers and food operators have the primary responsibility for food safety. National competent authorities enforce this responsibility through surveillance and control systems. The Commission is foreseen as evaluating the ability of the competent authorities to deliver these systems through audits and inspections at national level. Consumers must recognise that they are responsible for the proper storage, handling and cooking of food. This comprehensive policy is intended to cover the whole of the food chain from 'stable to table' including feed production, primary production, food processing, storage, transport and retail sale. The White Paper

---

[23] Other reasons include the transfer of regulatory power would have required a modification to the EC Treaty, a more decentralised decision-making process would not provide the same high level of accountability and transparency.

sets outs the case that this comprehensive, integrated approach will lead to a more coherent, effective and dynamic food policy.

Legislative measures foreseen

The establishment of this independent authority was foreseen to be accompanied by a wide range of measures aiming to both improve legislation but also to bring coherence at all levels in the food chain from 'farm to fork'. The Commission identified in the White Paper a large number of wide ranging measures that were necessary. Over eighty separate actions are identified to be carried out within the following few years.[24]

A new legal framework is proposed covering the whole of the food chain including animal feed production. The Commission intended to clearly attribute primary responsibility for safe food to industry, producers and suppliers. The suggested new legal framework is outlined in some detail and was seen to involve reforms in many aspects of food law including animal feed, animal health and welfare, zoonoses, BSE/TSE, hygiene, contaminant's and residues, novel food, additives, flavourings, packaging, irradiation, dietetic foods, food supplements and fortification.

The concept of traceability is highlighted in the White Paper, identifying the ability to trace products through the whole food chain as being essential to food safety. The precautionary principle is mentioned throughout the White Paper.

The rapid alert system

The Commission highlights that the ability to take effective safeguard measures in response to emergencies endangering human health throughout the food chain will be critical in the future. In particular, reference is made to the lessons learnt from the dioxin crisis in Belgium, that had happened shortly prior to the issue of the White Paper, which had highlighted the risks associated with food contamination.

The White Paper states that the Rapid Alert System for food functions well in respect of food intended to be sold to the final consumer. However, there were at that time other various types of notifications systems in different areas, for example, transmissible diseases or animal products stopped at the external EU borders. However the objectives and scope of the systems differ and therefore integrated use of that information is difficult. In addition animal feed is not covered. The White Paper envisaged the creation of a comprehensive and harmonised legal framework expanding the scope of the Rapid Alert System to cover all food and feed. It also foresaw an extension of the notification requirements put on economic operators, and additional measures ensuring appropriate information is passed to consumers and trade associations.

---

[24] See Annex 1 which lists the 84 proposed actions.

Enforcement

Legislation setting out controls at both the national and EU level have been established in different pieces of Community legislation over a 30 year period. There were, and still are, wide variations in the manner in which Member States implement and enforce Community legislation. This means that consumers could not be sure of receiving the same level of protection throughout the Community. The numerous food safety crises had highlighted deficiencies in national systems of control. The Commission in the White Paper expressed the view that the lack of a harmonised approach to the design and development of control systems was at the heart of the problem. In light of this, the Commission took the view that a Community framework for the development and approach of national control systems was necessary. In addition, more rapid, easier to use, enforcement procedures should be developed. Controls on imports at the borders of the Community were also to be extended to cover all feed and foodstuffs, and action should be taken in order to improve coordination between various inspections posts. The White Paper sets out three core elements that should be contained in the Community framework:

- *Operational criteria set up at Community level*: National authorities would be expected to meet these criteria. They would also form the basic reference points against which the competent authorities would be audited by the FVO.
- *Community control guidelines*: These would promote coherent national strategies and identify risk-based priorities.
- *Administrative co-operation*: This would allow the exchange of best practice between national authorities and would promote mutual assistance between Member States.

Consumer information

In terms of consumer information, the White Paper highlights that consumers must be kept well informed. The Commission, together with the new European Food Authority envisaged within the White Paper, was foreseen as establishing a continuous dialogue with consumers and encouraging their involvement in the formation of new food safety policy. It was thought to be important to keep consumers better informed of any emerging food safety concerns, and particular groups of consumers (e.g. pregnant women, infants or the elderly) informed of specific risks from particular foods. In addition, the White Paper states that consumers should receive information on food quality and constituents. However, this information should be helpful and clearly presented so that informed choices can be made.

Proposals on the labelling of food were foreseen in the White Paper. These included the removal of the possibility not to indicate the components of compound ingredients where they constitute 25 per cent or less of the final product. It also foresaw the specific labelling of known allergens. The Commission set out its intention to consider whether specific rules were needed to govern functional claims (e.g. claims that a nutrient has a beneficial effect on certain normal bodily functions) and nutritional claims (e.g. claims that describe the presence of a particular nutrient).

The international dimension

As previously identified in the Green Paper, the Commission highlighted the international dimension of EU food policy as being critical. It is important that all the measures proposed in the White Paper are effectively explained to trading partners and for the Community to be an active member in international bodies. The European Union is the world's largest importer/exporter of food products. It trades with countries all over the world in an increasingly diverse range of food products. Therefore food safety cannot be an internal issue alone. All the same safety issues apply to imported products. Consumers all over the world have the right to expect products, exported from the European Union, to meet the same high standards that apply within the European Union.

With increasing globalisation of markets an international approach to food safety is desirable. The international framework for food safety has developed considerably through organisations such as Codex Alimentarius and under the World Trade Organisation Agreements such as the application of Sanitary and Phytosanitary measures (the SPS Agreement). The European Union has obligations to fulfil in this international context.

Greater transparency and openness is the key to enhancing consumer confidence in the food safety policy. The White Paper calls for this increased openness from all those concerned in the food chain including the political institutions as well as industry who bear the prime responsibility for the daily application of the requirements of food safety.

What has been achieved so far?

The Commission made very clear its determination to implement the actions it set out in the White Paper. It provided a detailed action plan together with a timetable for action to be taken over a 3 year period (see Annex I). Following the issuing of the White Paper, there has been considerable momentum within the Commission's DG Health and Consumer Protection (SANCO). They have been vigorously pursuing their programme of adopting the measures identified in the action plan set out in the White Paper. Many of these initiatives will be considered during the course of this book.

Chapter 4

The Emergence of Food Law as an Autonomous Branch of Law

On the 21st of February 2002, the cornerstone Regulation,[25] which sets out the general principles of food law and establishes the European Food Safety Authority, came into force. This Regulation, foreseen in the White Paper, for the first time establishes food law as an autonomous branch of EU law and will become the basis for food and feed legislation in the foreseeable future. Historically, food law has emerged gradually as a separate branch of law. Originally, it was based on the free movement of goods rules contained in the Treaty of Rome, as explained in Chapter 2, but overtime a large body of food specific EU legislation has been adopted. In addition, there has been a substantial amount of case law produced by the European Courts.

Moreover, the Regulation also establishes an independent European Food Safety Authority (EFSA) with particular responsibilities for both risk assessment and communication of food safety issues. The EFSA is intended to be independent, based on best science, transparent and to have a high level of accountability to the European institutions.

The adoption of this key piece of legislation, marks agreement in record time between the Member States in the Council, all political groups in the European Parliament, and demonstrates the sheer political determination to achieve a major overhaul of the EU Food Safety system and the way scientific advice feeds into policy-making. The adoption of this Regulation is a significant phase of the reform of the EU food law as foreseen in the White Paper.

Regulation 178/2002 addresses three issues:

- the general principles and requirements of food law;
- the establishment of the European Food Safety Authority;
- the Rapid Alert System, crises management and emergencies.

This chapter will look at each of these issues in turn.

The General Principles and the Requirements of Food Law

The scope and definitions

The scope of the Regulation, as set out in Article 1, includes both food and feed issues. The principles governing food and feed in general, and food and feed safety

[25] Regulation 2002/178.

in particular, at both Community and national level are established. Food is defined as any substance or product, whether processed, partially processed, or unprocessed, intended to be, or reasonably expected to be, ingested by humans. It includes drink, and any substance intentionally incorporated into the food during its manufacture. Medicinal products within the meaning of Directive 65/65[26] are excluded from the definition, as is feed which is defined separately under Article 3. The definition of feed is any substance or product, including additives, whether processed, partially processed or unprocessed intended to be used for oral feeding to animals.

General objectives

The general objectives of food law (Article 5) include the protection of consumers' interests, such as fair practices in food trade, in addition to ensuring a high level of protection of human life and health. It also includes taking account of, where appropriate, the protection of animal health and welfare, plant health and the environment.

Article 8 of the Regulation protects consumers' interests. It aims to prevent: fraudulent or deceptive practices; adulteration of food; and any other practices which may mislead the consumers.

Safety requirements

There is general obligation (Article 14(1)) that food shall not be placed on the market if it is unsafe. In respect of feed (Article 15(1)), it should not be placed on the market or fed to any food-producing animal if it is unsafe. Competent authorities will be permitted to restrict the placing on the market or withdrawal of food or feed, in the absence of breaches of specific provisions, as long as there are 'reasons to suspect' that the food or feed is unsafe. The grounds which constitute 'reasons to suspect' upon which a competent authority can act are not set out. This could provide legal uncertainty for the food industry and give a very wide discretion to food authorities. In particular, they could impose restrictions despite the fact that the product is in conformity with the relevant specific provisions applicable to it. Once these requirements come into force it will mean the safety requirements in relation to food will be more stringent than the other requirements applicable to products in general as set out under the Product Safety Directives.

Labelling

Article 16 of the Regulation addresses the presentation and labelling of the food and feed. It sets out a general requirement that the labelling, presentation and advertising of food or feed, and information made available about the product, shall not mislead consumers. This requirement must be seen against the background of the

---

[26] OJ P 022, 09/02/1965 P. 369–373.

General Labelling Directive 2000/13[27] (see Chapter 5) as well as the general labelling review launched by Commissioner Byrne in the summer of 2002.

Risk analysis and the precautionary principle

Article 6 outlines how risk analysis should be addressed. Risk assessment is referred to separately from risk management. Risk assessment is to be based on the available scientific evidence and undertaken in an independent, objective and transparent manner. Risk management is to take into account: the results of the risk assessment; 'other factors legitimate to the matter under consideration'; and the precautionary principle 'where the conditions are relevant'. The phrase 'other factors legitimate to the matter under consideration' is not defined.

The Precautionary Principle is dealt with in Article 7 of the Regulation. The fact that it is dealt with in a distinct article gives it a great deal of emphasis, in comparison with other fundamental principles of EC law such as the principle of proportionality. Some would argue that this over emphasis, could result in double precaution and arbitrary decisions. The article remains broadly in line with the Commission's Communication on Precautionary Principle.

Traceability

Article 18 deals with the traceability of any food, feed, food-producing animals, or any other substance intended to be, or expected to be, incorporated into a food or feed. It applies at all stages of production, processing and distribution. However, it only requires food and feed business operators to be able to identify any person from whom, and to whom they have supplied food, feed, food-producing animal or substance expected to be incorporated into a food or feed. In other words: 'one step up, one step down'. This information must be stored so that it can be made available to the relevant authorities.

The application of these principles

In general terms the definitions and principles laid down in the Regulation applied from 20 days from its publication at the beginning of 2002, that is, 22 February 2002. However, Articles 11 and 12 and 14–20 which deal with the food safety requirements do not apply until 1 January 2005.

THE EUROPEAN FOOD SAFETY AUTHORITY

The EFSA's mission

Article 22 of the Regulation sets out the mission of the EFSA. It is to provide scientific advice, and scientific and technical support for the Community's legislation

[27] OJ L 109, 06/05/2000 P. 29–42.

and policies in all fields, which have a direct or indirect impact on food and feed safety. The information it provides should be independent. It is also to be responsible for risk communication. The EFSA is to aim to contribute to a high level of protection of human life and health, and in this respect take into account animal health and welfare, plant health and the environment, in the context of the operation of the internal market.

The most pressing task of the EFSA is to help restore consumer confidence in food safety. The focus of the EFSA is food safety. This is emphasised through its name, which was amended to include the word 'safety' (rather than the 'European Food Authority' as initially proposed) by Mr Philip Whitehead, the European Parliament's Rapporteur. The concern was that if the EFSA had been given a remit and competence that was too wide this could serve to undermine its ability to deliver the necessary scientific excellence in all areas. Moreover, its budget and personnel are relatively small compared to other authorities, for example, the UK's Food Standards Agency, and there is a fear that it could be overstretched. In addition, the forthcoming enlargement of the European Union will present additional important challenges in respect of ensuring a consistent level of food safety and consumer protection across the expanded EU.

Risk communication

One of the key functions of the EFSA is risk communication. This involves letting consumers know about risks in easily understandable language. Explaining what the risk means for the consumer, in other words, putting it into context. The EFSA will also communicate about nutrition within the context of food safety. However, it must not stray into the public health dimension of nutrition as this is not within its remit.

It will also be key to ensuring consistent messages are delivered in a rational way to consumers throughout the European Union. The timing of the delivery of these messages will be a key factor. For example, the information should be reviewed and should not panic consumers unnecessarily. However, it is essential that consumers have all the relevant information to minimise the effect of any potential risks. It will be interesting to see how this area of competence develops.

The EFSA will be responsible for risk assessment and communication. However, in communicating a risk, identified by scientists to the public, it will be essential to outline what measures are to be taken by the risk managers in order to address that risk. There is a need to ensure coherence and consistency in the messages delivered to the public by the EFSA and the national food authorities in order to establish the confidence of both consumers and trading partners.

The EFSA will act as an arbiter between diverging scientific opinions, between the European Agencies, and between the European and National Agencies. The EFSA will be a 'go-between' for the national food authorities. It will be the central authority to which all Member States must send relevant information, including information of potential risks and/or food scares. In other words it will not just communicate information it will also receive communications and then be responsible for co-ordination.

It is anticipated that the EFSA will have a key role in the rapid alert system. It will assist in any crisis situation. However, it should not take any management decisions in either the rapid alert system or a crisis situation. It will be for the Commission and the other institutions, as appropriate, to take such decisions in line with the separation of responsibility for risk assessment and risk management (see below for consideration of the rapid alert system in more detail).

The Structure of the EFSA

The EFSA comprises of:

- a management board;
- an executive director and his staff;
- an advisory forum;
- a scientific committee and scientific panels.

Management Board

The Management Board is composed of 14 members appointed by the Council, in consultation with the European Parliament, from a list drawn up by the Commission, which included a number of candidates substantially higher than the number of members to be appointed. A representative of the Commission also sits on the board. The Regulation specifically states that four members of the Management Board should have their backgrounds in organisations representing consumers and other interests in the food chain. Normally the mandate of members of the Management Board will be for 4 years. However, in the first mandate half the members were appointed for 6 years. This is to hopefully achieve consistency in the work of the Management Board. The first mandate of the Management Board was granted by the Agriculture Council on the 15 July 2002. The Council appointed the 14 members. The Council is of the opinion that four of the members of the Management Board have their background in organisations representing consumers and other interests in the food chain. The list of appointed members from 1 July 2002 to 30 June 2008 is as follows:

- Giorgio Calabrese (Professor at the University of Cattolica, Italy),
- Catherine Geslain-Laneelle (Director General at the Ministry of Agriculture, France),
- Matthias Ludwig Horst (Director General of the Federal Association of the German Food and Drink Industry),
- Deirdre Hutton (President of the National Consumer Council, UK),
- Joao Pedro Machado (President of the Confederation of Farmers, Portugal),
- Pirkko Marjatta Raumenaa (Finland),
- Patrick Gerard Wall (Director General of the Food Safety Authority, Ireland).

The list of appointed members from 1 July 2002 to 30 June 2006 is as follows:

- Angeliki Assimakopoulou (former Director General of the State Chemical Laboratory, Greece),
- Ernst Bobeck (Federal Ministry of Social Security, Austria),
- Carlos Escribano Mora (Director General for stock farming at the Ministry of Agriculture, Spain),
- Peter Gaemelke (President of the Agriculture Council, Denmark),
- Bart Sangster (Unilever Vice-President, The Netherlands),
- Alexander Stuart Slorach (Deputy Director General of the National Food Administration, Sweden),
- Roland Vaxelaire (Managing Director of Carrefour, Belgium),

Many of these members have links with Governmental organisations. It could be that the Governmental organisation, or a Government of a Member State, could be represented on both the Management Board and in the Advisory Forum which is in fact the official body on which the Member States are represented (see below). At Council level, the UK and Italy initially blocked approval of the Management Board because of the lack of representation of consumer organizations.

The Management Board's role is to ensure that the EFSA carries out its mission and performs the tasks assigned to it as set down in Regulation 178/2002.[28] The Management Board is to adopt the EFSA's programme of work annually as well as a revisable multi-annual programme. The Management Board is to ensure that these programmes are consistent with the Community's legislative and policy priorities in the area of food safety. The Management Board is also responsible for the budget of the EFSA. It is not, however responsible for the day-to-day running of the EFSA which is the role of the Executive Director and his staff.

Executive Director

The Executive Director is appointed by the Management Board on the basis of a list of candidates proposed by the Commission following an open competition. Before the appointment the candidate put forward by the Management Board is required to make a statement before the European Parliament. The Executive Director may be removed from office by a majority of the Management Board.

The Executive Director is the legal representative of the authority and is responsible for the day-to-day administration of the EFSA. Together with the Commission he draws up a proposal for the work of the EFSA, and implements the work programmes and decisions finally adopted by the Management Board.

---

[28] OJ L 031, 01/02/2002 P. 01–24.

The first Executive Director, Geoffrey Podger, the former Chief Executive of the UK Food Standards Agency, began work in February 2003.

The Advisory Forum

The Advisory Forum is composed of representatives from competent bodies in the Member States which undertake tasks similar to those of the EFSA. There is one representative designated by each Member States to attend the Advisory Forum. Representatives may be replaced by an alternate appointed at the same time. The Regulation expressly states that members of the Advisory Forum may not be members of the Management Board. The Advisory Forum advises the Executive Director in the performance of his duties as set down under the Regulation. In particular, it advises on the drawing up of the proposal for the EFSA's work programme. The Executive Director may also ask the Advisory Forum for advice on the prioritisation of requests for scientific opinions. The Advisory Forum is designed to be a mechanism for exchange of information on potential risks and the pooling of knowledge. It is also designed to ensure close co-operation between the EFSA and the competent bodies in the Member States. This is designed to avoid the duplication of a scientific work and to promote the European network and thereby help to identify emerging risks. The Advisory Forum is chaired by the Executive Director. A Representative of the Commission may also attend the Advisory Forum.

Scientific committee and scientific panels

A scientific committee and scientific panels are responsible for the provision of the scientific opinions of the EFSA. The scientific committee is responsible for the general coordination necessary to ensure the consistency of the scientific opinion procedure. This is particularly in relation to the adoption of working procedures and harmonisation of working methods. The EFSA will provide opinions on multi-sectorial issues falling within the competence of one or more scientific panels. The scientific committee will also provide opinions on issues which do not fall within the competence of any of the scientific panels. The scientific committee is to be composed of the chairs of the scientific panels and six independent scientific experts who do not belong to any of the scientific panels.

The scientific panels are composed of independent scientific experts and at the time of writing, the newly appointed Executive Director, Geoffrey Podger, had recently appointed them. The scientific panels are as follows:

- the panel on food additives, flavourings, processing aids and material in contact with food;
- the panel on additives and products intended to be used in animal feed;
- the panel on plant health, plant protection products and their residues;
- the panel on genetically modified organisms;
- the panel on dietetic products, nutrition and allergies;

- the panel on biological hazards;
- the panel on contaminants in the food chain;
- the panel on animal health and welfare.

Scientific opinions

The EFSA is to issue a scientific opinion either at the request of the Commission or on its own initiative. The Parliament or a Member State may request the EFSA to issue a scientific opinion on matters falling within its mission. If the EFSA has already delivered a scientific opinion on the specific topic of a request, the EFSA may refuse if it can prove that there are no new scientific developments justifying re-examination. Although there is no specific time-limit set down in Community legislation the EFSA, will be expected to issue scientific opinions within a time-limit specified in the request for the opinion. However, this can be delayed in duly justified circumstances.

The EFSA will exercise vigilance to identify any potential source of divergence between its scientific opinion and the scientific opinions issued by other bodies carrying out similar tasks, for example, Member State authorities. If the EFSA identifies a potential source of divergence it is to contact the body in question to ensure that all relevant scientific information is shared in order to identify potentially contentious scientific issues. When a divergence has been identified the body in question should co-operate, with the EFSA's scientific committees, to resolve the divergence or to prepare a joint document clarifying the contentious scientific issues and identifying the relevant uncertainties in the data. Such a document would be made public.

The EFSA also has other roles, for example, scientific and technical assistance as requested by the Commission, conducting scientific studies and the collection of scientific and technical data in the fields within its mission, particularly in relation to food consumption and the exposure of individuals to risks related to the consumption of food, the incidents and prevalence of biological risk, contaminants in food and feed, and residues. The EFSA is also required to monitor the systems for searching, collating, collecting and analysing information and data with a view to identifying emerging risks.

Dispute over the location of the EFSA

The permanent location of the EFSA has not been decided. In order to ensure that the EFSA is up and running as soon as possible temporary office space was made available in Brussels from the beginning of 2002. Certain stakeholders believe that the EFSA should be located as closely as possible to the European Commission and DG Sanco. This is particularly the view of many members of DG Sanco and the European Parliament. David Byrne in the summer of 2002 suggested that the EFSA provisionally remained in Brussels for 2 or 3 years before a decision is made on the merits of the various candidate cities. The candidates appear to be Barcelona

(Spain), Parma (Italy), Lille (France) and Helsinki (Finland). The seat of the EFSA has provoked much political debate and it is unlikely that it will be resolved easily. At the time of writing, no political agreement could be reached. Initially the EP had withheld approximately half the EFSA's budget foreseen for 2003 in an attempt to force a decision. However in April 2003 this money was released in order not to hinder the work of the EFSA.

Rapid Alert System, Crisis Management and Emergencies

Regulation 178/2002 establishes a rapid alert system for the notification of a direct or indirect risk to human health deriving from food or feed. It is established as a network involving Member States, the Commission and the EFSA. This builds on a system that was already operational within DG Sanco but takes a more holistic and comprehensive approach, for example, including animal health issues. When a member of the network has any information relating to a serious direct or indirect risk to human health from food or feed, the information is to be immediately notified to the Commission under the rapid alert system. The Commission shall transmit this information immediately to the other members of the network. The EFSA may supplement the notification with any scientific or technical information which will facilitate rapid appropriate risk management action by the Member States. Member States are to immediately notify the Commission under the rapid alert system of:

- measures which they adopt aimed to restrict the placing on the market or the withdrawal from the market or recall of food or feed in order to protect human health; or
- of any recommendation or agreement with professional operators which is aimed at preventing, limiting or imposing specific conditions on the placing on the market or with the eventual use of food and feed, on account of a serious risk to human health; or
- any rejection related to an indirect or direct risk to human health of a container or cargo of food or feed by a competent authority at a border post of the EU.

Information available to the members of the network relating to a risk to human health posed by food and feed shall in general be available to the public. Therefore, in general the public will have access to the information on a product identification, the nature of the risk and the measures taken. There is a provision in Regulation 178/2002 that obliges the members of the network to take care not to reveal information that is covered by professional secrecy. However, that information can be released if necessary in order to protect human health.

The Regulation provides for emergency measures for food and feed of community origin or imported from third countries. These include the suspension of the placing of the product on the market or preventing its importation, and laying down special conditions for the food or feed. Member States are also permitted to take into protective measures in the event that the Commission has not yet acted.

The Commission in co-operation with the EFSA and the Member States is to draw up a general plan for crisis management in the field of food and feed safety. The plan should specify different types of situations, and the practical procedures necessary to manage a crisis including the principles of transparency and communication strategies. The Regulation also makes provision for the Commission to set up a crisis unit in which the EFSA shall participate.

Chapter 5

Food Labelling

During the 1970s (see Chapter 11 on vertical directives) the EC developed several compositional laws relating to foodstuff. However it was also necessary to introduce a new system of labelling, presentation and advertising of foodstuffs throughout the Community, in order to allow the consumer to have adequate and necessary information to choose between products whilst ensuring free movement of foodstuffs. Differences and variations between national labelling laws, regulations and administrative procedures in the Member States impeded the free movement of foodstuffs and therefore prevented the completion of a single market. The original Framework Directive 79/112/EEC[29] on food labelling was designed to meet the two aims of consumer protection and the single market. However, it was amended on several occasions with the objective of improving consumer protection. In 2000, these labelling directives were consolidated (and repealed) through the adoption of Directive 2000/13/EC[30] on the approximation of the laws of Member States relating to the labelling, presentation and advertising of foodstuffs. Member States may still decide to implement additional laws relating to food labelling provided that they do not conflict with EC law.

General Food Labelling Directive 2000/13/EC

Definition

The Directive applies to the labelling of foodstuffs that are to be delivered to the ultimate consumer or intended to be supplied to restaurants, hospitals, canteens and other similar mass caterers. Labelling is defined as:

> 'any words, particulars, trademarks, brand name, pictorial matter or symbol relating to a foodstuff and placed on any packaging, document, notice, label, wing or collar accompanying or referring to such foodstuff.'

Pre-packaged foodstuff means:

> 'any single item for presentation as such to the ultimate consumer and to mass caterers, consisting of a foodstuff and the packaging into which it is put before

[29] OJ L 033, 08/02/1979 P. 01–14.
[30] OJ L 109, 06/05/2000 P. 29–42.

being offered for sale, whether such packaging encloses the foodstuff completely or only partially, but in any case in such a way that the contents cannot be altered without opening or changing the packaging.'

Misleading labelling prohibited

Labelling must not be such as will mislead the purchaser, in particular, as to the characteristics of the foodstuff and as to its nature, identity, properties, composition, quantity, durability, origin or provenance, method of manufacture or production (Article 2). It must not mislead the consumer by attributing to the foodstuff effects or properties which it does not possess, or by suggesting the foodstuff possess special characteristics when in fact all similar foodstuffs possess such characteristics. The duty not to mislead applies to all aspects of the labelling including the product name, description, pictures or graphics, colours used on-packs, etc. In addition, these prohibitions and restrictions apply equally to the presentation of the foodstuffs, including their shape, appearance or packaging, the packaging materials used, the way they are displayed and arranged and the setting in which they are displayed, as well as the advertising of the foodstuffs.

What should be on the label

Article 3 of the Directive sets out compulsory particulars which should generally be included on the labelling of foodstuffs.[31] They are as follows:

- the name under which the product is sold;
- the list of ingredients;
- the quantity of certain ingredients or category of ingredients in certain cases;
- in the case of pre-packaged foodstuffs, the net quantity;
- the date of minimum durability 'best before date', or in the case of foodstuffs which, from the micro-biological point of view, are highly perishable, the 'use by date';
- any special storage conditions or conditions of use;
- the name or business name and address of the manufacturer or packager, or of the seller established within the Community (although there are special provisions in relation to butter);
- particulars of the place of origin or provenance where failure to give such particulars might mislead the consumer to a material degree as to the true origin or provenance of the foodstuff;

---

[31] Please note that different requirements apply to certain products, for example, designations (e.g. chocolate) or products subject to processes (e.g. irradiation) among other exceptions, exemptions and additional rules.

- instructions for use where it would be impossible to make appropriate use of the foodstuff in the absence of such instructions;
- with respect to beverages containing more than 1.2 per cent by volume of alcohol, the actual alcoholic strength by volume.

Member States may retain national provisions requiring the indication of the factory or packaging centre in respect of home production. These provisions are without prejudice to more extensive and precise regulations relating to weights and measures.

The name under which a product is sold

Article 5 of Directive 2000/13 deals with the name under which the product should be sold. It begins from the premise that if there is a name provided for the foodstuff in Community provisions, then it must be sold under that name. In the absence of any name in Community provisions, the name under which the product should be sold is the name provided for in the laws, regulations and administrative provisions applicable in the Member States. Failing this, the product should be sold under the name customary in that Member State. In the event that it does not have a customary name, it can be sold under a name which is a description of the foodstuff, and if necessary of its use, which is clear so as to allow the purchaser to know the true nature of the foodstuff and to distinguish it from other products.

The product can be sold under a 'sales name'. However, if this sales name would not enable the consumer to know the true nature of the foodstuff or to distinguish it from foodstuffs with which they could confuse it, the sales name shall be accompanied by other descriptive information which must appear in the proximity of the sales name. It is clearly stated that no trade mark, brand name or fancy name may be substituted for the name under which the product is sold.

The name under which the product is sold should also include, or be accompanied by, the particulars as to the physical condition of the foodstuffs or the specific treatment which it has undergone, for example, powdered, freeze-dried, deep frozen, concentrated, smoked, in all cases where the omission of such information could create confusion in the mind of the purchaser. If the foodstuff has been treated with ionizing radiation it must bear a specified indication. In English this is either 'irradiated' or 'treated with ionizing radiation'. In practice, use of irradiation, as a treatment to ensure the safety of food, is generally prevented by negative public perception.

List of ingredients

An ingredient is defined as 'any substance, including additives, used in the manufacture or preparation of foodstuffs and still present in the finished product, even if in altered form'. Article 6 of the Directive provides that ingredients need not be listed for fresh fruit and vegetables, cheese, butter, fermented milk and cream, or for products comprising of a single ingredient where the trade name is the same as the ingredient name or the trade name enables the nature of the ingredient to be clearly identified.

Additives whose presence in a given foodstuff is solely due to the fact that they were contained in one or more ingredients of that foodstuff, provided that they serve no technological function in the finished product, do not need to be included in the ingredients list. This is more commonly known as the 'carry over principle'. Neither is it necessary to include in the ingredients list processing aids; in practise many enzymes are used as processing aids. Substances that are used as solvents or media for additives or flavourings, and are strictly necessary for that or other purposes, do not need to be included on the ingredients list.

Additives (see also Chapter 6) must be designated by the name of their category, followed by their specific name or EC number: categories of additives include colours, preservatives, thickeners, gelling agents, etc. An explanation of how flavourings should be referred to on the food label is set out in Chapter 7. Certain categories of ingredients may be referred to by the name of the category they belong to rather than the specific name, for example, sugar.

The ingredients list should include all the ingredients of the foodstuff and should be displayed in descending order of weight, recorded as at the time of their use in the manufacture of the foodstuff (in other words, when they were added to the mixing bowl). As an exception to this, added water and volatile products shall be listed in order of their weight in the finished products. Ingredients used in concentrated or dehydrated form and reconstituted at the time of manufacture should be listed in order of weight as recorded before their concentration or dehydration. In the case of concentrated or dehydrated food which are intended to be reconstituted by the addition of water, the ingredients may be listed in order of proportion in the reconstituted product provided that the list of ingredients makes this clear by the inclusion of an expression such as 'ingredients of the reconstituted product' or 'ingredients of the ready-to-use product'.

Mixtures of fruit or vegetables where no particular fruit or vegetable significantly predominates in proportion by weight, do not have to be listed in order of weight provided that the ingredients list is accompanied by an expression such as 'in variable proportion'. Mixtures of spices and herbs may also be listed 'in variable proportion'.

A compound ingredient can currently be included in the ingredients list, without detailing its ingredients, where it constitutes less than 25 per cent of the finished product. Please note, there is a proposal for EU legislation that would amend Directive 2000/13 and amend this rule. This proposal would also make it obligatory for food manufacturers to include in the list of ingredients a specific reference to ingredients known to be allergenic. When adopted, this law is expected to include a number of technical exceptions that should make it practical for manufacturers to implement the new law. The new law is expected to be adopted at EU level in autumn 2003. Once adopted, Member States will have 1 year to implement the law at national level.

The declaration of quantity of certain ingredients – quid labelling

Where the presence of a particular ingredient or category of ingredients is emphasised in the labelling of a foodstuff, the quantity of that ingredient or category of ingredients must be indicated on-pack. An ingredient or category of ingredient could be emphasised in a number of ways, including:

- when an ingredient or category of ingredients concerned appear in the name under which the foodstuff is sold or is usually associated with that name by the consumer; or
- where the ingredient or category of ingredients is emphasised on the labelling in words, pictures or graphics; or
- where the ingredient or category of ingredients concerned is essential to characterise the foodstuff and to distinguish it from products with which it might be confused because of its name or appearance.

Generally, the quantity is indicated on the label as a percentage and corresponds to the quantity of the ingredient or category of ingredients at the time of its use (i.e. at the time of adding the ingredient to the 'mixing bowl'). The Quantitative Ingredients Declaration (QUID) appears either next to the name under which the food is sold or, more usually, in the ingredients list. However, a QUID is not required in certain circumstances, such as:

- where the drained net weight is already indicated;
- where the quantities of the ingredient are already required to be given by another provision of Community law;
- in relation to an ingredient which is used in small quantities and for the purposes of flavouring; or
- in relation to an ingredient which, while appearing in the name under which the foodstuff is sold, is not such as to govern the choice of the consumer in the country of marketing because the variation in quantity is not essential to characterise the foodstuff or does not distinguish it from similar foods.

Net quantity of pre-packaged foods

The Directive requires that the net quantity of pre-packaged food must be expressed either in litres, in the case of liquids, or in kilograms in the case of the solids. If indication of a certain type of quantity, for example, a nominal quantity, minimum quantity or average quantity, is required elsewhere in Community law, in relation to a specific foodstuff, that quantity is regarded as a net quantity for the purposes of food labelling. If a solid foodstuff is presented in a liquid medium (e.g. water, brine, vinegar), the drained net weight of the foodstuff should be indicated on the label.

Where a pre-packaged item consists of two or more individual pre-packaged items containing the same quantity of the same product, the net quantity should be indicated by mentioning the net quantity contained in each individual package and then the total number of packages. However, if the total number of packages can be clearly seen from outside the pack, these particulars do not need to be displayed where at least an indication of the net quantity contained on each individual package can be seen from the outside of the pack. Where the pre-packaged item consists of two or more individual packages which are not regarded as units of sale, the net quantity should be given by indicating the total net quantity and the total number of individual packages. If the foodstuff is normally sold by number, Member States do not need to require the indication of net quantity provided that the number of items can be clearly seen and easily counted from the outside. Alternatively, the number could be indicated on-pack.

A common practical problem manufacturers face is having systems in place that ensure any piece count on-pack is accurate. Occasionally, they qualify any piece count or quantity declaration by words such as 'average', 'approximate' or 'at least'. However, any number on-pack should be accurate. The indication of any number on-pack that is not accurate, risks being considered incompatible with the legal requirements. However, if a manufacturer does choose to qualify a number, the qualification should not itself be misleading, so, for example, if a piece count is declared to be an average it must be a true average. In other words some packs will contain more than the declared average and some less. If the qualification is 'at least' all the packs should contain more than the number declared.

Please note, that, as an exception to this rule, tolerances are provided at EU level in relation to weight marking and therefore some variation is permitted. No such provision is made in relation to other information indicated on-pack. However, at EU level it is acknowledged that the declared values in relation to nutrition labelling are averages (although please note that Member States authorities may recognise different testing and calculation methods).

It is not compulsory to indicate the net quantity of a foodstuff if that foodstuff is subject to considerable losses in their volume or mass and which are sold by number or weighed in the presence of the purchaser. Neither is it compulsory to indicate the net quantity which is less than 5 g or 5 ml. However, this exception does not apply to herbs or spices. Please note that Member States can lay down higher thresholds than 5 g and 5 ml in relation to specified foods provided that this does not result in the purchaser being inadequately informed.

Date of minimum durability

In general, the 'best before date' or 'best before end of a month' should be indicated on-pack. Either the words should be accompanied by the date itself or a reference to where the date is given on the labelling, for example, 'see base of jar'. The date shall be given in days, months and years. However, if the foodstuff would not keep for more than three months the indication of the day and the month is acceptable. Foodstuff that will keep more than 3 months but not more than 18 months, an indication of the month and year will suffice, and for food which will keep more than 18 months, an indication of the year will suffice. Foodstuff which is highly perishable and therefore likely after a short period to constitute an immediate danger to health must carry the date of minimum durability by indicating the 'use by'.

The date of minimum durability is not required for:

- fresh fruit and vegetables;
- wines, liqueur wines, beverages containing 10 per cent or more by volume of alcohol;
- soft drinks, fruit juices, fruit nectars;
- alcoholic beverages in individual containers of more than 5 litres intended for supply to mass caterers;
- bakers' or pastry cooks' wares which given the nature of their content are normally consumed within 24 h of manufacture;
- vinegar;
- cooking salt;
- solid sugar;
- confectionary products consisting almost solely of flavoured or coloured sugars;
- chewing gums and similar chewing products;
- individual portions of ice cream.

Instructions for use

The instructions for use of a foodstuff should be indicated such that they are clear to a consumer. These may also affect the safety of the product, for example, if a cooking time is insufficient, the food may not be cooked, or if it is not specified to remove a product from outer packaging before cooking, the packaging could explode. There should also be clear instructions for any special storage conditions.

Name or business name and address of the manufacturer or seller or packager

The name or business name and address of the manufacturer or packager or seller established within the European Union must be indicated on-pack. The requirement that the seller be established within the European Union is generally because sellers are usually smaller enterprises and in the event that the authorities wish to locate them or a consumer contacts them, they would be harder to locate when they are outside the EU. However, manufacturers and packagers tend to be larger businesses which are easily identifiable by authorities or consumers.

Particulars of the place of origin or provenance

It is only necessary to indicate the particulars of the place of origin or provenance if failure to do so may mislead the consumer to a material degree as to the true origin or provenance of the foodstuff, for example, Chinese crackers produced in Italy. In this case, the fact that they have been manufactured or packed in Italy should be indicated on-pack as the consumer could be misled into believing that the crackers originate from China. It could be that they are produced in the same style or recipe as a traditional dish originated from a certain country or region and this should be explained. However, some Member States, in particular the United Kingdom, have guidance on when words such as authentic and traditional should be used. The use of such descriptions is being considered at EU level as part of the General Labelling Review announced by the European Commission in the summer of 2002 (see below). There are also strict rules in respect of products that have been registered under the protected designation of origin, geographical indication and traditional speciality guaranteed legislation (see Chapter 13).

Exemptions and exceptions

Limited particulars must be given on the label, to comply with the requirements of this Directive, where a product is intended to be sold to the ultimate consumer but is being marketed at a stage prior to sale to the ultimate consumer (and where it is not sold to mass caterer at that stage) or is intended for supply to a mass caterer for preparation, processing, splitting or cutting up. Moreover, small packages, and in certain circumstances glass bottles, need not carry all the particulars normally required.

There are also exemptions for foodstuffs that are packaged on the premises at the consumer's request or are pre-packaged for direct sale. Provisions are made for national laws to provide exemptions for the labelling of foodstuffs presented in fancy packaging such as figurines or souvenirs. These exemptions and exceptions are broadly worded at EU level and must be implemented and given force at Member State level.

Language

Under the Directive Member States have to ensure that the particulars of foodstuffs are provided in a language easily understood by the consumer. Obviously, the official language of Member State will probably be the most easily understood by the consumer. However, Member States are not permitted to prohibit particulars by virtue of the fact they are not in the national language. Multi-lingual labelling is permitted and is often used by multinationals.

In particular, it is noted that the ECJ has confirmed that a requirement by a Member State for a particular language to be used on-pack, for example, for the product name, is disproportionate and is not in accordance with EC law because it can inhibit the free movement of goods. At the time of writing the European Commission had recently announced that it has sent a reasoned opinion to France for its requirement that the product name always be in French (this is the infamous Loi Tourbon). The Commission is of the view that, for example, 'Chicken Wings' labelled as such in English, and pictured on-pack will be easily understood by the French customer, yet this is prohibited by French law. If France does not respond and amend its laws adequately, this could result in the European Commission taking the French Government to court.

Nutrition Labelling

Council Directive 90/496[32] sets out the requirements for nutrition labelling (including the declaration of vitamin and mineral content). Nutrition labelling is optional unless a nutrition claim appears in the labelling, presentation or advertising, in which case it is compulsory. A nutrition claim means any representation and advertising message which states, suggests or implies that a foodstuff has particular nutrition properties. Nutrition labelling consists of either:

- 'the big four' – energy value, protein, carbohydrate and fat; or
- 'the big eight' – energy value, protein, carbohydrate, sugars, fat, saturates, fibre, and sodium.

Generally, a declaration of 'the big four' will be sufficient. However, 'the big eight' declaration is required where a nutrition claim is made for sugars, saturates, fibre or sodium. The declaration should relate to the food as sold.

Nutrition labelling may also include amounts of one or more of the following: starch, polyols, mono-saturates; polyunsaturates, cholesterol and certain vitamins and minerals. Where the amount of polyunsaturates and/or mono-saturates and/or cholesterol rate is given, the amounts of saturates should be declared.

The information should be given per 100g or per 100ml. In addition, this information may be given per serving or per portion. Information on vitamins and minerals should be expressed as a percentage of the recommended daily allowance.

Where sugars and/or polyols are declared, the declaration shall immediately be followed by a declaration as to the carbohydrate content detailing sugars, polyols and starches. Where the amount and/or type of fatty acid and/or cholesterol rate is declared, there shall be a declaration of the amount of total fat detailing saturates mono-unsaturates, polyunsaturates and cholesterol.

Article 6(8) provides that the declared values that appear on-pack shall be 'average values' and should be based on one of the following:

- the manufacturer's analysis of the food;
- a calculation from the known or actual average values of the ingredients used; or
- a calculation from generally established and accepted data.

---

[32] OJ L 276, 06/10/1990 P. 40–44.

The relevant authorities in the Member States sometimes prefer particular methods of analysis to be used to calculate the nutrient levels when the manufacturer is analysing the food (under the point (a) above). For example, the AOAC method for calculating fibre (which includes other types of fibre in addition to polysaccharides) content is normally the preferred method of analysis (although until recently it was the Englyst method, which includes polysaccharides but excludes cellulose and resistant starch, preferred in the United Kingdom).

At EU level, it is acknowledged that the declared values in relation to nutrition labelling are averages. However, it is important to ensure that the declared amounts are true averages (and not, for example, estimations or approximate numbers) and that any variations are reasonable. If this is not the case, not only will the declarations be in breach of Directive 90/496,[33] but they could also be considered to be misleading. As discussed above, Article 2 of the Labelling Directive 2000/13 requires that a label should not mislead the consumer. For example, if testing shows that a large proportion of a product consistently contains less than the quantity of vitamin C declared on-pack, then the declared value will not be a true average.

The Commission is currently reviewing nutrition labelling requirements. They are concerned that currently consumers do not find the nutrition information provided to be meaningful. A proposal to reform the requirements for nutrition labelling is expected at the end of 2003.

The Future of Food Labelling

In the summer of 2002, Commissioner Byrne, the EU Commissioner for Health and Consumer Protection, launched a fundamental review of the labelling of foodstuffs. The first stage of this review will be a report to be prepared by external consultants which could be finished by the end of 2003. The review is designed to consider what information should be given on labels. Commissioner Byrne is concerned that adequate, clear and meaningful information is made available to consumers. This would enable them to make informed choices. However, they should not be overloaded with information and the labelling requirements should not be disproportionately burdensome on industry.

[33] OJ L 276, 06/10/1990 P. 40–44.

Chapter 6

Additives

Introduction

In the 1980s concerns were raised that the differences between Member States' legislation covering food additives were barriers to trade. As a result of this and to further protect consumers' health, it was agreed that the legislation concerning food additives should be harmonised at EU level. In 1988 the Framework Directive 89/107[34] was adopted paving the way for further directives for specific categories of food additives and thereby harmonising at Community level food additives' legislation.

Directive 89/107, the Framework Directive, provides a definition of food additives, a comprehensive list of categories of food additives and the criteria for their approval. Under the Framework Directive three specific directives have been adopted covering sweeteners, colours and 'other food additives'. These specific directives have set out lists of authorised food additives which can be used within the European Union and must be accepted by the Member States. Only those food additives which have been included in these authorised lists may be used in the manufacture or preparation of foodstuffs within the European Union.[35] Maximum limits for most authorised food additives have been prescribed, and for a number of food additives restricted use is permitted in only specified foodstuffs.

The Commission has recently proposed amending the existing directives. In the White Paper on food safety[36] the Commission suggested that it should be given powers to maintain Community lists of authorised food additives. Moreover, the Commission has also suggested that the authorised lists of colours, sweeteners and other food additives need to be updated.

It is important to note that flavourings are not considered as food additives for the purpose of these Directives. However, flavour enhancers is one of the categories set out in Directive 89/107 and is defined in Directive 95/2.[37]

There are four main directives that legislate at EU level food additives:

- Council Directive 89/107, as amended by Directive 94/34,[38] provides a framework for the authorisation of food additives;

---

[34] OJ No L 040, 11/02/1989 P. 2–33.

[35] The situation for flavourings is currently different, see Chapter 7.

[36] Com (1999) 719 Final.

[37] OJ L 061, 18/03/1995 P. 1–40.

[38] OJ No L237, 10/09/1994 P. 1–2.

- European Parliament and Council Directive 94/36[39] lays down rules for colours;
- European Parliament and Council Directive 94/35,[40] as amended by Directive 96/83,[41] lays down rules for the use of sweeteners;
- European Parliament and Council Directive 95/2, as amended by Directives 96/85,[42] 98/72[43] and 2001/5,[44] lays down rules for the authorisation of food additives other than colours and sweeteners.

This chapter will look at the requirements of each of these directives in turn.

Directive 89/107 – Food Additives Authorised for use in Foodstuffs Intended for Human Consumption

Directive 89/107 was adopted to harmonise the laws of the Member States concerning food additives. The Directive provides a framework for the subsequent specific Directives on food additives. It provides a definition of food additives:

- a substance that is not normally consumed as a food and not normally used as an ingredient of food whether or not it has a nutritive value;
- it is deliberately added to food for a technological purpose in the manufacture, processing, preparation, treatment, packaging, transport or storage of such food;
- the food additive or its by-products may become directly or, could reasonably be expected to become, indirectly a component of the food.

The Directive does not apply to: processing aids; flavourings that are covered by Directive 88/388;[45] nutrients that are added to foodstuffs; and substances that are used to protect plants and plant products.

Categories of food additives

In Annex I of the Directive, a comprehensive list of 24 categories of food additive is set out.

Preservative	Stabilizer	Modified starch
Anti-oxidant	Colours	Glazing agent
Enzymes	Raising agent	Anti-foaming agent

[39] OJ L 237, 10/09/1994 P. 13–29.
[40] OJ L 237, 10/09/1994 P. 3–12.
[41] OJ No L104, 22/04/1997 P. 39.
[42] OJ No L086, 28/03/1997 P. 4.
[43] OJ No L 307, 17/11/1998 P. 30.
[44] OJ No L 055, 24/02/2001 P. 59–61.
[45] OJ No L184, 15/07/1988 P. 61–66.

Emulsifier	Flavour enhancer	Flour treatment agent
Emulsifying salt	Acid	Firming agent
Thickener	Acidity regulator	Humectant
Gelling agent	Anti-caking agent	Sequestrant
Bulking agent	Propellent gas and packaging gas	Sweeteners

A food additive is included in a particular category based on the principal function normally associated with the food additive. This does not prevent a food additive from being authorised for several functions, for example, carrageenan can be used as a stabiliser or a thickener, and sorbitol can be used as a sweetener or as a humectant. It is therefore always necessary to determine the purpose or function of the additive in the particular product to assess which specific directive and provisions would apply in each case.

General criteria

Food additives can only be authorised if they comply with the general criteria set out in Annex II of the Directive:

- a food business must demonstrate that there is a reasonable technical need for the food additive;
- the purpose of the food additive cannot be achieved by other means which are economically and technologically practical;
- the food additives must present no hazard to consumer health at the levels set in the specific directives;
- the food additive must not mislead consumers.

In addition, a food additive can only be authorised if a need for the additive has been shown and the use of the food additive would serve one of the following purposes:

(a) to preserve the nutritional quality of the food;
(b) to improve the keeping quality or stability of a food or its organoleptic properties; the additives cannot be used to change the nature, substance or quality of the food in such a way that it would deceive the consumer;
(c) to assist in the manufacture, processing, preparation, treatment, packing, transport or storage of the food; food additives cannot be used to disguise faulty raw materials or undesirable practices by food businesses.

Directive 89/107 provides that to ensure that additives are not harmful, they must undergo toxicological tests. In particular, the possibility of any cumulative effect must be considered. Food additives must also be 'under continuous observation' and comply with approved purity criteria (considered later on in this chapter).

The Directive sets out the information that must be given when a food additive is approved including the circumstances in which the food additive could be used, and the foodstuffs to which it could be added. Only the lowest level of the additive that will fulfil its purpose can be permitted. Account is taken of acceptable daily intakes when acceptable levels are set.

A Member State can, if it has received new information or the existing information has been reassessed, temporarily suspend or restrict the use of a food additive even though it complies with the additives directives. The Member State must have detailed grounds for believing that the food additive, if used in food, would 'endanger human health'. In such circumstances the Member State must inform the other Member States and the Commission. The Commission then investigates the allegation and if it considers that the authorisation of the food additive should be amended, the comitology procedure will be followed to adopt these amendments.

To enable food businesses to take advantage of scientific or technical developments, a Member State is allowed to provisionally authorise, within its territory, a food additive that falls within one of the specified categories of food additives. These 'authorised additives' must be monitored. The Member State must inform the other Member States and the Commission within two months, and can only authorise the 'new' food additive for a maximum of 2 years during which time the Member State can request that the food additive is authorised throughout the Community under the appropriate directive. If a request is made and the Commission fails to initiate proceedings to amend the list of authorised additives within 2 years or the Council does not act within 18 months, after having received the proposal from the Commission, the authorisation in the specific Member State would be cancelled.

Derogations for traditional foodstuffs

The framework Directive was amended in 1994 by Directive 94/34/EC to allow Member States to prohibit certain food additives in the production of traditional foods. Member States were only permitted to 'maintain' a prohibition that was already in place on 1 January 1992, without prejudice to Regulations 2081/92[46] and 2082/92[47] (see Chapter 13 on Agricultural Products). Member States were obliged to send to the Commission a list of traditional foodstuffs that they wanted to be covered by Directive 94/34.

Decision 292/97/EC[48] sets out a list of traditional foodstuffs in which Member States can continue to prohibit the use of certain food additives. The list contains 14 foodstuffs from nine Member States. In Annex II the Member State, the foodstuff and the categories of additives which may continue to be banned are listed in a table. For example, France can continue to ban the use of all food additives in traditional French bread.

---

[46] OJ No L208, 24/07/1992 P. 1–8.

[47] OJ No L208, 24/07/1992 P. 9–14.

[48] OJ No L048, 19/02/1997 P. 13–15.

Labelling requirements

The Directive sets out detailed provisions for the labelling of food additives. Member States are not allowed to adopt more stringent provisions relating to the indication of the prescribed particulars. These particulars must be set out in the 'language most easily understandable to purchasers'. An alternative language can only be used if other measures are taken to ensure that the purchaser understands the information. The Directive confirms that the prescribed information can be indicated in various languages.

Different labelling requirements are given for food additives intended for sale to the ultimate consumer, and those food additives not intended for sale to the ultimate consumer. However, all prescribed particulars must be clearly set out legible and indelible on the container or packaging of the food additive.

Food additives intended for sale to businesses. Food additives that are not intended for sale to the ultimate consumer must carry prescribed information including:

- (a) for each food additive the name given to the food additive in Community provisions and its EEC number, where this does not exist, then a description of the food additive must be used so that the particular food additive cannot be confused with other food additives; the information must be given in descending order of weight;
- (b) the statement 'for use in food', or 'restricted use in food', or a statement as to its intended food use;
- (c) conditions of storage and use, if necessary;
- (d) directions for use, if necessary to ensure that the food additive is appropriately used;
- (e) the batch or lot mark;
- (f) the name or business name and address of the manufacturer or packager, or of a seller established in the Community;
- (g) the net quality;
- (h) any other information required by the specific directives.

To reduce the amount of information set out on the packaging or containers of food additives, the Directive does allow some information, including requirements (d)–(f) set out above, to appear on the documents supplied before or on delivery of the additives instead of on the packaging or containers. However, if businesses take advantage of this provision the statement 'intended for the manufacture of foodstuffs and not for retail sale' must also appear on a conspicuous part of the packaging or container.

Food additives intended for sale to the ultimate consumer. Food additives intended for sale to the ultimate consumer must carry prescribed information including:

- (i) the name under which the product is sold, that is, the name provided in Community provisions, plus its EEC number, for example, 'Colour-Curcumin' or 'Colour E100', where this does not exist a precise description of the product is required;

(ii) the information set out above for food additives intended for businesses.

Directive 2000/13[49] lays down the rules for Member States relating to the labelling, presentation and advertising of foodstuffs (see Chapter 5). It does however specifically refer to the labelling of food additives. In Annex II of the Directive, a list of categories of food additives is given. The list gives the same categories as those set out in Directive 89/107, except for sequestrates, enzymes and packaging gas. Directive 2000/13 requires that ingredients belonging to one of the categories given in Annex II must be designated (in the ingredients list) by the name of the category followed by the specific name or EEC number of the ingredient. It clarifies that if an ingredient belongs to more than one of the categories the appropriate category should be selected based on the principle function of the ingredient in the particular foodstuff.

Processing aids. As explained above, processing aids are expressly excluded from the scope of the framework Directive. Processing aids are defined in the Directive as:

- any substance not consumed as a food ingredient by itself;
- intentionally used in the processing of raw materials, foods or their ingredients, to fulfil a technological purpose during treatment or processing;
- which may result in the unintentional but technically unavoidable presence of residues of the substance or its derivatives in the final product.

Residues that remain in the final product must not present any health risk and must not have any technological effect on the finished product.

Unlike additives, there is no obligation on manufacturers to include processing aids in the list of ingredients for foodstuffs. The main differences between a processing aid and a food additive are that a processing aid:

- fulfils a technological purpose only during treatment or processing whereas a food additive can, in addition, perform a technical purpose in the manufacture preparation, packaging, transport or storage of a foodstuff;
- can only remain in the finished product 'unintentionally as a residue' whereas a food additive may become a component of the foodstuff;
- remaining in the finished product must not have a technological effect on the finished product.

It is important to note that both food additives and processing aids cannot be a substance that is 'normally consumed as a food ingredient itself'. A substance may

---

[49] OJ No L109, 06/05/2000 P. 29–42.

comply with the definition of either an additive or a processing aid (i.e. it fulfils a technological function) and still be labelled as an ingredient if it is normally consumed as a food ingredient itself.

Specific Directives on Sweeteners, Colours and 'Other Food Additives'

Three specific Directives on food additives have been adopted as provided for in the framework Directive 89/107:

- European Parliament and Council Directive 94/36 lays down rules for colours;
- European Parliament and Council Directive 94/35, as amended by Directive 96/83, lays down rules for the use of sweeteners;
- European Parliament and Council Directive 95/2, as amended by Directives 96/85, 98/72 and 2001/5, lays down rules for the authorisation of food additives other than colours and sweeteners.

In the recital of each of the three Directives, it states that the prime consideration for rules on food additives is the need to protect and inform the consumer. Member States are also required under each of the Directives to monitor the consumption and usage of food additives.

Directive 94/35 on sweeteners for use in foodstuffs

Directive 94/35 was the first of the specific directives to be adopted in compliance with Directive 89/107. As prescribed under Directive 89/107, this Directive establishes an exclusive authorised list of sweeteners. For a sweetener to be authorised it must comply with the general criteria set out in Directive 89/107. The sweetener must perform a useful purpose, be safe and not mislead consumers. In the recital to the Directive the use of sweeteners is justified for the production of:

- energy-reduced food;
- non-cariogenic foodstuffs or food without added sugars;
- for the extension of shelf life through the replacement of sugar;
- dietetic products.

The Directive applies to food additives which are used to impart a sweet taste to foodstuffs or are used as a table-top sweetener. Foodstuffs with sweetening properties such as honey or sugar fall outside the scope of the Directive. If an additive has sweetening properties but is being used to serve a different function, such as sorbitol being used as a humectant rather than as a sweetener, it would fall outside the scope of Directive 94/35 and would fall within the scope of Directive 95/2 (see below). When deciding which provisions apply to an additive it is the function of the additive in the particular foodstuff that is decisive.

Sweeteners are prohibited from being used in food for infants and young children as set out in Directive 89/398[50] (see Chapter 9).

Authorised sweeteners

The Directive establishes an exclusive list of authorised sweeteners that can be sold to the ultimate consumer or used in the manufacture of foodstuffs.

Many of the foodstuffs and compound foods that are allowed to contain sweeteners are described as 'energy-reduced' products or products 'with no added sugar'. The Directive provides definitions for both of these types of products. No added sugar is defined as 'without any added mono- or disaccharides or any other foodstuff used for its sweetening properties'. Energy reduced products are defined as having 'an energy value reduced by at least 30 per cent compared with the original foodstuff or a similar product'.

There are currently 12 authorised sweeteners.

Sorbitol (E420)	Mannitol (E421)
Isomalt (E953)	Maltitol (E965)
Lactitol (E966)	Xylitol (E967)
Acesulfame K (E950)	Aspartame (E951)
Cyclamic acid and its Na and Contracting authority salts (E952)	Saccharin and its Na, K and Contracting authority salts (E954)
Thaumatin (E957)	Neohesperidine DC (E959)

Set out in the Annex to the Directive for each authorised sweetener is the designated EEC number, the name of the sweetener, the maximum usable dose, and the particular foodstuffs in which the sweetener is permitted to be used. For example aspartame (E 951) can only be used in chewing gum that contains no added sugar with a maximum useable dose of 5500 mg/kg.

Maximum useable dose. For the purposes of the Directive, maximum useable dose refers to ready-to-eat foodstuffs prepared according to the 'instructions for use'. There is no maximum useable dose indicated for a group of authorised sweeteners often referred to as polyols. The dose indicated for these sweeteners is 'quantum satis'. In 1996 the Directive was amended by Directive 96/83[51] to clarify that quantum satis means that no maximum dose is specified. However where 'quantum satis' is indicated manufacturers are obliged to use the authorised food additives:

- in accordance with good manufacturing practice;

---

[50] OJ No L 186, 30/06/1989 P. 27–32.
[51] OJ L 048, 19/02/1997 P. 16–19.

- the dose level must not be higher than is necessary to achieve the intended purpose;
- consumers must not be misled.

Carry over principle/compound foodstuffs. The Directive (amended by Directive 96/83) permits the presence of an authorised sweetener in a compound foodstuff insofar as the sweetener is allowed in one of the ingredients of the compound foodstuffs and the compound foodstuff:

- does not contain added sugar or is energy reduced; or
- is a dietary foodstuffs intended for a low calorie diet; or
- has a long shelf life.

A sweetener is also permitted in a foodstuff if the foodstuff is intended to only be used in the preparation of a compound product where the compound product complies with this Directive.

Labelling of sweeteners. The Directive sets out strict labelling obligations on those who are placing tabletop sweeteners on the market in addition to the labelling obligations set out in the framework Directive described above. A tabletop sweetener must be labelled using the name of the sweetening substance '… -based tabletop sweetener', for example, 'saccharin-based tabletop sweetener'. The label must also carry additional warnings if the tabletop sweetener contains aspartame or polyols:

- aspartame – 'contains a source of phenylalanine';
- polyols – 'excessive consumption may induce a laxative effect'. Approved polyols include sorbitol, mannitol, isomalt, maltitol, lacitol and xylitol.

Labelling of compound foodstuffs containing sweeteners. Council Directive 96/21[52] sets out prescribed labelling for foodstuffs containing sweeteners. Foodstuffs containing a sweetener or sweeteners authorised under Directive 94/35 must bear the following descriptions accompanying the name of the product:

- 'with sweeteners'; or
- 'with sugars and sweeteners' for foodstuffs that contain both added sugars and sweeteners.

Additional warnings must be set out on the label of the foodstuffs if it contains aspartame or more than 10 per cent added polyols:

- aspartame – 'contains a source of phenylalanine';
- polyols – 'excessive consumption may produce laxative effects'.

---

[52] OJ L 088, 05/04/1996 P. 5–6.

Comitology procedure. The Directive provides a procedure for determining future labelling and warning requirements. The same procedure is also used for solving differences of opinion which may arise as to whether a foodstuff belongs to one of the categories listed in the Annex, and whether a sweetener can be used in a given foodstuff under the terms of the Directive. Where such issues arise, the matter is referred to the Standing Committee for Foodstuffs by its chairman on his own initiative or at the request of a Member State. The Commission submits to the Committee a draft of the measures that it believes should be taken. The Committee gives its opinion on these proposed measures. The Commission can adopt the measures if they are in accordance with the opinion of the Committee. However, if the Committee does not agree with the measures proposed by the Commission, the matter is referred to the Council. If the Council fails to act within 3 months, the measures proposed can be adopted by the Commission.

The Directive does not set out a procedure for determining whether a substance is a sweetener within the meaning of the Directive (see section on 'Proposals').

Directive 94/36 on Colours for use in Foodstuffs

Directive 94/36 on colours for use in foodstuffs was the second specific directive to be adopted as prescribed in Directive 88/107. Colours are defined for the purpose of the Directive as substances which 'add or restore colour in a food'. These additives can include natural constituents of foodstuffs and natural sources however they cannot be a substance that is normally consumed as foodstuffs, nor used as characteristic ingredients of food. Colours also include preparations that are obtained from foods and other natural source materials obtained by physical and/or chemical extraction resulting in a selective extraction in the pigments relative to the nutritious or aromatic constituents.

The following substances are not considered to be colours for the purpose of the Directive:

- Foodstuffs, dried or in a concentrated form, and flavourings incorporated during the manufacture of compound foodstuffs for their aromatic, sapid or nutritious properties together with a secondary colouring effect, for example, paprika, turmeric and saffron.
- Colours used for the colouring of the inedible external part of foodstuffs, for example cheese coatings do not fall within the scope of this Directive. However, only colours set out in Annex I of the Directive may be used for the decorative colouring of eggshells or for the stamping of eggshells (Regulation 1274/91[53]).

---

[53] OJ L 121, 16/05/1991 P. 11–24.

There are five Annexes to the Directive. Annex I of the Directive establishes an exclusive list of over 40 authorised additives that can be used to colour foodstuffs. Only those 'colours' included in the list can be used as colours in foodstuffs. The Directive also determines which colours can be sold directly to consumers. Eight of the authorised colours set out in Annex I cannot be sold directly to consumers.

Colours can only be used in the foodstuffs specified in Annexes III, IV, and V part 2 in accordance with the conditions set out in the annexes. Annex II provides a list of over 30 foodstuffs that cannot contain added colours unless a specific exception is given in Annex III, IV or V. This list includes unprocessed foods, honey, and oils and fats of animal or vegetable origin.

Unprocessed foodstuff is defined as 'not having undergone any treatment resulting in a substantial change in the original state of the foodstuffs'. However foodstuffs that have been divided, parted, severed, boned, minced, skinned, pared, peeled, ground, cut, cleaned, trimmed, deep-frozen, frozen, chilled, milled, packed or unpacked are not considered to have been processed.

Annex III establishes a list of foodstuffs which may only contain prescribed colours, for example, the only colour that can be used in butter is carotenes (E160a). Annex IV sets out a list of 10 colours that may only be used for certain foodstuffs, for example, gold (E 175) can only be used in the external coating of confectionary, the decoration of chocolates and in liqueurs.

Annex V is divided into two parts. Part one gives a list of 15 colours that can be used in the foodstuffs set out in Part two of the annex, and all other foodstuffs except those listed in Annexes II and III. Part two gives a list of colours that can be used singly or in combination in the prescribed foodstuffs up to the maximum level given, for example, for mustard the maximum level given is 300 mg/kg. However for five foodstuffs colours can be used up to the limit given in the table but quantities for each of four prescribed colours, including Brown HT (E 155), cannot be more than 50 mg/kg.

Carry over principle/compound foodstuff. Colours are permitted in a compound foodstuff, except those mentioned in Annex II, where the colour is permitted in one of the ingredients of the compound foodstuff. A colour is also allowed in a foodstuff if the foodstuff is to be used in a compound product and the compound foodstuff complies with the Directive.

Comitology procedure. The Directive provides a procedure for deciding whether a particular foodstuff belongs to a category of foods mentioned in the annexes, and whether a substance is deemed to be a colour for the purposes of the Directive. The matter is referred to the Standing Committee for Foodstuffs by its chairman on his own initiative or at the request of a Member State. The Commission submits to the Committee a draft of measures that should be taken. The Committee gives its opinion on these proposed measures. The Commission can adopt the measures if they are in accordance with the opinion of the Committee. However, if the Committee does not agree with the measures proposed by the Commission, the matter is referred to the Council. If the Council fails to act within 3 months, the measures proposed can be adopted by the Commission.

Directive on Food Additives other than Colours and Sweeteners (95/2)

Directive 95/2 is the most recent specific directive to have been adopted forming part of the comprehensive Directive 89/107. The Directive applies to additives that fall within the 21 categories set out below and provides definitions for each of the categories:

Preservative	Flavour enhancer	Glazing agent
Anti-oxidant	Acid	Flour treatment agent
Emulsifier	Acidity regulator	Firming agent
Emulsifying salt	Anti-caking agent	Humectant
Thickener	Modified starch	Sequestrant
Gelling agent	Raising agent	Bulking agent
Stabilizer	Anti-foaming agent	Propellent gas and packaging gas

Originally flour treatment agents, other than emulsifiers, were excluded from the scope of the Directive. However, in 1998 the Directive was amended, by Directive 98/72,[54] to include flour treatment agents.

The Directive sets out a list of substances that are not food additives for the purpose of this Directive:

- substances used for treatment of drinking water as provided for in Directive 80/778/EEC;[55]
- products containing pectin and derived from dried apple pomace or peel of citrus fruits, or from a mixture of both, by the action of dilute acid followed by partial neutralization with sodium or potassium salts ('liquid pectin');
- chewing gum bases;
- white or yellow dextrin, roasted or dextrinated starch, starch modified by acid or alkali treatment, bleached starch, physically modified starch and starch treated by amylolitic enzymes;
- ammonium chloride;
- blood plasma, edible gelatin, protein hydrolysates and their salts;
- milk protein and gluten;
- amino acids and their salts other than glutamic acid, glycine, cysteine and cystine and their salts and having no additive function;
- caseinates and casein;
- insulin.

---

[54] OJ L 295, 04/11/1998 P. 18–30.

[55] OJ No L229, 30.8.1980, P. 11–29.
Directive as last amended by Directive 91/692/EEC (OJ No L 377, 31.12.1991, P. 48).

Only those additives listed in the annexes to the Directive may be used in foodstuffs for the purposes indicated in the Directive, such as, preservatives, anti-caking agents and thickeners. Annex I establishes a list of food additives that are generally permitted in foodstuffs. However, there are derogations to this rule: certain foodstuffs including unprocessed foodstuffs, honey, and butter may only contain seven specified additives set out in Annex I.

Again unprocessed foodstuff is defined as 'not having undergone any treatment resulting in a substantial change in the original state of the foodstuffs'. However foodstuffs that have been divided, parted, severed, boned, minced, skinned, pared, peeled, ground, cut, cleaned, trimmed, deep frozen, frozen, chilled, milled, packed or unpacked are not considered to have been processed.

Annex II of the Directive sets out a list of foodstuffs in which only a limited number of the additives given in Annex I can be used with a specified maximum level for example, refined olive oil may only contain the additive alpha-tocopherol (E307) with a maximum level of 200 mg/1.

Annex III refers to permitted preservatives and antioxidants. It sets out which preservatives and antioxidants can be used in specified foods. It also gives the maximum levels allowed.

Annex IV sets out 'other permitted additives'. The additives listed in Annex IV can only be used in the specified foodstuffs under the conditions given. For example, the additive carbamide (EU 927B) is only permitted in chewing gum that does not contain added sugars. The maximum levels indicated in Annex IV refer to foodstuffs that are ready for consumption after having been prepared in compliance with the manufacturer's instructions.

Only those food additives specified in Annex VI are permitted in foods for infants and young children as referred to in Directive 89/398/EEC including foods for infants and young children not in good health.

Carrier and carrier solvents. Directive 89/107 requested rules to be adopted in respect of additives' carriers and carrier solvents. Annex V of the Directive 95/2 solely concerns permitted carriers and carrier solvents. Carriers, including carrier solvents, are defined as:

> substances used to dissolve, dilute, disperse or otherwise physically modify a food additive without altering its technological functions (and without exerting any technological affect themselves) in order to facilitate its handling, application or use.

Only those additives listed in Annex V may be used as carriers or carrier solvents for food additives. Certain permitted carriers and carrier solvents can only be used in restricted circumstances, for example, ammonium phosphaditdes (E 442) can only be used with anti-oxidants.

The list of permitted carriers and carrier solvents excludes:

- substances generally considered as foodstuffs;

- those substances referred to previously that are not considered as food additives including ammonium chloride;
- substances having primarily an acid or acidity regulator function, such as citric acid and ammonium hydroxide.

Carry-over additives in compound foodstuffs. Carry-over additives are permitted in a compound foodstuff, other than those expressly exempt, to the extent that the food additive is permitted in one of the ingredients of the compound foodstuff.

Comitology procedure. The Directive provides a procedure for deciding whether:

- a foodstuff that was not categorised at the time the Directive was adopted belongs to one of the categories referred to in the Directive;
- a food additive is being used in accordance with the prescribed criteria;
- a substance is a food additive for the purposes of the Directive.

The matter is referred to the Standing Committee for Foodstuffs by its chairman on his own initiative or at the request of a Member State. The Commission submits to the Committee a draft of measures that should be taken. The Committee gives its opinion on these proposed measures. The Commission can adopt the measures if they are in accordance with the opinion of the Committee. However, if the Committee does not agree with the measures proposed by the Commission, the matter is referred to the Council. If the Council fails to act within three months, the measures proposed can be adopted by the Commission.

Konjac (E 425) – a case study. Konjac (E 425) is an authorised food additive under Directive 95/2. It is authorised for restricted use under Annex IV of Directive 95/2. Konjac which is a derivative of yam has been used in the manufacture of 'jelly mini-cups'. The substance has allegedly been linked to 'death by suffocation caused by a solid ingredient'. In third countries, 18 deaths have allegedly been linked to the use of Konjac gum.

Several Member States and third countries had temporarily prohibited the use of Konjac and on 27 March 2002, the Commission adopted a Decision suspending the placing on the market and import of jelly confectionery containing the food additive E 425 Konjac. The Decision was adopted under Article 53(1) Regulation 178/2002[56] laying down the general principles and requirements of food law and procedures in matters of food safety (see Chapter 4). The use of Konjac in jelly confectionery was also suspended.

The Commission decided to take these measures because it felt that warnings given on labels were not sufficient to protect consumers, in particular, with regards to children. The Commission decided that in addition to the shape and size of the

---

[56] OJ L 031, 01/02/2002 P. 1–24.

jelly mini-cups containing Konjac, the chemical and physical properties of Konjac were causing the jelly mini-cups to constitute a serious risk to human health.

On 5 August 2002, the Commission adopted a proposal to amend Directive 95/2 as regards the conditions for use of Konjac as a food additive. Annex IV of the Directive would be amended so that Konjac would not be permitted to be used in 'foodstuffs in general (except those referred to in Article 2(3) and jelly confectionery including jelly mini-cups'. On 18 June 2003 Directive 2003/52 was adopted as drafted. Member States will have to implement the Directive before 17 January 2004.

Purity Criteria

The comprehensive Directive 89/107 required the adoption of purity criteria for additives. Three directives have been adopted setting out in detail the purity criteria that authorised food additives have to comply with:

- Directive 95/31[57] laying down specific criteria of purity for sweeteners used in foodstuffs as amended by Directives 98/66,[58] 2000/51[59] and 2001/52;[60]
- Directive 95/45[61] laying down specific purity criteria for colours used in foodstuffs as amended by Directives 1999/75[62] and 2001/50;[63]
- Directive 96/77[64] laying down specific purity criteria for food additives other than colours and sweeteners as amended by Directives 98/86,[65] 2000/63,[66] 2001/30[67] and 2002/82.[68]

Request for Authorisation of a Food Additive

Requests for the authorisation of a new food additive, the modification of the conditions for use of an authorised additive and/or the modification of the purity criteria for

---

[57] OJ No L178, 28/07/1995 P. 1–19.
[58] OJ L 257, 19/09/1998 P. 35–36.
[59] OJ L 198, 04/08/2000 P. 41–43.
[60] OJ L 190, 12/07/2001 P. 18–20.
[61] OJ No L226, 22/09/1995 P. 1–45.
[62] OJ L 206, 05/08/1999 P. 19–21.
[63] OJ L 190, 12/07/2001 P. 14–17.
[64] OJ No L339, 30/12/1996 P. 1–69.
[65] OJ L 334, 09/12/1998 P. 01–63.
[66] OJ L 277, 30/10/2000 P. 01–61.
[67] OJ L 146, 31/05/2001 P. 01–23.
[68] OJ L 292, 28/10/2002 P. 01–28.

food additives are sent to the European Commission. The processing of a request for the authorisation of a food additive takes place in three stages:

- the additive must be evaluated by the Scientific Committee on Food to ensure that it is safe as laid down in Directive 89/107;
- if it is evaluated as safe, it follows the co-decision procedure after which it can be included in the relevant specific directive according to the general criteria set out in Annex II of Directive 89/107;
- the Commission adopts purity specification for the additive after reaching an agreement in the Standing Committee on the Food Chain and Animal Health.

Report on Dietary Food Additives Intake

The Commission presented a report on the intake of dietary food additives in the European Union on 1 October 2001. The report gives an overview of the intake of food additives based on information received from Member States.

Under the three specific Directives Member States are required to monitor the consumption and usage of food additives. The Commission is required to submit a report on this monitoring exercise. The Commission stresses in the report that the results 'must be regarded as a very preliminary indication of the dietary intake of food additives'. The report indicates that the intake of the majority of food additives permitted in the European Union is below the acceptable daily intake set by the Scientific Committee on Food.

The report concludes that there is a need for Member States to apply agreed harmonised methodology to post-marketing monitoring to ensure a consistency of approach. The Commission recommends that a new report should be drawn up by October 2004.

Proposals for Reform

The White Paper on Food Safety indicated the intention of the Commission to propose amendments to the Directive 89/107 to confer on the Commission implementing powers to maintain the list of food additives and also to clarify the status of enzymes by laying down specific provisions. It is anticipated that the proposal will be for one Regulation to replace the four main Directives in this area, and will contain provisions for the re-assessment of authorised additives every ten years. The Commission is said to be considering a general revision of the levels of certain additives and possibly the deletion of others.

Enzymes. It is currently being discussed how enzymes should be regulated at EU-level. The Commission has prepared a discussion paper which is being sent to Member States asking for their views on this issue. In particular, the Commission is considering regulating them as a separate category irrespective of their function. This could lead to the labelling of many enzymes that currently do not require labelling when used as processing aids. It is possible that the EFSA would be required to carry out mandatory risk assessments of enzymes before they can be used in food, or alternatively that a positive list of enzymes would be created together with conditions for their use in foods. Discussions on legislating for enzymes are likely to include the criteria for their authorisation and labelling provisions.

Proposed amendments for sweeteners. On 11 July 2002 the Commission issued a proposal for a Directive of the European Parliament and the Council amending Directive 94/35 on sweeteners for use in foodstuffs. The Commission proposal puts forward three main amendments to Directive 94/35:

- the authorisation of two intense new sweeteners, sucrose and the salt of aspartame and acesulfame;
- the reduction of the maximum useable dose for cyclamates by banning or reducing its use in certain food categories;
- to confer on the Commission the power to decide according to the procedure laid down in Article 7 of the Directive whether a substance is a sweetener within the meaning of the Directive.

At the time of writing the proposals was following the co-decision procedure and had just entered second reading.

Additives used with flavourings. In November 2002 the Commission adopted a proposal to amend Directive 95/2 on food additives other than colours and sweeteners. The aim of the proposal is to authorise only those food additives that are strictly necessary for the storage and use of flavourings. As with other processed products food additives are used for the preservation and in the production of flavourings. For example, emulsifiers are used with flavourings to ensure that an oily flavouring is equally dispersed in a water-based product. If the proposal is adopted as drafted the number of authorised food additives which can be used in flavourings would be greatly reduced. These food additives would have to comply with the general criteria set out in the framework Directive 89/107 on food additives (see Chapter 7 on flavourings).

Chapter 7

Flavourings

INTRODUCTION

As flavourings are treated separately from other food additives there is a separate body of Community legislation on this subject. Directive 88/388[69] is the framework Flavourings Directive which (as amended by Directive 91/71[70]) sets out the definition of different types of flavourings and labelling requirements. It also provides for further provisions to be adopted where necessary, for example in respect of flavouring substances, smoke flavourings, and additives used in flavourings. Community legislation for flavouring substances is contained in several regulations and Commission decisions including:

- Regulation 2232/96[71] – Community procedure for flavouring substances used in or intended to be used in or on foodstuffs;
- Commission decision 1999/217[72] – Setting up a register of flavouring substances;
- Regulation 1565/2000[73] – Measures for the adoption of the evaluation programme;
- Regulation 622/2002[74] – Establishing deadlines for the submission of information for the evaluation of chemically defined flavouring substances used in or on foodstuffs.

This legislation aims to establish an exclusive list of authorised flavouring substances, which is anticipated in 2005.

The Commission is considering a review of Directive 88/388. It has also adopted proposals for legislation on smoke flavourings and additives used in flavourings as provided for in Directive 88/388.[75]

---

69 OJ L 184, 15/07/1988 P. 61–66.
70 OJ L 042, 15/02/1991 P. 25–26.
71 OJ L 299, 23/11/1996 P. 01–04.
72 OJ L 084, 27/03/1999 P. 01–137.
73 OJ L 180, 19/07/2000 P. 08–16.
74 OJ L 095, 12/04/2002 P. 10–11.
75 OJ L184, 15/07/1988 P. 61–66.

Directive 88/388 Flavourings for Use in Foodstuffs and Source Materials for their Production

Directive 88/388 (as amended by Directive 91/71) sets out: the definition of flavourings; types of flavourings; general rules for their use; requirements for labelling; and the maximum units permitted for certain undesirable substances. Only flavourings that comply with the rules set out in the Flavourings Directive can be marketed or used in the Community. This also applies to flavourings intended for use in foodstuffs imported into the Community but does not apply to flavourings intended for export outside the Community. Member States are obliged to ensure that flavourings are not marketed unless they comply with the labelling and maximum limits set out in the Directive.

Only flavourings used, or intended for use, in or on foodstuffs to impart odour and/or taste fall within the scope of the Directive. The Directive does not apply to: edible substances and products which are in intended to be consumed; substances which have a taste which is exclusively sweet, sour or salt; and material which is of vegetable or animal origin which has inherent flavouring properties but are not being used as flavouring sources. Flavour enhancers do not come within the scope of this Directive. They are regulated by the Additives Directives (see Chapter 6).

The legislation for flavourings used in foodstuffs is based on the premise that human health should be the primary requirement, however once this has been assured, economic and technical needs should also be taken into account.

The Directive separates flavourings into five categories flavouring substances, flavouring preparations, process flavourings, smoke flavourings or mixtures of flavourings that fall within any or all of the previous categories. The Directive proceeds to define each category of flavourings.

Definitions of flavourings

A flavouring substance is defined as a chemical substance with flavouring properties which is obtained:

(i) by appropriate physical processes (including distillation and solvent extraction) or enzymatic or microbiological processes from material of vegetable or animal origin either in the raw state or after processing for human consumption by traditional food-preparation processes (including drying, torrefaction and fermentation). This type of flavouring substance is referred to as 'natural';

(ii) by chemical synthesis or isolated by chemical processes and which is chemically identical to a substance naturally present in material of vegetable or animal origin as described in (i); This type of flavouring substance is referred to as 'natural identical';

(iii) by chemical synthesis but which is not chemically identical to a substance naturally present in material of vegetable or animal origin as described in (i); This type of flavouring substance is referred to as 'artificial'.

A flavouring preparation is defined as a product of animal or plant origin other than a flavouring substance. A process flavouring is defined as a product which is obtained by heating a mixture of ingredients of which at least one contains nitrogen and another is a reducing sugar. Smoke flavouring is defined as a smoke extract used in traditional foodstuffs smoking processes.

Labelling requirements

The Directive sets out detailed labelling requirements for flavourings not intended for sale to the final consumer, and in Directive 91/71 for flavourings intended for sale to the final consumer which include:

- the name or business name and address of the manufacturer or packer or of a seller established within the Community;
- either the word 'flavouring' or a more specific name or description of the flavouring;
- either the statement 'for foodstuffs' or a more specific reference to the foodstuffs for which the flavouring is intended.

All prescribed particulars must be clearly set out, legible and indelible, on the container or packaging of the food additive. They must be given in 'terms' (for flavourings not intended for the final consumer) or 'language' (for flavourings intended for the final consumer) easily understood by the purchasers unless other measures have been taken to ensure that the purchaser is informed. The Directive allows the prescribed information to be indicated in various languages.

Directive 2000/13[76] also sets out provisions for the labelling of flavourings (see Chapter 5). Directive 2000/13 lays down provisions for the approximation of the laws of Member States relating to the labelling presentation and advertising of foodstuffs. Annex 3 of the Directive contains strict provisions for the labelling of flavourings. It states that flavourings are to be 'designated either by the word flavourings or by a more specific name or description of the flavouring'.

'Natural' claims

Specific labelling provisions are set out for the use of the word 'natural', or 'any other word having substantially the same meaning'. These words may only be used for flavourings in which the flavouring component contains exclusively:

- 'natural' flavouring substances that are obtained by appropriate physical, enzymatic or microbiological processes (see point (i) of the definition for flavouring substances set out above); and/or
- flavouring preparations.

[76] OJ L 124, 25/05/2000 P. 66–66.

The term natural, or words implying natural, can also be used where the sales description of the flavouring refers to a foodstuff, or a flavouring, and the flavouring component has been isolated by appropriate physical, enzymatic or microbiological processes or traditional food-preparation. This flavouring component should have been derived solely or almost solely from the foodstuff or the flavouring source referred to. For example, if it is claimed that it is 'an apple flavouring' the flavouring component should have been isolated by one of the processes referred to and should have been obtained only from apples or almost entirely from apples. However some Member States may permit nature-identical to be labelled as natural.

Undesirable substances/toxicologically dangerous substances

Flavourings must not be toxicologically dangerous. The Directive prescribes the quantities of arsenic, lead, cadmium and mercury that can be used in flavourings. In addition, annexed to the Directive is a table setting out the maximum amounts permitted for undesirable substances. Currently the table only contains the maximum limits for 3,4-benzopyrene.

Comitology procedure

The Directive provides a procedure for the amendment of the Directive where as a result of new information or a reassessment of existing information a Member State has detailed evidence that a flavouring whilst complying with the Directive constitutes a danger to human health. In such circumstances a Member State can temporarily suspend or restrict the use of the flavouring. However, the Member State is obliged to inform immediately the other Member States and the Commission of its actions. The Commission first consults the Standing Committee on Foodstuffs. The Standing Committee is made up of Member State representatives and Chaired by a Commission official. If after consulting the Standing Committee on Foodstuffs the Commission believes that the Directive should be amended it refers the matter to the Standing Committee for Foodstuffs. The Commission submits to the Committee a draft of the measures that it believes should be taken. The Committee gives its opinion on these proposed measures. The Commission can adopt the measures if they are in accordance with the opinion of the Committee. However, if the Committee does not agree with the measures proposed by the Commission, the matter is referred to the Council. If the Council fails to act within 3 months, the measures proposed by the Commission can be adopted by the Commission.

This procedure is also used to determine other issues such as the purity criteria for flavourings and the microbiological criteria for flavourings. However in these circumstances the matter can be referred to the Standing Committee on Foodstuffs by the chairman on his own initiative or at the request of a Member State.

The Directive provides for further EU legislation to be adopted in respect of smoke flavourings, additives used in flavourings, flavouring sources, source materials and flavouring substances. The Commission has recently adopted proposals to cover smoke flavourings and food additives used in flavourings which will be considered later on in this chapter. There is, however, already a significant body of Community legislation in respect of flavouring substances.

Regulation 2232/96 – Community Procedure for Flavouring Substances

The Regulation only applies to flavouring substances as defined in Directive 88/388 set out above and does not apply to other flavourings such as flavouring preparations, flavouring sources or source materials.

General criteria

The aim of the Regulation is to create an exclusive list of authorised flavouring substances that can be used in foodstuffs within the European Union. The Regulation provides a 'general use' criteria, set out in the annex, that flavouring substances must comply with before they can be authorised. Flavouring substances can be authorised provided that:

- they present no risk to the health of the consumer; and
- their use does not mislead the consumer.

The flavouring substances must be evaluated for their toxicological effects to ensure that they do not present a risk to the health of consumers. Where a flavouring substance contains or consists of a genetically modified organism (as defined in Directive 90/220[77] see Chapter 12 on GMOs and Novel Foods) the evaluation for safety purposes must also take into account environmental safety issues. The Regulation provides that all flavouring substances must be constantly monitored, and re-evaluated whenever necessary.

Authorisation procedure

The Regulation sets out a procedure for establishing an exclusive list of authorised flavouring substances. The procedure consists of three stages:

(i) Member States notify the Commission of the flavouring substances that they allow to be used in their territory and which comply with Directive 88/388;
(ii) a Register of these flavouring substances is then created;
(iii) the flavouring substances entered in the Register are evaluated.

---

[77] OJ L 117, 08/05/1990 P. 15–27.

The Regulation also lays down a procedure for adopting a programme for the evaluation of the flavouring substances set out on the Register. The same procedure must also be followed for the authorisation of new flavouring substances that were not initially included in the Register.

Evaluation process

The Commission is assisted in the evaluation of the flavouring substances by the Standing Committee on Foodstuffs (this will be transferred to the scientific panel on food additives, processing aids and materials in contact with food under the EFSA). The Commission representative submits a draft proposal to the Committee regarding a flavouring substance and the Committee can give its opinion on the draft proposal. If the Committee agrees with the measures set out in the draft proposal the Commission can then adopt the measures. If however the Committee does not give an opinion or does not agree with the proposal set out by the Committee, the Commission must take the proposal to the Council. If the Council does not act within 3 months of receiving the proposal the Commission can adopt the measures proposed.

It is conceivable that a flavouring substance, which has been considered in accordance with the scientific assessment and has been shown to present no risk to the health of the consumer, could still be refused authorisation because, for example, some enzymes that are currently on the Register have a very low degree of taste or smell. It is therefore possible that the Standing Committee on Foodstuffs could decide that the substance is safe but is not a flavouring substance.

After the evaluation programme is completed an exclusive list of authorised flavouring substances will be adopted under a slightly amended procedure from that described above so that the Commission can adopt the proposed measures where the Council fails to act within 3 months of receiving the proposal from the Commission except where the Council has decided against the measures by a simple majority.

It was envisaged when adopting the Regulation that the evaluation programme would be completed by 2001. However, the evaluation programme has taken much longer than was initially predicted and is still not complete. Several Regulations have been adopted setting deadlines for the collection of information and the evaluation programme as a whole. These Regulations will be considered in more detail later on in this chapter. The first stage of the procedure was to establish a Register of flavouring substances.

Commission Decision 1999/217 – A Register of Flavouring Substances

In 1999 a Register was established of flavouring substances used in or on foodstuffs that are authorised at national level within the Member States and comply with Directive 88/388. The Register was last amended by Commission Decision

2002/113.[78] Under Commission Decision 2002/113 a number of additives which were found to be genotoxic were deleted from the Register. In addition, the Register was divided into two parts: Part A sets out the flavouring substances in accordance with their FL numbers; and Part B contains flavouring substances for which the Member States have requested confidentiality to protect the intellectual property rights of the of the manufacturer.

Commission Regulation 1565/2000 – Measures for the Adoption of the Evaluation Programme

In July 2000, Regulation 1565/2000 was adopted laying down the necessary measures for adopting a programme for the evaluation of flavouring substances contained in the Register. In light of the large number of flavouring substances that were entered in the Register it was decided by the Commission that in order not to 'waste scientific resources' use should be made of the safety assessments already produced by the Committee of Experts on Flavouring Substances of the Council of Europe (CEFS), the Scientific Committee of Food of the European Commission (SCF), and the Joint FAO/WHO Expert Committee on Food Additives (JECFA).

The first step in the evaluation programme was to attribute FL-numbers as defined in the Flavis data base to each flavouring substance entered in the Register. The flavouring substances contained in the Register were subdivided into the 34 chemical groups set out in the Annex to the Regulation.

Flavouring substances were divided into categories and then prioritised for evaluation. It was decided that certain flavouring substances that had already been classified by the SCF, CEFS or JECFA as safe for use in foodstuffs did not need to be re-evaluated unless:

- the necessary purity and chemical specification information was not provided;
- the Scientific Committee on Foodstuff received new information which would or could change the results of the previous evaluations.

For flavouring substances that must be evaluated the person responsible for ensuring that the Commission receives the required information to enable the evaluation to take place is the person placing the flavouring substance on the market. The Regulation also prescribes the information that must be given to the Commission and the form in which the information must be presented.

It is the role of the Scientific Committee on Foodstuff to evaluate the flavouring substances for their compliance with the 'general use' criteria set out in Regulation 2232/96. A Member State or the Commission can ask for the re-evaluation of a substance that has been evaluated as complying with the general use criteria if new data has become available.

---

[78] OJ L 049, 20/02/2002 P. 01–160.

The first results of the evaluation programme under Regulation 1565/2000 are not available. However, the results will be used to establish a positive list of flavouring substances by 2005. In this respect the Commission has contracted a consultant to build and maintain a database of flavourings.

Regulation 622/2002 – Establishing Deadlines for the Submission of Information

Regulation 622/2002 was adopted in April 2002 establishing deadlines for the submission of the information required under Regulation 2232/96 for the evaluation programme. Under Regulation 1565/2000 the responsible person was obliged to provide the required information within 1 year of the adoption of the Regulation. However, the Commission did have the discretion to allow extensions to this time limit if a reasoned request was received.

To ensure the smooth running of the evaluation process, the Commission decided to set out deadlines for the submission of the information. The Regulation gives four categories of flavouring substances with four deadlines. The final deadline is 30 June 2004. The Commission is hopeful that the evaluation process will be completed by 2005.

Labelling of Quinine and Caffeine Used as Flavourings

The Scientific Committee for Food published an opinion on 21 January 1999 on caffeine and other substances used in 'energy drinks'. The opinion concluded that for children and pregnant women an increase in the daily intake of caffeine may bring about temporary changes in behaviour, such as increased excitability, irritability, nervousness or anxiety. The Committee advised that pregnant women should moderate their intake of caffeine. As a result of this opinion it was decided that it is necessary to provide labelling which gives consumers clear information that a foodstuff contains quinine or caffeine, and in the case of caffeine to provide a warning message.

Directive 2000/13 allows the term 'flavourings' to be included in the list of ingredients in place of the name of the particular flavouring. It is therefore possible or indeed likely, that a product would contain quinine or caffeine without this being indicated specifically in the ingredients list.

Directive 2002/67[79] was adopted in response to the Scientific Committee on Food's opinion to ensure that consumers are aware of the presence of quinine or caffeine. It provides that where quinine or caffeine has been used as a flavouring in the

[79] OJ L 026, 30/01/2002 P. 17–17.

production or preparation of a foodstuff, it must be mentioned by its name in the list of ingredients immediately after the term 'flavouring'.

PROPOSALS FOR CHANGE

It is understood that the Commission is planning to amend the Framework Directive 88/388. It is likely that the aim of proposal will be to change the definition of flavouring and possibly update the maximum levels of toxicological substances contained in flavourings. It is understood that the key elements will be:

- The definition of six categories of flavourings – flavouring substances, flavouring preparations, thermal process flavourings, smoke flavourings, flavour precursors (new) and other flavourings (a new category comprising all flavourings not covered by one of the other previous categories).
- The division of flavourings into two categories:
  (a) flavourings which do not need to be evaluated;
  (b) flavourings which need to be evaluated and explicitly authorised.
  It is understood that the evaluations would be carried out by the EFSA.
- Clarification that the use of the word 'natural', should be restricted to flavourings which are exclusively obtained from natural flavouring substances and/or flavouring preparations.

Proposals have been recently adopted by the Commission on smoke flavourings and additives used in flavourings.

Proposed regulation on smoke flavourings used or intended for use in or on food

On 15 July 2002 the Commission adopted a proposal for a regulation on smoke flavourings used or intended for use in or on foods. It was announced by the Commission in the White Paper on Food Safety that a proposal for a Regulation on smoke flavourings would be produced as provided for under Directive 88/388.

National legislation for the authorisation of smoke flavourings throughout the European Union is diverse and the objective of the proposal is to harmonise at EU level procedures for the safety assessment and authorisation of smoke flavourings.

Smoke flavourings are produced from condensed smoke. Smoked foods in general have given rise to health concerns. However, smoke flavourings are generally considered to be of less of a health concern because of the purification process carried out when the smoke is condensed.

The proposal sets out procedures for the safety assessment and authorisation of smoke condensates and primary tar fractions. A positive list of products authorised to the exclusion of all others in the Community would be produced. Authorizations for smoke flavourings would be restricted to an initial period of 10 years after which their authorizations would need to be renewed. This is to ensure that products are regularly re-evaluated using the latest scientific knowledge.

The European Food Safety Authority will carry out the evaluation of the smoke flavourings. The Commission would within 3 months of receiving the opinion of the European Food Safety Authority, prepare a draft regulation amending the list, or a draft decision refusing authorisation. If the Commission's decision is not in line with the opinion of the European Food Safety Authority the Commission would have to provide an explanation for the differences.

The Commission has estimated that approximately 20 products will need to be evaluated for the positive list of products as there are few companies inside and outside the European Union that produce smoke flavourings for the Community market.

Concerns have been raised about the legal basis for the proposal. The proposed Regulation is based on Article 95 of the Treaty, which refers to the approximation of laws. Proposed legislation based on this Article is adopted under the co-decision procedure. However, the proposed Regulation is seen by some to be an attempt to create a centralised authorisation system and not just the harmonisation of national laws. It has therefore been argued that the correct legal basis would be Article 308 of the Treaty:

> If action by the Community should prove necessary to attain, in the course of the operation of the common market, one of the objectives of the Community, and this Treaty has not provided the necessary powers, the Council shall, acting unanimously on a proposal from the Commission and after consulting the European Parliament, take the appropriate measures.

On 9 October 2003 the Council and European Parliament reached an agreement in respect of this Regulation which is expected to be published shortly in the Official Journal.

Additives used with flavourings

Directive 88/388 provided that a list of food additives that are necessary for the storage and use of flavourings should be adopted. Food additives are used in the preservation and production of flavourings, for example, anti-caking agents may be needed to ensure that a flavouring in powdered form can be evenly dispersed in the foodstuff.

In November 2002 the Commission adopted a proposal to amend Directive 95/2[80] on food additives other than colours and sweeteners (see Chapter 6). The aim of the proposal is to authorise only those food additives that are strictly necessary for the storage and use of flavourings. Currently the provisions vary between the Member States, and if the proposal is adopted as drafted the number of authorised food additives which can be used in flavourings would be greatly reduced. These food additives would have to comply with the general criteria set out in the framework Directive 89/107[81] on food additives.

---

[80] OJ L 061, 18/03/1995 P. 01–40.

[81] OJ L 040, 11/02/1989 P. 27–33.

Chapter 8

Claims

In the White Paper on Food Safety the Commission suggested that consideration should be given as to whether Community legislation was required to govern 'nutritional claims' and 'functional claims'. 'Nutritional claims' describe the presence, absence or level of a nutrient contained in a food or its value compared to similar products and 'functional claims' relate to the beneficial effects of a nutrient on certain normal bodily functions.

Consequently, the Commission produced a discussion paper on functional and nutritional claims which was put on the Commission's website in May 2001. The paper outlined issues that need to be considered and addressed in future legislation and asks for comments and suggestions. At that time, the Commission envisaged that a separate discussion on the potential regulation of 'health claims', would be held at a later date. The Commission received a large number of comments on the discussion paper. Some Member States and many stakeholders (including consumers and industry) expressed their disappointment that 'health claims' were not addressed and called for this type of claim to be regulated at a Community level. The motivation for this is that 'health claims' are already found on the market. Due to the lack of harmonisation Member States have legislated on the different types of claims to a greater or lesser extent. In light of this, the Commission has produced a single proposal addressing 'nutrition' and 'health' claims (including 'functional' claims within 'health' claims). The proposal was published in July 2003.

This chapter will look at the issues surrounding nutrition, functional and health claims as well as outlining some of the possible provisions that are contained in the proposal for legislation at EU level.

Recent History

Over recent years food production has become more complicated. This is combined with the fact that consumers are becoming increasingly interested in their diet and its relationship to their health. They are aware of the composition of the foodstuffs that they are selecting. In light of this, they often take account of the information relating to the nutritional value of food appearing on labelling when selecting their purchases. Consequently, manufacturers have been keen to provide additional information as to the benefits of their particular product. This often involves highlighting the nutritional value of products through claims in their labelling, presentation and advertising. Some would argue that this development is positive as it provides relevant information to the consumer. It also provides companies with the opportunity to make claims as marketing devices. However, some argue that some of the information could be unsubstantiated or confusing.

Due to the increased number and types of claims appearing on labels and the absence of harmonisation at the EU level, Member States have adopted legislation and other measures to regulate claims to greater and lesser extents. Consequently, varying approaches have been taken by the different Member States and there are discrepancies, for example, in relation to the definitions of the terms and conditions and circumstances in which such claims can be made. These discrepancies can hinder the aim of a high level of consumer and public health protection and also can constitute an obstacle to the free movement of foodstuffs and the proper functioning of the internal market. In light of this the Commission believes that it is necessary to harmonise the regulation of claims at the EU level.

The International Level

General guidelines exist at the international level on the use of claims. They were adopted by Codex Alimentaries in 1979 and revised in 1991. In general, these guidelines follow two principles. First, no food should be described or presented in a manner that is false, deceiving or deceptive and they should not create an erroneous impression regarding their character in any way. Second, the person marketing the food should be able to justify the claim made. The guidelines also set out claims made on foods that should be prohibited including false claims that cannot be substantiated, claims that a balanced diet or ordinary foods cannot supply adequate amounts of all nutrients, and claims as to the suitability of food for prevention, treatment or cure of diseases.

Specific guidelines on the use of nutrition claims have been adopted by Codex Alimentaries since 1997. These guidelines provide definitions for 'nutrient content claims', for example, low fat, source of calcium, 'comparative claims' such as reduced fat, increased calcium and 'nutrient function claims' such as calcium aids in the development of strong bones and teeth. These guidelines also set out conditions in which these claims should be permitted. Initially, it was intended that health claims should be included in these guidelines. However, the discussions surrounding health claims proved to be much more difficult and controversial and therefore no definition or conditions for health claims have been adopted at the international level.

Issues

The definition of nutrients

The definition of nutrients is not clear. Traditionally, nutrients include protein, carbohydrate, fat, fibre, sodium, vitamins and minerals but other substances with a nutritional or physiological effect, for example, anti-oxidants or lactic bacteria may be also included within the definition. In fact, many claims concerning these other substances are already visible on products throughout the European Union. Therefore the general view is that if these substances are not included within the scope, claims relating to them would continue to be regulated by differing national rules as is currently the case and consequently the free movement of the foodstuffs would continue to be impeded.

Nutrition profiling

Some have suggested that products that are not considered to be good foods, in other words those that have a less desirable nutritional profile, for example, high salt and high fat foods, should not be permitted to carry claims. In other words, a low fat claim should only be made on a product if, not only it is low fat but also it is not high in sugar or salt. Another example is a high calcium claim could not be permitted on a product with high fat content. However, if this approach were adopted it would lead to the situation where the calcium content of full fat milk could not be drawn to the attention of the consumer. Previously the attitude in the European Union has been to concentrate on the overall diet of individuals. General nutrition advice recommends consumption in moderation of certain products but accepts a varied diet is desirable in the long term.

Nutrition labelling

Some argue that providing the consumer with more information on the nutritional profile of a food on its label empowers the consumer. However, there is also concern that labels should not be over burdened and should not confuse the consumer by bombarding them with too much information. It is therefore a question whether nutrition labelling should be required on foods bearing a nutrition, functional or health claim. It is also under debate whether statements relating to the importance of a varied diet should be placed on certain products. Other methods of communicating these claims are being considered, such as leaflets at the point of sale or websites access available in store (see Chapter 5).

Presentation of Claims

Legislation already exists prohibiting misleading advertising or labelling. Claims must be presented in a way that is easily understood by consumers. In some cases, logos or images can be meaningless to the consumer. Indeed, in the United Kingdom the Food Standards Authorities are currently investigating quality assurance schemes such as ‘Red Tractor’. The appearance of the ‘Red Tractor’ does not clearly explain to the consumer what criteria the product has met. Moreover, some claims can be misleading because they are unclear. They may be true, yet are explained in a confusing manner. For example, '90 per cent fat-free'. This may be true, but it means that 10 per cent of the product is actually fat. Highly technical and specialized claims may also be unclear to the consumer, for example, 'folate may help normalize plasma homocystine'. This may be true, but not many people on the street would understand the claim.

There is also a debate surrounding non-specific benefit claims, for example, general well being and normal functions of the body. In other words, claims such as 'help support your body's natural defences', 'boosts your immune system' and 'helps your body resist stress'. In some Member States, it is felt that these claims are vague and not verifiable. However, it has also been argued that it would be disproportionate to prohibit generalized claims because they are not necessarily misleading. Whether or not a particular claim is misleading should be judged on a case-by-case basis in reference to the particular product and how the claim is made.

The Commission's Proposal

The Commission's proposal was published in July 2003. It begins by laying down general principles relating to all claims. It requires that in accordance with the General Food Labelling Directive (see Chapter 5) nutrition and health claims in the labelling, presentation and advertising of foods must not be false or misleading; give rise to doubt about the safety and/or the nutritional adequacy of other foods; or state or imply that a balanced and varied diet cannot provide appropriate quantities of nutrients in general. Nutrition and health claims would only be permitted if the substance for which the claim is made has been proven to have a beneficial nutritional or physiological effect. Moreover, according to the proposal such a claim would only be permitted if the substance for which the claim is made is contained in the final product in significant quantity as defined in Community legislation or where such rules are not already in existence for a quantity that will produce the nutritional or physiological effect claimed. The substance would also have to be available in the foodstuff in a form that is bio-available to humans. In addition, the claim would only be permitted to be made if the quantity of the product, that can be reasonably expected to be consumed provides, a significant quantity of the substance that is the subject of a nutrition, functional or health claim. A significant quantity could be specified in Community legislation or where rules do not exist in a significant quantity that will produce nutritional or physiologically effect as that claimed as established by generally accepted scientific data. The use of any claims should only be permitted if the beneficial effects, as expressed in the claim, can be understood by the average consumer. Any claims should refer to the food ready for consumption as instructed by the manufacturer.

In relation to comparative claims, pursuant to the proposal a nutrition claim would only be permitted to compare the level of a nutrient and all the energy value of a food with similar foods only if the other foods being compared are easily identifiable by the average consumer or clearly indicated. The difference in the level of a nutrient and/or energy value shall be stated and it shall relate to the same quantity of the food. Member States could require food business operators to justify the choice of the 'similar food' that is chosen for comparison.

If adopted as drafted the proposal, would require nutrition and health claims to be based on substantiated generally accepted scientific data. It is for the food business operator making the claim to justify and substantiate it. The competent authority of any Member State would have to require the food business operator or the person placing the product on the market to produce scientific work and data established in compliance with these rules.

Prohibited claims

The proposal, if adopted as drafted, would mean that certain claims that made reference to general non-specific benefits of a nutrient or food for overall good health, well being and normal functions of the body would be prohibited. All claims making reference to physiological and behavioural functions would be prohibited. Beverages containing more than 1.2 per cent by volume of alcohol would be prohibited from carrying any health claims. The proposal would also allow foods or categories of foods to be determined, in respect of which claims or categories of claims may be restricted or prohibited.

Where a nutrition or health claim appeared on the labelling or in the advertising, nutrition labelling would be required if the proposal eventually became law (see Chapter 5).

The proposal sets out requirements for different types of claims: nutrition and health claims.

Nutrition claim

Conditions which would warrant specific nutrition claims set out in the annex to the draft. At the time of writing, the nutrition claims the proposal suggests to permit are as follows:

Low energy. A claim that a food is low in energy, and any claim likely to have the same meaning for the consumer, would only be allowed where the product contains less than 40 kcal/100 g and less than 20 kcal/100 ml.

Energy-reduced. A claim that a food is energy-reduced, and any claim likely to have the same meaning for the consumer, may only be made where the energy value is reduced by at least 30 per cent, with an indication of the characteristic(s), which make(s) the food reduced in its total energy value.

Energy-free. A claim that a food is energy-free, and any claim likely to have the same meaning for the consumer, would only be allowed where the product contains less than 4 kcal/100 ml.

Low fat. A claim that a food is low in fat, and any claim likely to have the same meaning for the consumer, would only be allowed where the product contains no more than 3 g of fat per 100 g and 1.5 g of fat per 100 ml.

Fat-free. A claim that a food is fat-free, and any claim likely to have the same meaning for the consumer, would only be allowed where the product contains no more than 0.5 g of fat per 100 g or 100 ml. However, claims expressed as 'X per cent fat-free' would be prohibited.

Low saturates. A claim that a food is low in saturates, and any claim likely to have the same meaning for the consumer, would only be allowed where the product contains no more than 1.5 g of saturates per 100 g for solids, 0.75 g of saturates per 100 ml for liquids and also saturates must not provide more than 10 per cent of the energy of the food.

Saturates-free. A claim that a food does not contain saturates, and any claim likely to have the same meaning for the consumer, would only be allowed where the product contains no more than 0.1 g of saturates per 100 g or 100 ml.

Low sugar(s). A claim that a food is low in sugar(s), and any claim likely to have the same meaning for the consumer, would only be allowed where the product contains no more than 5 g of sugar(s) per 100 g or 100 ml.

Sugar(s)-free. A claim that a food is sugar(s)-free, and any claim likely to have the same meaning for the consumer, would only be allowed where the product contains no more than 0.5 g of sugar(s) per 100 g or 100 ml.

With no added sugar. A claim stating that sugar has not been added to a food, and any claim likely to have the same meaning for the consumer, would only be allowed where the product does not contain any added mono- or disaccharides or any other food used for its sweetening properties.

Low sodium/salt. A claim that a food is low in sodium, and any claim likely to have the same meaning for the consumer, may only be made where the product contains no more than 0.12 g of sodium, or the equivalent value for salt, per 100 g or per 100 ml.

In the case of foods naturally low in sodium, the term 'naturally' may be used as a prefix to this claim.

Very low sodium/salt. A claim that a food is very low in sodium, and any claim likely to have the same meaning for the consumer, may only be made where the product contains no more than 0.04 g of sodium, or the equivalent value for salt, per 100 g or per 100 ml.

In the case of foods naturally very low in sodium, the term 'naturally' may be used as a prefix to this claim.

Sodium-free or salt-free. A claim that a food is sodium-free, and any claim likely to have the same meaning for the consumer, may only be made where the product contains no more than 0.05 g of sodium, or the equivalent value for salt, per 100 g.

In the case of foods naturally sodium-free, the term 'naturally' may be used as a prefix to this claim.

Source of fibre. A claim that a food is a source of fibre, and any claim likely to have the same meaning for the consumer, would only be allowed where the product contains at least 3 g of fibre per 100 g or at least 1.5 g of fibre per 100 kcal.

High fibre. A claim that a food is high in fibre, and any claim likely to have the same meaning for the consumer, would only be allowed where the product contains at least 6 g of fibre per 100 g or at least 3 g of fibre per 100 kcal.

Source of protein. A claim that a food is a source of protein, and any claim likely to have the same meaning for the consumer, would only be allowed where at least 12 per cent of the energy value of the food is provided by protein.

High protein. A claim that a food is high in protein, and any claim likely to have the same meaning for the consumer, would only be allowed where at least 20 per cent of the energy value of the food is provided by protein.

Source of vitamins and/or minerals. A claim that a food is a source of vitamins and/or minerals, and any claim likely to have the same meaning for the consumer, would only be allowed where the product contains at least 15 per cent of the recommended allowance specified in the Annex of Council Directive 90/496/EEC[82] per 100 g or 100 ml.

Enriched or fortified in vitamins and/or minerals. A claim that a food is enriched or fortified in vitamins and/or minerals, and any claim likely to have the same meaning for the consumer, may only be made where the product contains the vitamins and/or minerals in at least a significant amount as defined in the Annex of Directive 90/496/EEC.

---

[82] OJ L 276, 06/10/1990 P. 40–44.

High vitamins and/or minerals. A claim that a food is high in vitamins and/or minerals, and any claim likely to have the same meaning for the consumer, would only be allowed where the product contains at least twice the value of 'source of vitamins and minerals'.

Contains (name of the nutrient or other substance). A claim that a food contains a nutrient or another substance, or any claim likely to have the same meaning for the consumer, may only be made where the product complies with all the applicable provisions of this Regulation.

In the case of foods that naturally contain the named nutrient or other substance, the term 'naturally' may be used as a prefix to this claim.

Increased (name of the nutrient). A claim stating that the content in one or more nutrients has been increased, and any claim likely to have the same meaning for the consumer, would only be allowed where the product meets the conditions for the claim '*source of*' and the increase in content is at least 25 per cent compared to a similar product, except for micronutrients where a 10 per cent difference in the reference values as set in Council Directive 90/496/EEC shall be acceptable.

Reduced (name of the nutrient). A claim stating that the content in one or more nutrients has been reduced, and any claim likely to have the same meaning for the consumer, would only be allowed where the reduction in content is at least 25 per cent compared to a similar product, except for micronutrients where a 10 per cent difference in the reference values as set in Council Directive 90/496/EEC shall be acceptable.

Light/lite. A claim stating that a product is 'light' or 'lite', and any claim likely to have the same meaning for the consumer, would have to follow the same conditions as those set for the term 'reduced'; the claim would have to be accompanied by an indication of the characteristic(s) which make the food 'light' or 'lite'.

Conditions for claims relating to a low content of sodium are set out under Directive 89/398[83] on foods intended for particular use. The term diet which implies a food contains less energy or nutrients would not be used as a prefix or suffix in any manner other than in the name or the designation of a food.

Health Claims

Health claims, according to the proposal, would be permitted provided that, in addition to the general requirements laid down by the Regulation, the following information

[83] OJ L 186, 30/06/1989 P. 27–32.

would also have to appear on the label:

- the statement indicating the importance of a balanced diet and healthy life style;
- the quantity of the food and the pattern of consumption required to obtain the beneficial effect;
- as the case may be, a statement addressed to persons who should avoid using the food;
- as the case may be, a warning not to exceed quantities of the product that may represent a risk to health.

If a competent authority of a Member State had detailed grounds for considering that a health claim may not be in conformity with the proposed regulation or that the scientific substantiation of functional claim is not satisfactory that Member State would be able to temporarily suspend the use of the claim. In the event that such a suspension is in place, the Member State would have to inform the Commission and the other Member States giving reasons for the decision. The Commission would then examine these grounds and then take a decision as to the acceptability of the claim after having obtained opinion from the European Food Safety Authority (see Chapter 4). If the Commission is concerned about a claim it would be able to use its own initiative to begin an investigation.

Health claims that would be permitted under the draft would include enhanced functional claims and reduction of disease risk factor claims. Enhanced functional claims are claims that a nutrient has a beneficial effect on physiological, psychological or biological functions beyond their established role in growth development and other normal functions of the body including in relation to mild abnormal conditions such as indigestion. Reduction of disease-risk claims are claims that consumption of a food might help to reduce the risk of a specific disease or condition, for example, sufficient calcium intake may help to reduce the risk of osteoporosis, or a product that contains soluble fibre may help reduce the risk of bowel cancer. There would be a prior approval before a claim would be permitted. An application would be made to the EFSA by the producer or the person responsible for placing the product on the market. The application would include scientific substantiation as well as details of the claims in the various Community languages. The authorities would acknowledge receipt of the claim within 14 working days, and then inform the Member States and the Commission of the application and any information supplied by the applicant. A summary of the dossier would be made available to the public. The EFSA would give its opinion within 3 months if possible from the receipt of a valid application. This time limit could be extended whenever the EFSA required supplmentary information. The EFSA would forward its opinion to the Commission, the Member States and the applicant. The EFSA would also makes its opinion public and the public would have 30 days to comment. The Commission would then submit a draft decision. At this stage the Commission can consider other legitimate factors that it considers relevant as well as the opinion of the EFSA. A decision would be published in the Official Journal of the European Communities as well as being notified to the applicant. All approved health claims would be included in the register referred to below.

All modifications or revocations or approvals would follow the same procedure used in involving the co-ordination of the EFSA, Member States and the Commission.

Register. Under the draft proposal for a regulation the Commission would have to establish and maintain a Community register of functional and health claims. The register would be a public document.

Comment

The harmonisation of Member State legislation concerning health claims appears to be generally welcomed. This would allow pan-European labelling and promotions of certain products. However, it is argued by some that any claims made should be based on sound science and other legitimate factors should not be considered, in particular there should be no distinction or restriction of the use of health claims to certain kinds of food.

Some of the definitions set out in the proposal lack clarity, for example, it is unclear what is meant by 'generally accepted scientific data', 'bio-availability of a substance', and 'the need for beneficial effects to be understood by the average consumer'.

Making a prescriptive list of nutritional claims is restrictive and may inhibit other genuine nutrition claims from being made. In relation to the procedure for pre-market approval and supply of proprietary information to the Commission, there are various concerns of confidentiality. Moreover, any lengthy prior-approval, which a new claim is to be subject to, could stifle innovation. The Commission proposal will follow the co-decision legislative procedure.

Chapter 9

PARNUTS – Foodstuffs Intended for Particular Nutritional Uses

Introduction

Foodstuffs intended for particular nutritional uses, more commonly referred to as PARNUTS, are foodstuffs which because of their special compositional or manufacturing process are suitable for their claim of a nutritional purpose. These types of products are produced to satisfy specific groups of the population that have particular nutritional requirements, for example, infants and young children or food for special medical purposes such as that for diabetics. Foodstuffs intended for particular nutritional requirements are also known as dietetic or dietary foods.

Strict rules are set out in a number of directives for the composition, marketing and labelling of dietetic foods. Legislation at EU level covering foodstuffs for particular nutritional uses was first adopted in 1976. However, because Council Directive 77/94[84] had been amended on a number of occasions, it was decided that to improve its quality, the Directive should be re-drafted and replaced by Directive 89/398.[85]

Framework Directive on Foods Intended for Particular Nutritional Uses

Council Directive 89/398 as amended by Directive 96/84[86] sets out the general rules for the composition, marketing and labelling requirements of PARNUT products. It also includes provisions to ensure that the foodstuffs are safe. The Directive gives a definition of foodstuffs for particular nutritional uses:

> 'foodstuffs which, owing to their special composition or manufacturing process, are clearly distinguishable from foodstuffs for normal consumption, which are suitable for their claimed nutritional purposes and which are marketed in such a way as to indicate such suitability.'

---

[84] OJ L 026, 31/01/1977 P. 55–58.

[85] OJ L 186, 30/06/1989 P. 27–32 amended by Directive 96/84 OJ L048 p. 20.

[86] OJ L 048, 19/02/1997 P. 20–21.

The Directive goes on to state that a 'particular nutritional use' must fulfil the particular requirements of:

(i) certain categories of persons whose digestive processes or metabolism are disturbed; or
(ii) certain categories of persons who are in a special physiological condition and who are therefore able to obtain special benefit from controlled consumption of certain substances in foodstuffs; or
(iii) infants or young children in good health.

The products referred to in categories (i) and (ii) are categorised in the Directive as 'dietetic' or 'dietary'. The use of the words dietetic or dietary is permitted in the labelling, presentation and advertising of such a product. 'Dietetic' or 'dietary' are only permitted in the labelling, presentation and advertising of PARNUT foodstuffs. It is possible for foods for normal consumption, which are also suitable for a particular nutritional use, to indicate such suitability provided they follow the procedure laid down in the Directive to designate a product as either category (i) or (ii) referred to above. The labelling and presentation of foodstuffs for normal consumption shall not give the impression that the food could be classed as dietetic or dietary. The nature or composition of dietetic or dietary foodstuffs must be such that the product is appropriate for the intended particular nutritional use. PARNUT products must also comply with all mandatory requirements to foodstuffs in general.

Annex I of Directive 89/398 sets out a list of groups of foods for particular nutritional uses in respect of which specific directives should be adopted. Initially, there were nine groups of foods, however, the Directive was amended in 1999 by Directive 1999/41[87] which amended the Annex and reduced the original categories/groups to six:

(i) infant formulae and follow-on formulae;
(ii) processed cereal based foods and baby foods for infants and young children;
(iii) food intended for use in energy restricted diets for weight reduction;
(iv) dietary foods for special medical purposes;
(v) foods intended to meet the expenditure of intense muscular effort, especially for sportsmen; and
(vi) foods for persons suffering from carbohydrate-metabolism disorders (diabetics).

Directive 1999/41 also amended Directive 89/398 to allow for two additional categories in respect of which specific directives could be adopted:

- the reduction or absence of sodium or salt (sodium chloride, table salt) content;
- the absence of gluten.

---

[87] OJ L 172, 08/07/1999 P. 38–39.

The specific Directives that have been adopted in respect of PARNUTS are as follows:

- Commission Directive 91/321[88] on infant formulae and follow-on formulae, as amended by Commission Directives 96/4[89] and 1999/50;[90]
- Commission Directive 96/5[91] on processed cereal based foods and baby foods for infants and young children, as amended by Directives 98/36[92] and 1999/39;[93]
- Commission Directive 96/8[94] on foods intended for use in energy restricted diets for weight reduction;
- Commission Directive 99/21[95] on dietary foods for special medical purposes.

Dietetic food was considered in the White Paper on Food Safety, the Commission referred to four intended proposals which at the time of writing had not been adopted:

- a proposal for a directive on foods intended to meet the expenditure resulting from intense muscular effort;
- a report on foods intended for persons suffering from diabetes;
- to define the conditions for making the claims on 'low sodium' or 'sodium free' and 'gluten free';
- new purity criteria to be laid down for nutritional substances which are added to food for particular nutritional uses.

Certain specific Directives have already been adopted, for example, in respect of infant formulae and follow-on formulae, however certain groups or dietetic foods are still being considered, for example, foods for sports people and foods for people who are suffering from diabetics. At the time of writing the Commission was expected to soon present the proposal for a specific directive for persons suffering from diabetes.

It is understood that the Commission does not currently intend to put forward a proposal on 'low sodium' but is considering amending the framework directive. It is understood that the Commission is delaying making any proposal on 'gluten free' until the discussion at Codex has developed further. The Commission is expected to bring a proposal forward on sports food in the near future.

---

[88] OJ L 175, 04/07/1991 P. 35–49.
[89] OJ L 049, 28/02/1996 P. 12–16.
[90] OJ L 139, 02/06/1999 P. 29–31.
[91] OJ L 049, 28/02/1996 P. 17–28.
[92] OJ L 167, 12/06/1998 P. 23–24.
[93] OJ L 124, 18/05/1999 P. 08–10.
[94] OJ L 055, 06/03/1996 P. 22–26.
[95] OJ L 091, 07/04/1999 P. 29–36.

Directive 89/398 suggests some of the issues that could be covered by a specific directive:

- essential requirements of the nature of the composition the products;
- provisions regarding the quality of raw materials;
- hygiene requirements;
- a list of additives;
- provisions regarding labelling, presentation and advertising;
- permitted differences to the mandatory labelling requirements of foodstuffs for normal consumption because of the PARNUT nature of the product;
- sampling procedures and analysis to check compliance with the specific directive.

The conditions under which reference may be made in the labelling, presentation and advertising to either a diet or a category of persons for which a PARNUT product is intended can be adopted in accordance with a procedure specified under the Framework Directive 89/398. The Directive prohibits PARNUTS from being labelled, presented or advertised by attributing properties to the product for the prevention or treatment or curing of human disease or to imply that product has such attributes. Derogations from this prohibition can only be permitted after a prescribed procedure set out in Directive 89/398 has been followed.

Directive 89/398 requires the establishment of a list of substances with specific nutritional purposes such as vitamins, mineral salts and amino acids that are intended to be added to foodstuffs intended for particular nutritional uses. It also requires the establishment of purity criteria applicable to these substances and if necessary conditions for their use. This was in fact established by Directive 2001/15.[96] The annex to Directive 2001/15 is a list of substances that may be added to PARNUT products. The list is divided into six categories including vitamins, minerals and amino acids. In respect of the six categories, only the substances listed in the annex may be used in PARNUT products. However, other substances added for specific nutritional purposes that do not belong to one of the categories may be used. Under Directive 2001/15, the competent authorities of Member States are empowered to require the manufacturer or the importer of the product to produce scientific data establishing the use of substances fulfils the particular nutritional requirements of the persons for whom they are intended and that the product is safe. If this information is contained in a readily available publication reference to this document may suffice.

Directive 2001/15 provides that purity criteria for substances listed for their use in the manufacture of foodstuffs for general consumption, also applies to their use in PARNUT products. For substances for which no purity criteria are specified at Community legislation the Directive requires that generally acceptable purity criteria recommended by international bodies should apply, and reference is made to any of such criteria or international body. Additionally, national purity criteria are

---

[96] OJ L 052, 22/02/2001 P. 19–25.

expressly allowed to be maintained. Member States have until 1 April 2004 to prohibit the trade of products that do not comply with Directive 2001/15.

Safeguard Measures

Where a Member State has detailed grounds for establishing that a PARNUT which falls with that outside the scope of the Directive, does not comply with the Directive or endangers human health, it may temporarily suspend or restrict trade in the product within its territory. The Commission and other Member States must be informed immediately and reasons must be given for the restriction or suspension. The Commission must then produce an opinion after consulting with the other Member States and the Scientific Committee for Foodstuffs. There is a procedure set down in the Directive for the Commission to use if action is necessary.

Where a Member State, on a result of new information or of a reassessment of existing information made since one of the specific Directives was adopted has detailed grounds for establishing that a foodstuff intended for particular nutritional uses endangers human health although it complies with the specific Directive, then the Member State may temporarily suspend or restrict the application of the relevant implemented national rules. The Commission and the other Member States must be informed immediately with reasons. After consulting with the other Member States and the Scientific Committee for Foodstuffs, the Commission must produce an opinion. If appropriate, the relevant specific Directive can be amended in accordance with a procedure laid down in the Framework Directive.

In 1996, the Framework Directive 89/398 was amended by Directive 1996/84. Directive 1996/84 allows the Commission to authorise for a maximum of 2 years, PARNUTS foodstuffs which do not comply with the rules on composition established by the specific directives. The amendment was made to allow consumers to benefit from technological innovations quickly. The Commission is only permitted to authorise these products after consulting the Scientific Committee for food and following a prescribed procedure set out in Directive 89/398.

Labelling of Products that do not fall within a Specific Directive

PARNUT products that have not as yet had specific provisions set out in a specific directive must include in their labels:

- the particular elements of the qualitative and quantitative composition of the special manufacturing process which gives the product its particular nutritional characteristics;
- the available energy value expressed in kilojoules or kilocalories and the carbohydrate, protein and fat content per 100 g or 100 mm of the product as marketed and, if appropriate, the energy value for the quantity of the product proposed for consumption.

If the energy value of the product is less than 50kj (12kc) per 100g or 100mm, it is permitted to state on the label 'energy value less than 50kj (12kc) per 100g' or 'energy value less than 50kj (12kc) per 100mm' instead of the specific energy value of the product.

The particular labelling requirements for those products in respect of which a specific directive has been adopted are laid down in that specific directive (see below).

The Framework Directive lays down measures to permit efficient official monitoring of foodstuffs for a particular nutritional use which do not belong to one of the identified groups. Notably, when a product is placed on the EU market for the first time, the manufacturer (or the importer where appropriate) must notify the competent authority of the Member State where the product is to be marketed together with a model of the label to be used.

Specific Directives

Commission Directive 91/321 on infant formula and follow-on formula, as amended by Commission Directives 96/4 and 1999/50 and 2003/14[97]

This specific directive lays down compositional and labelling requirements for infant formula and follow-on formula intended for use by infants in good health. For the purposes of this directive, an infant is a child under the age of 12 months, and young children are children aged between 1 and 3 years. 'Infant formula' is defined as 'foodstuffs intended for particular nutritional use by infants during the first 4–6 months of life' whereas 'follow-on formula' means 'foodstuffs intended for particular nutritional use by infants aged over 4 months and constituting the principle liquid element in a progressively diversified diet of this category of person'.

The Directive requires Member States to allow free movement to products that meet the definitions and requirements laid down in this directive. However, no product other than infant formula within the definitions under this directive may be marketed or otherwise represented as suitable for satisfying, by itself, the nutritional requirements of normal healthy infants during the first 4–6 months of life. Infant formula shall be manufactured from protein sources as defined in the annexes to the Directive and other food ingredients who's suitability for particular nutritional use by infants from birth has been established by generally accepted scientific data. Specific compositional criteria are laid down in relation to infant formula. Follow-on formula must be manufactured from protein sources again defined in the annexes to the Directive and other food ingredients as the case may be who's suitability for particular nutritional use by infants aged over 4 months has been established by generally accepted scientific data. Follow-on formula must also comply with the compositional requirements set down in the annexes.

---

[97] OJ L 041, 14/02/2003 P. 37–40.

In order to make infant formula and follow-on formula ready for use, nothing more shall be required other than the addition of water. Prohibitions and limitations on the use of certain food ingredients, in both infant formula and follow-up formula, are laid down in the respective annexes. The Directive specifies minerals substances, vitamins, amino acids and other nitrogen compounds and other substances having particular nutritional purposes that can be included in infant formula and follow-on formula. Provision is made that infant formula and follow-on formula shall not contain any substance in such quantity as to endanger the health of infants and young children. Necessary maximum residue levels have been established along with microbiological criteria. Many of the amendments to this Directive have been about the maximum residue levels, in particular, in relation to particularly toxic pesticides.

In addition to the general labelling requirements (see Chapter 5) the Directive also lays down mandatory particulars which must be included in the labelling of infant formula and follow-on formula:

- in the case of infant formula, a statement to the effect that the product is suitable for particular nutritional use by infants from birth;
- in the case of infant formula, that do not contain added iron, a statement to the effect that, when the product is given to infants over the age of four months, their total iron requirements must be met from other additional sources;
- in the case of follow-on formula, a statement to the effect that the product is suitable only for particular nutritional use by infants over the age of 4 months, that it should form part of a diversified diet and that it is not to be used as a substitute for breast milk during the first 4 months of life;
- for both infant formula and follow-on formula, the available energy value, expressed in kilojoules and kilocalories, and the contents of proteins, carbohydrates and lipids expressed in numerical form, by 100 ml of the product ready for use;
- for both infant formula and follow-on formula, the average quantity of each mineral substance and of each vitamin mentioned in the annexes to the Directive and where applicable of choline, inositol, carnitine and taurine, expressed in numerical form by 100 ml of the product ready for use;
- for both infant formula and follow-on formula, instructions for appropriate preparation of the product and a warning against health hazards of inappropriate preparation.

The labelling is permitted to bear the average quantity of nutrients mentioned in the annexes to the Directive where such declaration is not required as a mandatory particular, see above. If such a declaration is given, it must be expressed in numerical form by 100 ml of the product ready for use. For follow-on formula in addition to numerical information, information on the vitamins and minerals included in the annexes to the Directive, can be expressed as a percentage of the reference values given under the Directive, per 100 ml of the product ready for use, provided that the quantities present are at least equal to 15 per cent of the reference value.

The labelling of infant formula shall, in addition, also bear the following mandatory particulars with the words 'important notice', or equivalent, in advance of them:

- a statement concerning the superiority of breastfeeding;
- a statement recommending that the product be used only on the advice of independent persons having qualifications in medicine, nutrition or pharmacy or other professionals responsible for maternal and child care.

Labelling of infant formula is not permitted to include pictures of infants and neither shall it include pictures or text which may in any way idolise the use of the product. It can have graphic representations for easy identification of the product and for illustrating methods of preparation. These restrictions also apply to the presentation of the product concerned, in particular their shape, appearance or packaging, the packaging material used, the way in which they are arranged and the setting in which they are displayed as well as their advertising.

Advertising of infant formula is restricted to publications specialising in baby care and scientific publications. Member States are permitted to further restrict or prohibit such advertising. Such adverts for infant formula must meet many of the labelling requirements set out above and contain only information of a scientific and factual nature. It should not imply or create any belief that bottle feeding is equivalent or superior to breastfeeding. Point of sale advertising is not be permitted and neither is the giving of samples or any other promotional devices to induce sales of infant formula directly to the consumer at the retail level, such as special displays, discount coupons, premiums, special sales, loss leaders and tie-in sales. Manufacturers and distributors of infant formula are not permitted to provide to the general public or to pregnant women, mothers or members of their family, free or low priced products, samples or other promotional gifts either directly or indirectly via health care workers or the health care system.

Member States are obliged to ensure that objective and consistent information is provided on infant feeding for use by families and those involved in the field of infant and young child nutrition. Moreover, Member States are obliged to ensure that information and educational materials on the feeding of infants and intended to reach pregnant women and mothers of infants and young children should include clear information on the following:

- the benefits and superiority of breastfeeding;
- maternal nutrition and the preparation for breastfeeding;
- the possibly negative effect on breastfeeding of introducing partial bottle feeding;
- the difficulty in reversing the decision not to breastfeed;
- where needed, the proper use of infant formula whether manufactured industrially or prepared, at home.

If such materials contain information about the use of infant formula they should include the social and financial implications of its use, the health hazards of inappropriate foods or feeding methods and, in particular, the health hazards of inappropriate use of infant formula. The Directive goes on to set rules about donations of information or educational material by manufacturers or distributors.

Commission Directive 96/5 on processed cereal based foods and baby foods for infants and young children as amended by Directive 98/36 and 1999/39

This Directive covers foodstuffs for particular nutritional use for filling the particular requirements of infants and young children in good health and are intended for use by infants while they are being weaned, and by young children as a supplement to their diet and/or for their progressive adaptation to ordinary food. 'Processed cereal-based foods' are divided into four categories:

- simple cereals which are or have to be reconstituted with milk or other appropriate nutritious liquids;
- cereals with an added high protein food which are or have to be reconstituted with water or other protein-free liquid;
- pastas which are to be used after cooking in boiling water or other appropriate liquids;
- rusks and biscuits which are to be used either directly or after pulverization with the addition of water milk or other suitable liquids.

Baby foods, other than processed cereal based foods are also covered by this directive for the purposes of this directive 'infants' refer to children under the age of 12 months whereas young children means children aged between 1 and 3 years.

Member States are to ensure that products covered by the scope of this directive is only to be marketed if they conform with the rules laid down in the Directive. Processed cereal based foods and baby foods must be manufactured from ingredients who suitability's for particular nutritional use by infants and young children has been established by generally accepted scientific data. Compositional criteria are set down under the Directive for processed cereal based foods and baby foods. There is a list of nutritional substances which may be added to such foods during the manufacturing process. No other nutritional substances can be added to cereal based foods and baby foods. Certain maximum residue levels have been established for substances that should not be present in processed cereal based foods and baby foods in such quantity as to endanger the health of infants and young children. Microbiological criteria has also been established as necessary. Many of the amendments refer to pesticides residues and the setting of maximum residue levels.

A further amendment also deals with maximum limits of vitamins and minerals and trace elements if added to processed cereal based foods and baby foods intended for infants and young children. The requirements concerning these nutrients refer to the products ready for use, marketed as such or reconstituted as instructed by the manufacturer except for potassium and calcium where the requirements refer to the product as sold.

In addition to the mandatory labelling requirements set down in the General Food Labelling Directive (see Chapter 5) the following mandatory particulars are required in respect of processed cereal based foods and baby foods:

- A statement as to the appropriate age from which the product may be used, regard of being had to its composition, texture and other particular properties. The stated age shall not be less than 4 months for any product. Products recommended for use from the age of 4 months may indicate that they are suitable from that age unless independent persons having qualifications in medicine, nutritional pharmacy or other professionals responsible for maternal and child care, advise otherwise.
- Information as to the presence or absence of gluten if the indicated age from which the product may be used is below 6 months.
- The available energy expressed in kilojoules and kilocalories, and the protein, carbohydrate and lipid content, expressed in numerical form, per 100 g or 100 ml of the product as sold and where appropriate, per specified quantity of the product as proposed for consumption.
- The average quantity of each mineral substance and of each vitamin governed by a specific level as set down in the annexes to the Directive expressed in numerical form per 100 g or 100 ml of the product as sold and, where appropriate, per specified quantity of the product as proposed for consumption.
- Instructions for appropriate preparation, where necessary a statement as to the importance of following those instructions.

Labelling may also bear, although it is not obligatory, the average quantity of nutrients covered in the annexes to the Directive where the declaration is not mandatory as set out in the particulars above. In addition to numerical information, information may also be given on the vitamins and minerals expressed as a percentage of the reference values set down in the annexes to the Directive. This can only be given provided that the quantities present are at least equal to 15 per cent of the reference value. The percentages can be expressed per specified quantity of the product as proposed for consumption or as per 100 g or 100 ml of the product sold.

Commission Directive 96/8/EC on foods intended for use in energy restricted diets for weight reduction

The Directive lays down composition and labelling requirements for foods of particular nutritional use intended for use in energy restricted diets for weight reduction and presented as such. Foods for use in energy restricted diets for weight reduction are specially formulated foods which, when used as instructed by the manufacturer, replace all or part of the total daily diet. They are divided into two categories:

(a) products presented as a replacement for the whole of the daily diet;
(b) products presented as a replacement for one or more meals of the daily diet.

The Directive lays down specific compensational requirements. Relating to the energy, protein, fat, dietary fibre, vitamins and minerals that must be provided by these products.

Products under bullet point (a) must be sold under the name 'total diet replacement for weight control'. Products sold that fall in bullet point (b) must be sold under the name 'meal replacement for weight control'.

In addition to the usual mandatory particulars (see Chapter 5) the following mandatory particulars are required for products covered by this directive:

- the available energy expressed in kilojoules and kilocalories and the content of proteins, carbohydrate and fat, expressed in numerical form, per specified quantity of the product ready for use as proposed for consumption;
- the average quantity of each mineral and each vitamin for which mandatory requirements are stipulated under the Directive expressed in numerical form per specified quantity of the product ready for use as proposed for consumption. In addition, for products mentioned in point (b) above, information on vitamins and minerals contained in the Directive shall also be expressed as a percentage of reference values set down in the Directives;
- instructions for appropriate preparation, when necessary and a statement as to the importance of following those instructions;
- if a product, when used as instructed by the manufacturer, provides a daily intake of polyols in excess of 20 g per day, there shall be a statement to the effect that the food may have a laxative effect;
- a statement on the importance of maintaining an adequate daily fluid intake;
- for products mentioned in point (a) above, a statement that the product provides adequate amounts of all essential nutrients for the day and a statement that the product should not be used for more than three weeks without medical advice;
- for products covered by point (b) above, a statement to the effect that products are useful for use as part of an energy restricted diet and other foodstuffs are necessary part of such a diet.

Labelling, advertising and presentation of the products concerned should not make any reference to the rate or amount of weight loss which may result from their use, or to a reduction to the sense of hunger or an increase in the sense of satiety.

Directive 1999/21 on dietary foods for special medical purposes

This directive sets down composition and labelling requirements for dietary foods for special medical purposes which are categories of food for particular nutritional uses specially processed or formulated and intended for the dietary management of patients and to be used under medical supervision. They are intended for the exclusive or partial feeding of patients with a limited, impaired or disturbed capacity to intake, digest, absorb, metabolize or excrete ordinary foodstuffs or certain nutrients contained therein or metabolites, or with other medically determined nutrient requirements, who's dietary management cannot be achieved only by modification of the normal diet, by other foods for particular nutritional use, or by culmination of the two. Dietary foods for special medical purposes are classified into three categories:

- nutritionally complete foods with the standard nutrient formulation which used in accordance with the manufacturers instructions may constitute the sole source of nourishment for the person for whom they are intended;
- nutritionally complete foods with the nutrient-adapted formulation specific for disease, disorder or medical condition, which, used in accordance with the manufacturers instructions may constitute the sole source of nourishment for the persons for whom they are intended;
- nutritionally incomplete foods with the standard formulation or nutrient adapted formulation specific for a disease, disorder or medical condition which are not suitable to be used as sole source of nourishment.

The Directive requires that dietary foods for special medical purposes must be based on sound medical nutritional principles. Their use, in accordance with manufacturers instructions, must be safe and beneficial and effective in meeting the particular nutritional requirements of the persons for whom they are intended, as demonstrated by generally accepted scientific data. Specific compositional requirements are set down in the annexes to the Directive. Including, for example, the provision of vitamins and minerals in the three different categories of dietary foods for special medical purposes.

The labelling should generally comply with the particulars provided for in Article 3 of Directive 2000/13 with the following additional mandatory particulars:

- The available energy shall be expressed in kilojoules and kilocalories, and the content of protein, carbohydrate and fat, expressed in numerical form, per 100 g or per 100 ml of the product sold and where appropriate per 100 g or per 100 ml of the product ready for use in accordance with the manufacturer's instructions. This information may also be given in relation to servings as quantified on the label or per portion, provided that the number of portions contained in the package is stated.
- The average quantity of each mineral substances and each vitamin mentioned in the Directive expressed in numerical form per 100 g or per 100 ml of the product as sold or where appropriate per 100 g or per 100 ml of the product ready for use in accordance with the manufacturer's instructions. This information may also be provided in relation to a serving as quantified on the label or per portion provided that the number of portions contained in the package is given.
- The content of components of protein, carbohydrate and fat and of other nutrients and their components the declaration of which will be necessary for the appropriate intent to use the product, expressed in numerical form, per 100 g or per 100 ml of the product as sold and where appropriate per 100 g or per 100 ml of the product ready for use in accordance with the manufacturer's instructions.

This information can also be given per serving or per portion provided that the number of portions contained in the pack is stated.
- Information on osmolality or osmolarity of the product where appropriate.
- Information on the origin and nature of the protein and/or protein hydrolysates contained in the product.

In addition, the labelling shall bear the following mandatory particulars and should be preceded by the words 'important notice' or the equivalent:

- a statement that the product must be used under medical supervision;
- a statement whether the product is suitable for use of as the sole source of nutrition;
- a statement that the product is intended for a specific age group if appropriate;
- whether the product possesses any potential health hazard being consumed by persons who do not have the disease, disorder or medical condition for which the product is intended.

The labelling should also include a statement 'for the dietary management of where the blank is filled in by the disease, disorder or medical conditions for which the product is intended, as well as a statement relating to the adequate precautions or contradictions as required. Additionally, a description should be given of the properties and/or the characteristics that may put as useful in particular relating to the nutrients which have been increased, reduced, eliminated or otherwise modified and the rationale of the use of the product. The labelling shall bear instructions for the appropriate preparation, the use and the storage of the product.

To enhance official monitoring of dietary foods for special medical purposes, the manufacturer or importer (as appropriate) must notify the competent authority of the Member State where the product is being marketed when a product is placed on a market. Member States may choose not to impose the obligation of notification if they can demonstrate that notification is not necessary in order to monitor those products efficiently.

Chapter 10

Food Supplements and Fortification

Food Supplements

In June 2002, the European Parliament and Council adopted for the first time a directive harmonising the laws of Member States relating to food supplements. Member States must bring their national laws into line by 31 July 2003, from the 1 August 2003 they must permit trade in products complying with the Directive, and by 1 August 2005 they must prohibit products that do not comply.

The scope of the Directive

Food supplements are defined as:

> 'foodstuffs for the purpose of which is to supplement the normal diet and which are concentrated sources of nutrients or other substances with a nutritional or physiological effect, alone or in combination, marketed in dose form, namely forms such as capsules, pastilles, tablets, pills and other similar forms, sachets of powder, ampoules of liquids, drop dispensing bottles and other similar forms of liquids and powders designed to be taken in measured small unit quantities.'

Nutrient for the purposes of the Directive include vitamins and minerals. The Directive only harmonises rules in relation to vitamins and minerals, and does not govern other nutrients as dietary supplements. The Commission intends to address the issue of the use of other substances with nutritional or physiological functions at a later date. The report on these other substances is expected no later than June 2007.

The Directive establishes a permitted list of vitamins and minerals for manufacturers of food supplements (see Annex IV for a full list of these substances). Only the vitamins listed may be used for the manufacture of food supplements. It is anticipated that purity criteria will be established for these substances. Where purity criteria, for purposes other than the use of food supplements, is already established they should apply. Where purity criteria has not been specified in relation to particular substances generally acceptable purity criteria recommended by international bodies is to be applicable and national rules setting stricter purity criteria may be maintained until such Community purity criteria is established. There are provisions set out in the Directive for the list of vitamins and minerals to be updated under a simplified procedure.

There is a derogation that allows Member States to permit in their territory the use of vitamins and minerals in forms not listed under the Directive until 21 January 2009 provided that:

- the substance in question is used in one or more food supplements marketed in the Community on the date the Directive entered into force;
- the European Food Safety Authority has not given an unfavourable opinion in respect of the use of that substance, or its use in that form;
- the manufacture of food supplements is on the basis of a dossier supporting the use of the substances in question to be submitted to the Commission by the Member State not later than December 2005.

Member States must permit the marketing of substances listed under the Directive in the forms listed in the Directive for use in food supplements. However, they may continue with these national restrictions or bans on the trade in food supplements containing vitamins and minerals not listed under the Directive or in forms not listed under the Directive.

Maximum and minimum limits

It is foreseen that the maximum permitted amount of vitamins and minerals present in food supplements per daily portion of consumption, as recommended by the manufacturers, will be set. These maximum amounts will take into account the upper safe levels of vitamins and minerals established by scientific risk assessments based on generally accepted scientific data and varying degrees of sensitivity of different consumer groups. In addition, to ensure that significant amounts of vitamins and minerals are present in the food supplements, minimum amounts per daily portion of consumption, as recommended by the manufacturer, will be set. The maximum and minimum amounts of vitamins and minerals will be set in accordance with the simplified procedure set out in the Directive.

The Standing Committee will decide on a case-by-case basis the permitted doses for each vitamin and mineral. Permitted doses will not purely be based on basic safety and therefore they, to some extent, will based on need as is indicated by the reference to the intakes of vitamins and minerals by the population. This goes away from the principles of sound science and could restrict innovation in the European food industry and the right of the consumer to choose.

The labelling of food supplements

Products covered by this Directive shall be sold as 'food supplements'. The labelling, presentation and advertising is not permitted to attribute to food supplements the property of preventing, treating or curing a human disease, as this would amount to a medicinal claim. In addition to the mandatory particulars referred to under Directive 2000/13[98] the labelling should also bear the following particulars:

- the name of the categories of nutrients or substances that categorise the product or an indication of the nature of those nutrients or substances;
- the portion of the product recommended for daily consumption;
- a warning not to exceed the stated recommended daily dose;
- a statement to the effect that the food supplements should not be used as a substitute for a varied diet;
- a statement to the effect that the product should be stored out of the reach of young children.

Labelling, presentation and advertising of food supplements should not include any mention, state or imply that a balanced and varied diet cannot provide the appropriate quantities of nutrients in general.

The amounts of the nutrients or substances with a nutritional or physiological effect present in the products must be declared on the labelling in numerical form. The Directive sets out units to be used in respect of vitamins or minerals. Information on vitamins and minerals must also be expressed as a percentage of the reference value mentioned in Directive 90/496/EEC[99] (see Chapter 5). Declared values mentioned must be average values based on the manufacturer's analysis of the product. Provision is made for further rules to be drawn up with regard to the differences between the declared value and those established during the course of official checks.

To facilitate effective monitoring of food supplements, Member States can require manufacturers or the person placing the products in the market in their territory to notify a competent authority and forward the label to be used on their product. Member States may not restrict the marketing of products complying with requirements of this directive at least when the reasons for such restrictions relate to their composition, manufacturing specifications, presentation or labelling.

A Member State that has, as a result of new information or of a reassessment of existing information made since this directive or one of the implementing Community Acts was adopted, detailed grounds for establishing that a product referred to under this directive endangers human health, although it complies with the requirements of the Directive, may temporarily suspend or restrict the application of the provisions in question within its territory. If it does so it should immediately inform the other Member States and the Commission of this, giving reasons for the decision. The Commission must then examine the grounds for such restriction or prohibition and consult with the Member States within the Standing Committee on the Food Chain and Animal Health before delivering an opinion and taking appropriate measures. If the Commission considers that amendments to the Directive or other Community Acts are necessary Member States may retain the safeguard measures adopted in the interim.

---

[98] OJ L 109, 06/05/2000 P. 29–42.

[99] OJ L 276, 06/10/1990 P. 40–44.

Conclusion. Harmonisation of the rules should allow companies to operate, to an extent, on a pan-EU basis. It remains to be seen if the Directive will be used to restrict the doses of vitamins and minerals on a base other than sound science. This would restrict the right of the consumer to choose as well as potentially stifling innovation in industry.

Fortification

Current situation

The rules relating to the extent to which foodstuffs can be fortified, and which substances can be used, have not yet been harmonised at Community level. Consequently they have developed at the national level. The approach of the different Member States has been varied. Some Member States, such as the United Kingdom, have generally permitted fortification of products provided they are safe and the labelling is not misleading. Other Member States have used a system of pre-notification, such as that in Germany whilst others, such as the Scandinavian countries, have only permitted fortification where a 'need' is identified in the population. Some Member States apply national rules requiring the mandatory addition of nutrients to certain foods. There are also a few Community rules requiring the mandatory addition of nutrients to a number of foods for particular nutritional use (see Chapter 9).

These discrepancies have hindered manufacturers' ability to place one product, labelled in one way, on the EU market. In light of this, the Commission has decided that harmonisation is needed to achieve free movement of goods. The proposal for this legislation was delayed whilst the Commission waited for the Directive on Food Supplements to be adopted. However, the Directive on Food Supplements has now been adopted, and the Commission has moved a proposal on the addition of vitamins and minerals to foodstuffs forward in the autumn of 2003. In view of this, the remainder of this chapter is based on the Commission's proposal. The text of a draft is by its nature fluid and it will continue to change until it is issued as a proposal. Once adopted as a proposal, the legislative process can then begin, during which the text of the proposal will continue to change.

Expected proposal for harmonisation

The objective of the proposed Regulation is to harmonise Community rules to facilitate free circulation of such products and to ensure a high level of consumer protection. The proposal only relates to the voluntary addition of vitamins and minerals to food. It permits the addition of certain vitamins and mineral to all foods for the purposes of: restoration; achieving nutritional equivalence; fortification or enrichment. Restoration is to ensure that in the final product offered to the consumer, the levels of nutrients (lost during storage, handling and manufacturing) are equal to the original levels. Substitution allows for the production of substitute foods that resemble the other foods in appearance, organicleptic properties and nutritional value. A good example is margarine which is a substitute for butter. Fortification or enrichment is the addition of vitamins or minerals to foods irrespective of whether these nutrients were present originally. Only certain vitamins and minerals would be permitted (see Annex III).

Maximum and minimum permitted levels of vitamins and minerals. Maximum amounts of vitamins and minerals present in foods as sold will be set for vitamins and minerals that have been added to those foods. For concentrated and dehydrated products the maximum amounts will be applied to the foods as prepared for consumption according to the manufacturers' instructions. The maximum amounts will be set taking the following into account:

- upper safe levels of vitamins and minerals established by scientific risk assessments based on generally acceptable scientific data, taking into account, as appropriate, the varying degrees of sensitivity of different consumer groups;
- intakes of vitamins and minerals from other dietary sources.

When the maximum levels are set, account will be taken of reference intakes of vitamins and minerals for the population. In cases where the reference intakes for the population are close to the upper safe levels, according to the proposal the following would also be taken into account, as necessary:

- the requirements for the addition of certain vitamins or minerals to food for the purpose of restoration and/or for the purpose of nutritional equivalence of substitute foods;
- the contribution of individual products to the overall diet of the population in general or of sub-groups of the population;
- the nutrient profile of the product (as established under the proposed claims legislation; see Chapter 8).

The addition of a vitamin or a mineral to food for the purpose of fortification would have to result in the presence of this vitamin or mineral in the food in at least a significant amount as is defined in the Annex of Directive 90/496/EEC[100] (see Chapter 5). In other words, there would have to be more than a minimum amount of a vitamin or mineral. The maximum and minimum amounts of vitamins and minerals would be set in accordance with a prescribed simplified procedure.

Labelling, presentation and advertising. Under the proposal the labelling, presentation and advertising, of foods to which vitamins and minerals have been added would not be permitted to mention or imply that a balanced and varied diet cannot provide appropriate quantities of nutrients. The labelling, presentation or advertising would be prohibited from misleading or deceiving the consumer as to the nutritional

[100] OJ L 276, 06/10/1990 P. 40–44.

merit of the food that may result from the addition of these nutrients. By derogation to Article 2 of Council Directive 90/496/EEC (see Chapter 5), nutrition labelling of products to which vitamins and minerals have been added would be compulsory. More specific rules for implementing these requirements relating to labelling, presentation and advertising may be specified in accordance with a simplified procedure.

Free movement and nutritional criteria. If a fortified product meets the requirements of the Regulation once adopted, it should benefit from free movement.

As currently drafted, the preliminary text offers Member States one area of flexibility in implementation: to require manufacturers or persons placing such foods on the market to notify the competent authority by forwarding a model of the label. The concern is that such a requirement could allow Member States to impede access of some products to their markets.

Currently only alcoholic drinks and fresh produce have been identified as a category of foods to which addition of nutrients would not be permitted. However it is not clear how the Commission will address the nutrient profiles that they are expected to outline. Such criteria could restrict the fortification of particular food categories.

Safeguard measures. Where a Member State, as a result of new information or of a reassessment of existing information has detailed grounds for establishing that a product to which vitamins or minerals have been added endangers human health, even though it complies with the Community rules, may temporarily suspend or restrict the application of the provisions in question within its territory. On doing so, it would have to immediately inform the other Member States and the Commission of this action along with its reasons. The Commission would examine, as soon as possible, the grounds adduced by the Member State concerned and consult the other Member States through the Standing Committee on the Food Chain and Animal Health. It will then deliver its opinion without delay and take appropriate measures. If the Commission considers that amendments to this Regulation or to the implementing Community acts are necessary it will follow a simplified procedure. The Member State that has adopted safeguard measures may in that event retain them until the amendments have been adopted.

Conclusion. Harmonisation of the rules on the addition of vitamins and minerals to foodstuffs should eliminate many of the discrepancies in the national laws. The possibility for Member States to impose notification requirements could impede the single market. Moreover, the proposal does not cover mandatory fortification so pan-EU marketing may continue to be difficult. A further concern is that the possibility to set nutritional criteria at EU level for foods to which vitamins and minerals may be added could restrict consumer choice and stifle industry innovation.

Chapter 11

Vertical Directives

Vertical Directives lay down particular compositional and labelling requirements for certain products including honey, chocolate, coffee, sugar, fruit juices, dried milk and jam.[101] Over the last few years, following the agreement at the Edinburgh Summit, about the need for simplification and transparency of EU legislation, these directives have been revised and updated. This chapter will look at the production and marketing requirements laid down in respect of each of these products.

Honey

Council Directive 74/409[102] on the harmonisation of the laws of Member States relating to honey was originally justified by the fact that differences between national laws could result in conditions of unfair competition, be likely to mislead consumers and inhibit the creation of a single market; thereby it could have a direct effect on the establishment and functioning of the Common Market. The Directive (as subsequently amended) established definitions and specified the different types of honey that could be placed on the market under particular names, laid down common laws on the composition and determined the main labelling information so as to ensure the free movement of honey products within the Community. However, it was decided that Directive 74/409 should be redrafted in order to make rules on the conditions for the marketing of honey more accessible. The Edinburgh Summit in December 1992 had decided that the vertical directives generally should be simplified in order to take account of the essential requirements to be met by the products in order to ensure the free movement of those products. In particular, it was necessary to ensure that the requirements relating to the conditions for the production and marketing of honey are in line with the general food labelling rules as laid down in Directive 2000/13[103] (see Chapter 5). Therefore the rules on honey have been modified and now are contained in Directive 2001/110.[104]

The composition of honey is defined as essentially different sugars, predominantly fructose and glucose together with organic acids, enzymes, and solid particles derived from honey collections. The colour of honey varies from nearly colourless

[101] Please note this list is not exhaustive.

[102] OJ L 221, 12/08/1974 P. 10–14.

[103] OJ L 109, 06/05/2000 P. 29–42.

[104] OJ L 010, 12/01/2002 P. 47–52.

to dark brown. The consistency can be fluid, viscose or partly to entirely crystallised. The flavour and aroma can vary.

The Directive only allows the term honey to be applied to products defined therein. Honey is defined as the natural sweet substance produced by *apis mellifera* bees from the nectar of plants, or from secretions of living plants, or excretions of plant sucking insects on the living parts of plants, which the bees collect, transform by combining with specific substances of their own, deposit, dehydrate, store and leave in honeycombs to ripen and mature. The following types of honey are identified in the annex to the Directive:

According to origin:

- blossom honey or nectar honey – honey obtained from the nectar of plants;
- honeydew honey – honey obtained mainly from excretions from plant sucking insects, the living parts of plants or secretions of plants.

According to mode of production and/or presentation:

- comb honey – honey stored by bees in the cells of freshly built, broodless combs, thin comb foundation sheets made solely of bees wax and sold in sealed, whole combs;
- chunk honey or cut comb in honey – honey which contains one or more pieces of comb honey;
- drained honey – honey obtained by draining decapped, broodless combs;
- extracted honey – honey obtained by centrifuging decapped, broodless combs;
- pressed honey – honey obtained by pressing broodless combs with or without the application of heat;
- filter honey – honey obtained by removing inorganic or organic matter in such as way as to result in the significant removal of pollen.

Baker's honey is honey which is either (a) suitable for industrial uses or as an ingredient in other foodstuffs which are then processed or (b) may have:

- a foreign taste or odour;
- begun to ferment or have fermented; or
- been overheated.

The product names described above can only be used in application to the products as described. The names can be replaced by the simple product name 'honey' except in the case of filtered honey, comb honey, chunk honey, or cut comb in honey and baker's honey. However, in the case of baker's honey the words 'intended only for cooking' must appear on the label in close proximity to the product name. Where baker's honey is used as an ingredient in compound food, the term honey can be used in the product name of the compound food instead of the term baker's honey, but bakers honey must be indicated in the ingredients list.

It is generally felt that given the close link between the quality of honey and its origin it is essential that full information on matters relating to its origin should be made available to the consumer so that they are not mislead as to the quality of the product. Therefore, the consumer interests are served by information relating to the geographical characteristics of the honey. The country or countries of origin where the honey has been harvested shall be indicated on the label. However, if the honey originates in one or more Member States or third country that indication may be replaced by either 'blend of EC honeys', 'blend of non-EC honeys', or 'blend of EC and non-EC honeys.

The Commission can adopt methods to permit verification of compliance of honey with the provisions of the Directive. However, until such time as methods are adopted Member States are required to use internationally recognised validated methods such as those approved by the CODEX Alimentarius. Member States must bring in laws to comply with this Directive before 1 August 2003.[105]

Chocolate

The now repealed 1973 Chocolate Directive 73/241[106] laid down common rules regarding the composition and labelling of chocolate. The addition of non-cocoa vegetable fats to chocolate. Products falling under this directive were subject to both the compositional and labelling requirements it sets down.[107] The General Labelling Directive did not apply to products that fall within the scope of this Directive.

For the purposes of Directive 73/241, cocoa and chocolate products meant cocoa beans, cocoa nib, cocoa dust, cocoa fines, cocoa mass, cocoa press cake, fat-reduced cocoa pressed cake, expeller cocoa pressed cake, cocoa, cocoa powder, fat-reduced cocoa, fat-reduced cocoa powder, sweetened cocoa, sweetened cocoa powder, drinking chocolate, sweetened fat-reduced cocoa, sweetened fat-reduced cocoa powder, fat-reduced drinking chocolate, cocoa butter, cocoa fat, chocolate, plain chocolate, vermicelli chocolate, chocolate flakes, gianduja nut chocolate, couverture chocolate, milk chocolate, milk chocolate with high milk content, milk chocolate vermicelli, milk chocolate flakes, gianduja nut milk chocolate, couverture milk chocolate, white chocolate, filled chocolate and a chocolate.

Each of these products had the compositional requirements laid down and the names, as listed above, could not be applied to any product that does not meet these designations. For example, chocolate was defined as the product obtained from cocoa nib, cocoa mass, cocoa powder, or fat-reduced cocoa powder and sucrose with or without added cocoa butter, having, without prejudice to the definition of chocolate vermicelli, gianduja nut chocolate and couverture chocolate, a minimum total dry cocoa solids content of 35 per cent – at least 14 per cent of dry non-fat cocoa

[105] Until that time they may continue to comply with Directive 74/409.

[106] OJ L 228, 16/08/1973 P. 23–35.

[107] Please note that as from 3 August 2003 Member States must comply with Directive 2000/36.

solids and 18 per cent of cocoa butter. These percentages must be calculated after the weight of the additions of ingredients (e.g. nuts) have been deducted. Only products complying with these requirements can be called chocolate.

The Directive set out standard sized bars/tablets that the products listed under the Directive led to. Each bar or tablet must not weigh less than 95 g and not more than 500 g. In particular, they had to be marketed in the following individual weights only: 85, 100, 125, 150, 200, 250, 300, 400 and 500 g. The labelling requirements under the Chocolate Directive were reduced as compared to the general labelling of foodstuffs. The reserve name of the product had to be indicated on-pack accompanied by an indication of any filling of the product. There had also normally to be a declaration of the total dry cocoa solids. For filled chocolate and chocolate obtained from chocolate products, other than chocolate and couverture chocolate, an additional indication of the type or types of chocolates used had to be given. Net weight must be indicated unless the product weighs less than 50 g. The name, or trade name, and address of the registered office of the manufacturer or packer or seller established within the Community, had to be indicated along with a declaration of dextrose or crystallised glucose and a declaration of a foodstuff having a flavouring effect, where a flavouring substance, other than ethnyl vanillin is used the name shall be added by '... taste' or '... flavour'. Any reference to a natural source had to be restricted to natural flavouring substances only. When ethnyl vanillin is employed the statement 'with ethnyl vanillin' or 'ethnyl vanillin' flavour had to be added. A declaration relating to the presence of edible substances added to the chocolate product had to also be indicated.

The 1973 Chocolate Directive laid down common rules on the composition and labelling of chocolate but it did not harmonise national laws concerning the addition of non-cocoa vegetable fats to chocolate. The United Kingdom does allow the addition of vegetable fat to chocolate, so many manufacturers have been able, in accordance with EU rules on the free movement of goods, to manufacture products containing vegetable fats in the United Kingdom and market them throughout the European Union under the name 'milk chocolate'. However, it has not been possible to manufacture such chocolate throughout the European Union. In addition, restrictions have been imposed by certain Member States on such products. Indeed the Commission instituted proceedings challenging Italy's and Spain's laws on chocolate implementing Directive 73/241 as being contrary to the completion of the internal market. The Spanish and Italian laws had required chocolate products containing vegetable fat to be labelled as 'substitute chocolate', giving the impression that the product was inferior.

The European Court of Justice (ECJ) in its judgements[108] found that Directive 73/241 did not harmonise the question of whether non-cocoa vegetable fat may be added to chocolate. This issue was left to the Member States to decide under national law. Second, the Court confirmed that national laws about the use of vegetable fat must comply with the EU rules of the free movement of goods. Therefore the Court

---

[108] C-12/00 and C-14/00.

concluded that the Italian and Spanish legislation was not compatible with EC rules on free movement because it forced manufacturers of chocolate products which have been lawfully produced in another Member State to either change the recipe or to label their products in a way that would lead the consumer to believe the product to be inferior to products labelled as 'chocolate'. The Court concluded that the Italian and Spanish authorities could have achieved their objective of safeguarding consumers by a labelling requirement.

However, the effect of these judgements is largely historic as Directive 2000/36 relating to cocoa and chocolate products intended for human consumption repealed Directive 73/241 with effect from 3 August 2003. It sets out simplified rules relating to the composition and labelling of chocolate products as well as dealing with the controversial question of the use of vegetable fat in chocolate. The new Directive was adopted in the summer of 2000. Because of ambiguous drafting, it is unclear if Member States were required to comply with the new legislation 'before' or 'with effect from' 3 August 2003.

Under the new Directive, Member States are obliged to permit the use of six authorised vegetable fats in chocolate products (illipe, palm-oil, sal, shea, kokum gugi and mango kernel). Use of these fats is permitted up to a maximum of 5 per cent of the weight of the product and provided they are clearly and conspicuously marked 'contains vegetable fats in addition to cocoa butter' in the same field of vision as the ingredients list. The United Kingdom and Ireland can continue to permit the labelling of 20 per cent cocoa/20 per cent milk fat product as 'milk chocolate', as long as this is labelled 'family milk chocolate' for export. Member States may, but are not obliged to, permit the use of coconut oil in chocolate ice-cream and similar frozen products.

Save for these changes, the majority of the same sales names, definitions and characteristics of the chocolate products remain the same as in the 1973 Directive. However, the labelling requirements are no longer reduced. The products have to be labelled in accordance with the General Food Labelling Directive (see Chapter 5) in addition to complying with the requirements of the designated names of the products in accordance with Directive 2000/36,[109] indicating the percentage of cocoa solids and in certain cases the percentage of cocoa butter and milk solids.

When chocolates are sold in assortments, the sales name may be replaced by 'assorted chocolates' or 'assorted filled chocolates' or similar names. For the sales name 'chocolate', 'milk chocolate' and 'couverture chocolate' additional information may be supplemented in respect of quality providing they meet certain criteria.

It is expected this new directive will allow manufactures to manufacture chocolate containing vegetable fat throughout the European Union. They will also be able to export milk chocolate, manufactured according to the requirements of the Directive. In the United Kingdom as milk chocolate manufactured in accordance with the Directive will be exported as 'milk chocolate', whilst milk chocolate manufactured in the United Kingdom or Ireland according to the

[109] OJ L 197, 03/08/2000 P. 19–25.

20 per cent cocoa/20 per cent milk fat recipe will be able to be exported as long as it is labelled as 'family milk chocolate'.

Coffee

Council Directive 77/436[110] harmonised the laws of the Member States relating to coffee extracts and chicory extracts. It was designed to define coffee extracts and chicory extracts, to determine which substances may be added during their manufacture, to lay down communal rules concerning the packaging and labelling of such extracts and to specify the conditions under which particular designations may be used for some of these products in order to ensure their free movement within the Community. However, following the European Councils held in Edinburgh and Brussels, it was felt that Directive 77/436/EEC should be brought into line with the general Community legislation of foodstuffs particularly relating to labelling and the methods of analysis. Consequently, Directive 1999/4/EC[111] relating to coffee extracts and chicory extracts was adopted on 22 February 1999. As from 13 September 2000, Directive 77/436/EEC was repealed.

Directive 1999/4/EC defines the following coffee products: 'coffee extract', 'soluble coffee extract', 'soluble coffee' and 'instant coffee'. In relation to chicory it defines: 'chicory extract', 'soluble chicory' or 'instant chicory'. The Directive also sets out the percentage of coffee- or chicory-based dried matter that must be contained in paste, dried extract and liquid extract. This directive does not apply to 'Café torrefacto soluble'. The product names may be supplemented by the term 'concentrated' provided that in the case of coffee, coffee-based dry matter content is more than 25 per cent by weight of the product and in the case of chicory, chicory-based dry matter content is more than 45 per cent by weight of the product.

The term 'decaffeinated' must be indicated on the label if the anhydrous caffeine content does not exceed more than 0.3 per cent weight of the coffee-based dry matter. This indication must appear within the same fields of visual of the sales description. In the case of liquid coffee extract and liquid chicory extract, the label must include the terms 'with ...', 'preserved with ...', 'with added ...' or 'roasted with ...' followed by the name of the types of sugars used as appropriate. In the case of paste and liquid coffee and chicory extract, the minimum coffee-based dry matter or chicory-based dry matter, respectively, must be indicated. This content shall be expressed as the percentage by weight of the finished product.

Provision is made for a procedure to bring the Directive into line with the general Community provisions applicable to foodstuffs.

---

110 OJ L 172, 12/07/1977 P. 20–24.

111 OJ L 066, 13/03/1999 P. 26–29.

Sugar

Council Directive 73/437[112] harmonised the laws of Member States concerning certain sugars intended for human consumption. It laid down definitions and common rules on manufacturing, characteristics, packaging and labelling of the products concerned so as to ensure free movement within the Community. It was decided that it was necessary to bring Directive 73/437 into line with general Community legislation on foodstuffs particularly legislation on labelling, colouring matter and other authorised additives, extraction solvents and methods of analysis. Consequently, Directive 2001/111/EC[113] was adopted relating to sugars intended for human consumption on 20 December 2001. Directive 73/437 is to be repealed with effect from 12 July 2003 by which time Member States must have brought laws and regulations into force to comply with this new Directive. Directive 2001/111 applies to the following types of sugar: semi-white sugar, sugar or white sugar, extra-white sugar, sugar solution, invert sugar solution, invert sugar syrup, glucose syrup, dried glucose syrup, dextrose or dextrose monohydrate, dextrose or dextrose anhydrous and fructose. It does not apply to icing sugars, candy sugars or sugars in low forms. Generally, the labelling requirements of Directive 2000/13 (see Chapter 5), apply to all these sugars. However, the product designation should only be applied to products as described within the Directive. Products defined under the Directive may also carry a qualifying term used in the various Member States. In addition to the compulsory product name, the products may sometimes bear qualifying terms used in the various Member States. Product designations may be used in product names made up to designate other products in accordance with customs, provided that neither of these product names are liable to mislead the consumer. For pre-packaged products weighing less than 20 g, net weight need not be indicated on the labelling. Labelling shall indicate dry matter and the invert content of sugar solution, invert sugar solution and invert sugar syrup. Labelling shall include the qualifying term 'crystallised' for invert sugar syrup incorporating crystals in the solution. If a product contains fructose in proportions greater than 5 per cent on a dry matter basis either glucose syrup or dried glucose syrup, they shall be indicated as 'glucose–fructose syrup' or 'fructose–glucose syrup' and 'dried glucose–fructose syrup' or 'dried fructose–glucose syrup' as appropriate.

Fruit Juices

Directives 75/726/EEC[114] and 93/77/EEC[115] had harmonized laws concerning fruit juices and nectars intended for human consumption. They had laid down common rules governing the composition, use of reserved descriptions, manufacturing

[112] OJ L 356, 27/12/1973 P. 71–73.
[113] OJ L 010, 12/01/2002 P. 53–57.
[114] OJ L 311, 01/12/1975 P. 40–49.
[115] OJ L 244, 30/09/1993 P. 23–31.

specifications and labelling in order to ensure their free movement within the Community. However, it was felt that these Directives should be brought into line with general Community legislation on foodstuffs particularly in relation to labelling, colouring matter, sweeteners and other authorised additives. Consequently, on 20 December 2001, Directive 2001/112/EC[116] relating to fruit juices and similar products intended for human consumption was adopted. The Directive applies to the following products which it goes on to define: fruit juice, fruit juice from concentrate, concentrated fruit juice, dehydrated/powdered fruit juice and fruit nectar. Currently, Member States are free to authorise or prohibit the addition of vitamins and minerals as far as the manufacturing process to fruit juices (see Chapter 10), however, the principles of free movement should be observed and in certain cases nutrition labelling will be required under Council Directive 90/496/EEC[117] as described in Chapter 5.

Directive 2000/13/EC (see Chapter 5) shall apply to the products covered by this directive. However, the product designations listed in this directive (see above) can only be used for products that meet the criteria set out in the Annex 2 of the Directive. If a product contains a single kind of fruit, the name of that single fruit shall be substituted for the word fruit, for example, orange juice. If a product is manufactured from two or more fruits (except when lemon juice is used under certain conditions), the product name shall be supplemented by a list of the fruits used in descending order of the volume of the fruit juices or purées included. However, if in the case of products manufactured from three or more fruits, the indication of the fruits used may be replaced by the words ‘several fruits’ or similar wording or by the number of fruits used.

The restoration of products defined under this directive to their original state by means or substances strictly necessary for this operation does not lead to an obligation to indicate on that label the ingredients used for this purpose. However, the addition to fruit juice of extra pulp or cells has to be indicated on the labelling. Mixtures of fruit juice and fruit juice from concentrate, and for fruit nectar obtained entirely or partly from one or more concentrated products, the labelling shall bear the words ‘made with concentrate’ or ‘partially made with concentrate’, as appropriate. This information must be near the product name standing out from the background in clearly visible characters. For fruit nectars the labelling shall indicate the minimum content of fruit juice, fruit purée or any mixture of those ingredients by declaring ‘fruit content: ... percentage minimum’. This information shall be located in the same field of vision as the product name.

However, labelling of fruit juice from concentrate as defined in the Directive which is not intended to be supplied to the final consumer must indicate the presence and quantity of added sugars, added lemon juice or acidifying agents. This reference can either appear on the packaging or a label attached to the packaging or in an accompanying document.

---

[116] OJ L 010, 12/01/2002 P. 58–66.
[117] OJ L 276, 06/10/1990 P. 40–44.

Dried Milk

Council Directive 76/118/EEC[118] of 18 December 1975 harmonised the laws of Member States relating to certain partly or wholly dehydrated preserved milk for human consumption. It laid down definitions and common rules defining the composition, manufacturing specifications and labelling of certain preserved milk, so as to ensure its free movement within the Community. It was decided that clarity was needed within the rules on the conditions for the products and the marketing of certain partly and wholly dehydrated preserved milks and to bring them into line with the Community legislation on foodstuffs, in particular, the labelling rules and rules relating to infant formulae and follow-on formulae (see Chapters 9 and 10). The Directive applies to the following types of partly dehydrated milk: condensed high-fat milk, condensed milk, condensed partly skimmed milk, condensed skimmed milk, sweetened condensed milk, sweetened condensed partly skimmed milk and sweetened condensed skimmed milk. It applies to the following totally dehydrated milks (i.e. where the water content does not exceed 5 per cent by weight of the finished product): dried high-fat or high-fat milk or high-fat milk powder, dried whole milk or whole milk powder, dried partly skimmed milk or partly skimmed milk powder and, dried skimmed milk or skimmed milk powder.

The addition of vitamins and minerals is permitted but there may be additional labelling requirements arising under Directive 90/496/EEC (see Chapter 5). The general labelling requirements set out in Directive 2000/13/EC apply, subject to following conditions:

- products names/designations as set out in Directive 76/118 should only be applied to products that meet the criteria designated to them under the Directive (e.g. evaporated milk, in English);
- as an alternative to the product's name, the Directive provides a list of designations which may be used in particular languages under the conditions laid down in the Directive;
- the labelling must state the percentage of milk fat expressed by the weight denomination to the finished product, except in the case of products defined as condensed or dehydrated skimmed milk when these particulars shall appear near the trade name;
- in the case of totally dehydrated milk the label must state the recommendations as the method of dilution or reconstitution including the fat content and the product as diluted or reconstituted;
- for products weighing less than 20g per unit which are packed in an outer packing, the particulars required only need appear on the outer packing as a general rule;
- the totally dehydrated milk should be marked as not intended as food for infants under 12 months.

---

[118] OJ L 024, 30/01/1976 P. 49–57.

Directive 76/118/EEC is repealed with effect from 13 July 2003, by which time Member States must have brought into force laws, regulations and administrative provisions necessary to comply with this new directive.

Jam

Council Directive 79/693/EEC harmonised laws of Member States relating to fruit jams, jellies, marmalade and chestnut purée. It laid down definitions and common rules governing composition, manufacturing specifications and labelling of the products concerned so as to ensure their free movement within the Community. It was decided that Directive 79/693/EEC should be brought into line with general Community legislation on foodstuffs in particular relating to labelling, colouring agents, sweeteners and other authorised additives. Consequently Directive 2001/113/EEC[119] relating to fruit jams, jellies and marmalade and sweetened chestnut purée intended for human consumption was adopted on 20 December 2001. The Directive applies to the following products as defined in the Directive: jam, extract jam, jelly, extract jelly, marmalade, jelly marmalade and sweetened chestnut purée. Only products meeting the criteria laid down in the Directive may use these product descriptions. The Directive however does not apply to products intended for the manufacture of fine bakery warehouses, pastries or biscuits.

Directive 2000/13 applies to the products defined within the Directive subject to the following conditions:

- product names listed in the Directive should only apply to products meeting the criteria designated within the Directive, however they may be used in addition to the name in accordance with practices used to designate the products provided the name can not be confused with those defined in the Directive;
- the products names shall be supplemented by an indication of the fruit or fruits used in descending order of weight of the raw materials used. However, for products manufactured from three or more fruits, an indication of the fruits used may be replaced by the words 'made of fruits' or similar wording or by the number of fruits used;
- the labelling shall indicate the fruit content by including the words 'prepared with... g of fruit per 100g' of the finished product, after deduction of the weight of water used in preparing the aqueous extracts, if appropriate. This declaration should appear in the same field of vision as the product name;
- the labelling shall indicate the total sugar content by the words 'total sugar content... g per 100g', the figure indicated representing the value determined by refractometer at 20°C for the finished product, subject to a tolerance of ±3 refractometric degrees. This declaration should appear in the same field of vision as the product name. The sugar content need not however to be indicated

[119] OJ L 010, 12/01/2002 P. 67–72.

where a nutrition claim is made for sugars on the labelling pursuing to Directive 90/496/EEC (see Chapter 5);
- when the residual content of sulphur dioxide is more than 10 mg/kg, its presence shall be indicated on the list of ingredients by way of derogation from Directive 2000/13/EEC.

Directive 79/693 is repealed with effect for 12 July 2003. From this date Member States must have put into force laws, regulations and administrative provisions necessary to comply with this new Directive. Measures shall be applied so as to authorise the marketing of products defined within the Directive if they comply with the definitions that will be laid down in the Directive from 12 July 2003 and prohibit the marketing of products which do not comply with this Directive with the effect from 12 July 2004. However, the marketing of products which fail to conform with this Directive which were labelled before 12 July 2004 in accordance with Directive 79/693/EEC shall be permitted until stocks run out.

Chapter 12

Novel Foods and Genetically Modified Organisms

INTRODUCTION

There is hardly a more controversial subject in the field of food law and policy than the issue of biotechnology, especially genetic modification (GM). Novel Foods are foods or ingredients which have not previously been used for human consumption within the Community and which fall within one of six prescribed categories. Genetically modified food is one example of novel foods, but the definition is wider also including other novel foods that have, for example, been developed using other scientific techniques.

Genetic modification is the alteration of genetic material (DNA) in a way that does not occur naturally. It permits selected individual genes to be transferred from one organism into another, including between species that are not related. In the US food produced using new scientific techniques, including GM is freely available on the market and it is considered by some good and wholesome to eat. In contrast, according to the EU Commissioner for Health and Consumer Protection, David Byrne speaking in November 2001, consumers in the European Union have developed a 'GM psychosis' apparently fearful of technical advances. In the European Union, concerns have been raised about the long-term health effects of eating GM food and of the potential impact on the environment of releasing genetically modified organisms (GMOs).

Despite the EU's scientific advisors signalling that GM plants and foods are safe for growing, marketing and consuming, the Member States have blocked authorisation since 1998. This has created a de facto moratorium on new approvals of GMOs which has had an impact on European industry, agriculture and research. It also creates legal uncertainty raising questions as to whether the European Union is in breach of its international obligations. The United States are taking the European Union to the WTO with the potential consequence of retaliatory measures.

RECENT HISTORY

Since 1998, EU Member States governments have been calling for a more stringent and transparent regulatory framework for authorisations to market GMOs and for labelling and traceability regimes for GMOs and for products produced from GM. Some Member States take the view that until such rules are in place new authorisations for growing and marketing GM products should be suspended. They justify this by referring to the preventative and precautionary principles. However, the

Commission believes the de facto moratorium is illegal and is determined that the authorisation process should be rekindled. In 2001 new environmental legislation was adopted and in July 2001 the Commission brought forward proposals for traceability and labelling and to improve the authorisation procedure for GM food and feed (which were adopted in July 2003). At the time of writing there is no clear timing or conditions for the restarting of authorisations. Even once the authorisations restart it will be some time before consumer confidence is regained.

Genetic Modification

Like many technologies GM can be used for many different things, GM can be used to increase the shelf life of a product or decrease the cost of production. It can improve the taste of a vegetable, increase its vitamin content, reduce the use of pesticides or increase yield.

Although any GMO released into the environment or used in food should have been approved as safe by the relevant EU authority, some fear the impact on human health of long term consumption or the long term impact on the environment.

This chapter will outline the current EU legislative framework for Novel foods including GM and then will go on to discuss the new package of legislation specifically relating to the authorisation, traceability and labelling of GMOs and GM food and feed, anticipated to enter into force at the beginning of 2004.

The Current Law

Overview of the current EU legislative

Directive 2001/13,[120] amending Directive 90/220,[121] provides for a Community authorisation procedure for the marketing of genetically modified raw materials and their release into the environment. This procedure does not however apply to processed products containing genetically modified ingredients. Up until now, authorisation for the marketing of processed products containing genetically modified ingredients has been under the Novel Foods Regulation 258/97.[122] However, this situation is further complicated because the Novel Foods Regulation did not apply to genetically modified foods or food ingredients which were already on the market prior to the Regulation coming into force and in any event its labelling requirements were of a very general nature. Consequently, a further Regulation 1139/98,[123] was adopted, which imposed specific and detailed labelling requirements for products derived from

[120] OJ L 075, 15/03/2001 P. 26–28.
[121] OJ L 117, 08/05/1990 P. 15–27.
[122] OJ L 043, 14/02/1997 P. 01–06.
[123] OJ L 159, 03/06/1998 P. 04–07.

genetically modified materials already authorised under, what was then, Directive 90/220. Labelling requirements were then incorporated in any subsequent authorisation under Regulation 258/97. Regulation 1139/98 was subsequently amended by Regulations 49/2000[124] and 50/2000[125] providing for the labelling of genetically modified ingredients and additives where GM DNA or protein is preset in the final foodstuff. Each aspect of the current legislative framework will now be briefly examined.

Novel foods regulation (258/97)

Under the current Novel Foods Regulation all Member States must ensure that foods that fall within the scope of the Regulation are not placed on the EU market without prior authorisation. Novel foods are defined as food that has not been used for human consumption to a significant degree within the Community before May 1997, and in addition fall into one of six categories:

- foods and food ingredients containing or consisting of GMOs within the meaning of Directive 90/220/EEC;
- foods and food ingredients produced from, but not containing, GMOs;
- foods and food ingredients with a new or intentionally modified primary molecular structure;
- foods and food ingredients consisting of or isolated from micro-organisms, fungi or algae;
- foods and food ingredients consisting of or isolated from plants and food ingredients isolated from animals, except for foods and food ingredients obtained by traditional propagating or breeding practices and having a history of safe food use;
- foods and food ingredients to which has been applied a production process not currently used, where that process gives rise to significant changes in the composition or structure of the foods or food ingredients which affect their nutritional value, metabolism or level of undesirable substances.

All such novel foods or food ingredients must be labelled as such if they:

- are no longer equivalent to a conventional food or ingredient;
- raise health implications for certain sections of the population;
- contain material which gives rise to ethical concerns; or
- contain live GMOs.

The Novel Foods Regulation does not currently apply to foods or food ingredients derived from genetically modified substances which were already on the EU market

---

124 OJ L 006, 11/01/2000 P. 13–14.
125 OJ L 006, 11/01/2000 P. 15–17.

prior to its entry into force. It also applies only to products that contain GM protein or DNA. In addition, the labelling provisions lay down only general principles, so that, in practice, it is extremely difficult to predict whether or not they apply.

The proposed package of legislation on GM (outlined below) does not cover the evaluation and authorisation of novel foods which are not genetically modified. Therefore the Novel Foods Regulation will remain in force for novel foods which are not genetically modified and is expected to be reviewed soon. The Commission has carried out a wide consultation of stakeholders. The results of this consultation are expected in the summer of 2003, and a proposal for an amendment could be brought forward before the end of 2003. Among other things, this review is likely to clarify the scope of the regulation as extending to whole animals and produce guidelines in respect of the 'production process' category of novel foods.

Genetically modified raw materials Directive (2001/18)

Directive 90/220 established a Community authorisation procedure for the marketing of genetically modified raw materials. It did not apply to processed products containing genetically modified ingredients.

After a lengthy legislative process, an amending Directive (2001/18[126]) was finally adopted by the European Parliament and the Council on 16 February 2001. It entered into force 17 October 2002. It strengthened the authorisation procedure by introducing better public access to information, mandatory consultation of the relevant Scientific Committees; mandatory labelling and traceability at all stages of the placing of GM materials on the market; a register of all places where GMOs are grown; a 10 year limitation on the renewal of authorisations; the application of the Precautionary Principle and setting out mechanisms for the analysis of the long-term cumulative effects of GMOs.

As mentioned above, no new GM products have been authorised since October 1998 because Member States have been applying a de facto moratorium on applications under Directive 2001/18. (For example, the Scientific Committee on Plants recently approved a new GM variety of oilseed rape but due to the moratorium, it will not be placed on the EU market.) Despite the initial hope that by strengthening the authorisation procedure, through the entering into force of the Directive 2001/18, the moratorium would be lifted, it now seems that this is not going to happen without further reform to the EU legislative framework.

Council regulation on the labelling of genetically modified soya and maize (1139/98) as amended by Commission Regulation 49/2000

Council Regulation 1139/98 (as amended by Commission Regulation (49/2000)) provides for detailed labelling provisions for products derived from genetically

[126] OJ L 106, 17/04/2001 P. 01–39.

modified soya and maize authorised under Directive 90/220 (Roundup Ready Soya and Bt maize). Foods and food ingredients produced from the genetically modified soya or maize in question have to comply with specific GMO labelling requirements, if protein or DNA resulting from genetic modification is present in the individual ingredients.

The labelling requirements are

- 'produced from genetically modified soya/maize' must appear in parentheses immediately after the name of the ingredient in the ingredients list or in a footnote to the list;
- only the words 'genetically modified' need to be used if an ingredient is already listed as already being produced from soya/maize;
- genetically modified ingredients included in an ingredient category or compound must be specifically mentioned with the addition of the words referred to above.

'May contain' labelling is not permitted.

Labelling is not however required if protein/DNA is detected at levels of less than 1 per cent. The purpose of this latter provision is to exempt products from labelling if the presence of genetically modified material is purely adventitious (e.g. from cross-contamination). However, manufacturers can only take advantage of the 1 per cent threshold if they can establish that the ingredient in question comes from a GMO-free source. It is therefore essential to trace ingredients back to the crop from which they were grown, in order to be able to make use of the threshold. The detailed requirements for establishing that ingredients come from a GMO-free source must be established by Member States at national level.

As explained below the Commission has now proposed a package consisting of two proposals; one dealing with traceability and the other with the authorisation and labelling of genetically modified food and feed. If these Proposals are adopted Regulations 1139/98 and 49/2000 would be repealed.

Commission Regulation on the labelling of GM additives (50/2000)

Commission Regulation 50/2000 on the labelling of food and ingredients containing genetically modified additives was adopted on 10 January 2000 and came into force on 10 April 2000.

Additives were not covered by Regulation 1139/98. The Commission Regulation relates to all additives and flavourings covered, by Directives 89/107[127] and 88/388,[128] which are GM, or contain or are produced from GMOs within the meaning of Directive 90/220. The Regulation requires labelling when either GM protein or DNA

[127] OJ L 040, 11/02/1989 P. 27–33.

[128] OJ L 184, 15/07/1988 P. 61–66.

is detectable in the final product. The labelling requirements for additives and flavourings are the same as those laid down for foods and food ingredients in Regulation 1139/98 (see above).

No threshold currently applies to the labelling of additives but a recital was included in the Regulation indicating the Commission's intention to deal with this issue in the future.

If the proposed legislative package (outlined below) is adopted Regulation 50/2000 will be repealed.

The Proposed Legislative Package

The proposed new legislative package consists of two proposed Regulations dealing with the authorisation, labelling and traceability of GMOs, and food and feed produced from GM. Both food and, now for the first time, feed products are covered by the proposal. This is illustrative of the Commission's new holistic approach, 'from farm to fork'. Below is the basic structure of the original proposals as put forward by the Commission. At the time of writing, the proposal had been through first reading at both the EU Parliament and Council and was about to enter second reading. The contents of the proposed package will continue to change until (if) final adoption takes place. Given the fluid nature of the proposal, it was decided to concentrate on the original proposal.

Products to be notified

Under the proposals (as presented by the Commission) prior authorisation will need to be obtained for:

- a GMO for food use;
- food containing or consisting of GMOs;
- food 'produced from' or containing ingredients produced from GM.

It is also worth noting that, because the draft uses the wording 'produced from', rather than the word 'with', arguably this means that processing aids that do not become part of the end food product, are not subject to the authorisation, traceability or labelling requirements. The proposal cites the example of a cheese produced with a GM enzyme that does not remain in the final product, may not be subject to the legislation.

A single authorisation

A single authorisation for a GMO or a product containing a GMO would be applicable to that substance and any of its derivatives. For example, a GM tomato, having received authorisation, would not require a further authorisation to be used in tomato puree or a tomato based sauce. A tomato puree using non-authorised GM tomatoes would require an authorisation, but on receipt of that authorisation the tomato puree could be used in tomato based sauce without further authorisation.

Effect on the existing regime

Upon these proposals entering into force the Novel Food Regulation will no longer be applicable to GM food or ingredients (it will remain in force in relation to non-GM Novel Foods) and Regulations 1139/98, 49/2000 and 50/2000 (see above) will all be repealed. Directive 2001/18 would still provide for an authorisation procedure for the deliberate release into the environment of GMOs as well as the placing on the market of genetically modified raw materials. However the authorisation procedure set out under 2001/18 will no longer be applicable to foods falling within the scope of the new procedure contained in these proposals.

Proposal for an EU Regulation on genetically modified food and feed (the authorisation and labelling proposal)

Basic obligation and adventitious contamination exemption. There would be a basic obligation on manufacturers not to place a product containing GMOs, produced from GMOs or containing GM ingredients on the market unless the product is covered by an authorisation or is a derivative of a product covered by an authorisation. The only exception to this general rule concerns the situation where a product has been inadvertently contaminated with minute quantities of unauthorised GMOs. No authorisation is required where

- a food contains GM material but this constitutes less than 1 per cent of the product (or such lower threshold as may in the future be set by the Commission following consultation with a regulatory committee);
- the presence of the GM material is adventitious or technically unavoidable;
- the GM material in question, although unauthorised, has been found by the Scientific Committee or the EFA not to present a risk to human health or the environment.

There are several points to note about this exception. First, it appears that the percentage threshold relates to the percentage the GM material represents in relation to the total product and not just the ingredient in question, but the drafting is unclear. Secondly, in order to take advantage of the exception, operators must be able to demonstrate that they have taken 'appropriate steps' to avoid the use of GM material (in order to prove that the presence of the material is adventitious or technically unavoidable). It seems it may be sufficient to demonstrate compliance with the certification requirements proposed in relation to traceability. It may be that the use of the words 'technically unavoidable' are intended to permit the presence of residues arising from the use of processing aids, but at the moment this is unclear and the subject of debate.

Length of authorisation and renotification of existing products. Each individual authorisation is granted for a period of ten years. Any existing authorisation granted under either the Novel Foods Regulation or Directive 2001/18 will initially continue in force, but additional information concerning the risk assessment process will have to be submitted to the European Food Authority within 6 months. Effectively, therefore, products already on the market will have to be re-notified within 6 months of the new Regulation entering into force.

Labelling. All products which require authorisation under the proposed Regulation will be subject to mandatory labelling. The proposed labelling requirements are very similar to those already imposed by Regulation 1139/98, as amended.

A foodstuff containing or produced from a GMO would be required to be labelled as follows:

(i) 'genetically modified'; or
(ii) 'produced from genetically modified [*name of organism*] but not containing a genetically modified organism'.

If adopted, the proposal would extend the current labelling provisions to all GM food and feed irrespective of the detectability of DNA or protein. Currently labelling is only required if DNA/protein is detectable. This is an important change that will result in the labelling of a large number of foodstuffs which are not currently required to be labelled. For example, refined oils of GM origin. Industry and enforcement agencies feel that such a paper-based system will be unenforceable and will lead to fraud. However consumer associations believe that the consumer has a right to this information.

Adventitious exemption. Again there is an exemption to the labelling requirements covering adventitious or technically unavoidable contamination with GM materials. This exemption is slightly different to the exemption provided for in relation to authorisation. It is simply stated that the labelling requirements are not applicable where:

- a food contains GM material but this constitutes a proportion of the food no higher than a threshold which is to be established by the Commission in the future following consultation with a regulatory committee;
- the presence of the GM material is adventitious or technically unavoidable.

The wording of the adventitious contamination exception is therefore different from that used in relation to the authorisation procedure, in a number of respects. First, the threshold is not fixed initially at 1 per cent. Second, there is no reference to the need to demonstrate that the GM material in question is without risk to human health. The implications of these differences are unclear but, theoretically, a product could benefit from the authorisation exemption but still be required to be labelled. If, for example, the labelling threshold is set at 0.5 per cent and the authorisation threshold remains at 1 per cent, a tomato based sauce containing 0.4 per cent of material derived from GM that is there due to adventitious contamination and meets all the necessary requirements, would be exempt from both the authorisation and labelling requirements. However, if the tomato based sauce contained 0.6 per cent of material derived from GM, the product would still be permitted on the market under the adventitious contamination exemption without a formal authorisation, but it would have to be labelled as containing GM material.

If no labelling threshold is agreed upon before the Regulation comes into force, then it may be that all products containing GM materials would have to be labelled even if its presence is adventitious, however it is noted that under the current legislation, the existing threshold has been set at 1 per cent through the same procedure.

Proposal for an EU legislation on the traceability of GMOs and products produced from GMOs

Traceability is the ability to trace or track GMOs and products produced from GMOs at all stages of their being placed on the market and throughout the distribution chain. The objective of imposing traceability obligations on GMOs is different from the objective as regards products produced from GMs. The information required to be transmitted and retained for each differs accordingly. The traceability of individual GMOs contained in a product requires the use of individual identification codes. However, traceability for products produced from GMOs on the other hand does not require identification of the individual GMOs from which they are produced.

Traceability of GMOs. In order to facilitate traceability of GMOs, the Proposal requires that operators transmit, to the operator receiving the product, specified information:

- that the product contains or consists of GMOs;
- the unique code relating to the GMO contained in a product.

The Proposal departs from the authorised transformation event 'from which the GMOs are developed'. A transformation event is when a conventional organism is transformed through the introduction of modified DNA sequences resulting in the formation of a GMO. The proposal therefore requires the Commission to establish a system to develop and assign simple numerical or alphanumerical unique codes to GMOs. The specified information would have to be retained for 5 years under the original draft.

Traceability of the products produced from GMOs. The Proposal builds upon the principles of traceability contained in the current Proposal for General Principles and Requirements of Food Law (see Chapter 4), with the aim of extending traceability requirements to include information on whether a food or feed contains GMOs or is produced from GMs. This would be achieved through an obligation on all operators to transmit specified information to the next operator in the distribution and production chain; one step up, one step down.

The Commission does not currently intend to stipulate how this should be done, although the original proposal does make specific reference to the use of lot and batch numbering. Each company could therefore be able to adapt any existing traceability system it has in place. However this approach could also permit each Member State to require different methods/levels of proof and thereby possibly impede free movement of goods.

Food produced from GMOs will be exempt from the traceability requirements if the same conditions are fulfilled as those required for the exemption applicable to the authorisation procedure (see above). In practice, this will mean that, if a product does not require authorisation, it will not be subject to the traceability requirement. However, as stated above, labelling requirements may still apply to such a product. It must, therefore, be assumed that if traceability of such products is not required, the labelling of such products will be upon a detection basis.

'GMO-free' labelling. In the White Paper on Food Safety, the Commission stated its intention to adopt a Proposal for a Regulation on the labelling of 'food and food ingredients produced without genetic engineering' by September 2000. However there would be little need for 'GMO free' labelling legislation if labelling based on certification was introduced (see paragraph (a) above). The idea of 'GMO free' labelling appears, for the time being, to have been dropped.

The Debate and the Future

This proposed package of legislation is of fundamental importance. In particular, it may end the de facto moratorium on placing any products on the EU market. As explained above, this proposed package is constantly changing, and will continue to do so until (if) it is finally adopted. The draft as proposed by the Commission, outlined above, has evoked heated debate on many subjects including:

- the correct legal basis for such a proposal. Some (including the Council legal service and the United Kingdom) take the view that the proposed legal base of Article 95 is incorrect for a centralised authorisation procedure, rather it should be Article 308. Consequently, should the proposal include a centralised procedure. The continuation of a decentralised authorisation procedure, as is currently in place, could allow the Member States the possibility to continue with the de facto moratorium. The legal basis would also affect the legislative procedure to be followed and consequently whether qualified majority (Article 95) or unanimity (Article 308) voting would be needed at Council. Given that it is extremely unlikely that unanimity will be reached, this could cause the proposal to lapse (fail). If the legal basis is not correct, then the possibility that the validity of the whole package could be challenged before the European Court of Justice who could annul the Regulations.

- whether products derived from animals fed with GM feed should be labelled, and, if yes, up to which generation should this be applied. In other words, if a pig is fed GM feed for a 1-month period with some GM feed and is slaughtered two years later, should meat from that pig, that is then processed into pepperoni and put on a pizza be labelled as being derived from GM? At the time of writing, the first readings at both the European Parliament and the Council had answered this question negatively.
- whether products that have not received EU approval, should be able to benefit from the exemptions, for adventitious contamination and technically unavoidable presence, to the authorisation, traceability and labelling requirements. In particular, adventitious is an inadvertent mixing, that is, by definition it is accidental. If a raw material or ingredient is being sourced from outside the European Union, it is impracticable for a producer to only have accidental mixing with products that have full EU approval. However, there is concern that if products do not have EU approval, they risk being unsafe. This could have severe consequences for the EU's trade with third countries, notably the United States. Any compromise currently appears to allow products that have received a positive opinion from the relevant EU Scientific Committee to benefit from this exemption for a limited period, say three years (the idea being that the backlog of approvals due to the de facto moratorium should have been worked through by then!).

Many other issues have been and continue to be debated. Indeed, there remains the possibility that there will be no agreement, that the proposed legislation will fail, and we will continue with the de facto moratorium. Alternatively, a practicable solution might be found to kick start the authorisation procedure, whilst ensuring the highest possible level of safety for consumers and the environment, as well as providing consumers with sufficient and clear information so enabling them to make an informed choice.

At the time of publication, the new package on the authorisation, traceability of labelling of GMOs and food and feed derived from GM was adopted and will enter into force in 2004.

Chapter 13

Agricultural Products

INTRODUCTION

In a move away from the Common Agricultural Policy (CAP) focusing almost entirely on productivity gains, and in acknowledgement that consumers want to be able to choose their products based on factors such as production processing methods, three Regulations were adopted in the early 1990s regarding the production of agricultural products.

In 1991, a regulation was adopted setting out the rules for organic products. In 1992, two regulations were adopted to harmonise the protection of geographical names for food products and for foodstuffs of specific character. These regulations were adopted to protect consumers so that they are given clear information regarding the products they are purchasing. The two regulations adopted in 1992 were also aimed at assisting rural economies, in particular less favoured or remote areas, by protecting and promoting products that have special characteristics from being copied or imitated. However concerns have been raised that the regime could also be seen as a form of protectionism.

Logos have been devised for each of these quality protection schemes so that consumers can easily identify products complying with the schemes:

PROTECTION OF GEOGRAPHICAL INDICATIONS AND DESIGNATIONS OF ORIGIN FOR AGRICULTURAL PRODUCTS OR FOODSTUFFS

Regulation 2081/92[129] on the protection of geographical indications and designations of origin for agricultural products or foodstuffs was adopted in July 1992. The Regulation was adopted to provide additional protection for agricultural products or foodstuffs from specified geographical areas. Some Member States had already

[129] OJ L 208, 24/07/1992 P. 1–8.

introduced registers for designations of origin, however, these were not uniform throughout the European Union. Concerns had been raised, that products that had become well-known outside their original region or Member State were in danger of being imitated and passed off as the genuine article, carrying the name of the product that had acquired the reputation for quality. This situation could lead to consumers being misled as to the quality and the origin of the product they are purchasing and also discourage the producers of the 'genuine article'.

The Regulation applies to foodstuffs that are referred to in Annex I of the Regulation. It also applies to agricultural products intended for human consumption referred to in Annex II of the Treaty and agricultural products referred to in Annex II of the Regulation. The Regulation does not apply to wine products or spirit drinks as there is already existing Community Legislation covering these products.

Products covered by the Regulation include:

- fresh meat (and offals);
- cheeses;
- beer;
- bread, pastry, cakes, confectionery, biscuits and other bakers' wares;
- natural mineral waters and spring waters (to be phased out);
- cochineal (raw product of animal origin);
- meat based products (cooked, salted, smoked, etc.);
- other products of animal origin including eggs, milk products;
- oils and fat including butter, margarine, oils, etc.;
- fruits, vegetables, cereals;
- fish, mollusc, fresh crustaceans;
- natural gums and resins.

The Regulation provides definitions of 'designation of origin' (PDO) and 'geographical indication' (PGI). Designation of origin is defined as:

> 'the name of a region, a specific place or, in exceptional cases, a country, used to describe an agricultural product or a foodstuff:
> - originating in that region, specific place or country, and
> - the quality or characteristics of which are essentially or exclusively due to a particular geographical environment with its inherent natural and human factors, and the production, processing and preparation of which take place in the defined geographical area.'

The geographical indication is defined as:

> 'the name of a region, a specific place or, in exceptional cases, a country, used to describe an agricultural product or a foodstuff:
> - originating in that region, specific place or country, and
> - which possesses a specific quality, reputation or other characteristics attributable to that geographical origin and the production and/or processing and/or preparation of which takes place in the defined geographical area.'

The differences between the two definitions do not appear to be great. The designation of origin includes 'natural' and 'human factors' of a particular geographical environment. It is also necessary for the production, processing and preparation to take place within the defined geographical area. However, to obtain a geographical indication 'reputation' is referred to and only one of three stages of production, processing or preparation must take place within the geographical area. Products that have obtained the geographical indication protection include Newcastle Brown Ale, Timoleague Brown Pudding, and Canard à foie gras du Sud-Ouest. Products that have obtained the protection of the designation of origin include White Stilton cheese, Noix de Grenoble and Beurre Rose de la marque Nationale Grand Duché de Luxembourg.

Application for registration

Generally only an association of producers and/or processors working with the agricultural product or foodstuff, referred to as 'the Group', can apply for registration of that particular product or foodstuff. However, a 'natural or legal person' may in certain prescribed circumstances also be allowed to apply for a product to be registered.

The Group sends an application to the relevant authority in the Member State. The Member State checks that the application contains the necessary information and forwards it to the Commission.

The Commission will investigate the merits of the application and will, where appropriate, conduct surveys and request the opinion of the Scientific Committee. If the Commission concludes that the application is valid and the product should be registered, it publishes a notification in the Official Journal of the European Communities to allow all interested parties to make a statement of objections. Member States have 6 months from the date of publication to object to the registration. If no statements of objections have been received by the Commission, it publishes the name of the product in the Official Journal of the European Communities. It will also enter in the Register:

- the name of the product;
- the name of the Group that applied for the product to be registered;
- the inspection bodies that have been authorised by the Member States to verify that the products meet the required specification.

Specification requirements

For a product to be eligible to use a PDO or PGI, it must comply with a product specification. Set out in the Regulation is a non-exhaustive list of criteria that the product specification must include such as:

- the name of the agricultural product or foodstuff, including the designation of origin or the geographical indication;
- the definition of the geographical area;

- evidence that the agricultural product or the foodstuffs originates in the geographical area;
- a description of the method of obtaining the product;
- details that show the link between the product and the geographical environment or the geographical origin.

Verification of products

It is the responsibility of the Member States to ensure that products that are registered meet the requirements laid down in the specifications. Each Member State designates inspection authorities or approves bodies to verify the products. The Commission publishes in the Official Journal of the European Communities, the inspection authorities or authorised bodies notified to them by the Member States. The most recent list at the time of writing was published in 2002.[130] Member States must ensure that the inspection bodies are objective and impartial, and have sufficient qualified staff and the necessary resources to carry out their tasks.

It falls to the producers using the protected names to bear the costs of the inspections required under the Regulation.

Protection obtained by registration

A product having been registered, obtains a high degree of protection against:

- the registered name being used for comparable products that exploit the reputation of the protected name;
- false or misleading indications as to the provenance, origin, nature or essential qualities of the product in the packaging advertising or documents relating to the product;
- any practice that might mislead the public as to the true origin of the product;
- any misuse, imitation or evocation of the protected product. This applies even if the true origin of the product is shown.

The Regulation specifically states that this also applies if the protected name is translated or accompanied by expressions such as ‘style’, ‘type’, ‘method’, or ‘as produced in’.

The Regulation does, however, allow a derogation to this protection in Article 13(2) of the Regulation. Under this article, a Member State is permitted, for a maximum

---

[130] Inspection structures notified by the Member States in accordance with Article 10(2) of Regulation (EEC) No 2081/92 on the protection of geographical indication and designations of origin for agricultural products and foodstuffs OJ C 069, 18/03/2002 P. 1–56.

of 5 years, to maintain its national system that permits the use of the name registered provided that:

- the products have been legally and continuously marketed by the undertakings using the name for at least five years prior to the name being registered;
- the labelling clearly indicates the true origin of the product.

The European Court of Justice recently considered a case concerning this derogation. Italy applied to the Commission for the registration of the name 'Parmigiano Reggiano'. The name was entered in the list of PDOs in 1996.[131] The Court considered in June 2002 whether or not a producer in the country that had applied for the registration of the name was able to take advantage of the derogation contained in Article 13(2) of the Regulation which allows Member States to permit for a transitional period, within its territory, producers to continue to market a product, under the registered name, that does not comply with the registered specifications. The Court found that at the time that the Member State makes the application to register the PDO, products that do not comply with the specifications of the name could not be marketed legally within its territory. The Court concluded that therefore the derogation only applies to the Member States that do not make the original application for the registration of the PDO.

Trade marks

It is possible for a product to have a registered trade mark as well as being entered on the Register of designation of origin or geographical indication. However, a designation of origin or geographical indication cannot be registered where, in light of a trade mark's reputation and renown and the length of time it has been used, the registration is liable to mislead the consumer as to the identity of the products.

Generic names

Names of products that have become generic cannot be registered under the Regulation. The Regulation defines generic as:

> 'the name of an agricultural product or a foodstuff which although it relates to the place or the region where this product or foodstuff was originally produced or marketed, has become the common name of an agricultural product or a foodstuff.'

When establishing whether or not a name has become generic, the Regulation states that all the factors of the case should be taken into account, in particular:

- the existing situation in the Member States in which the name originates and in areas of consumption;

---

[131] Commission Regulation No. 1107 96 of 12 June 1996.

- the existing situation in other Member States;
- the relevant national or Community law.

Initially, it was anticipated that a non-exhaustive list of the names of agricultural products or foodstuffs which would be considered as generic would be drawn up and published before the Regulation entered into force. The Commission drafted a proposal in 1993, however, the proposal was blocked and had still not been completed by January 1995. The Commission put forward a new proposal in March 1996. This second proposal was not adopted by the Council, however, it does provide some further clarification on how the Commission looks at this issue. The proposed decision incorporated a non-exhaustive list of names that the Commission considered have become generic. Interestingly, all the names proposed were for cheeses including Brie, Camembert, Cheddar, and Gouda. The Commission based its proposals on lists of names of products which it had received from the Member States that the Member States regarded as generic names.

There has been substantial case law as to whether or not a name is 'generic', for the purposes of the Regulation.

Feta Cheese – A Case Study

In January 1994, the Greek Authorities sent the Commission an application for the registration of the name, 'Feta'. As Feta is produced in other Member States, including Denmark and France, and has been produced for some time, the Commission conducted a Eurobarometer survey of consumers in the, then, 12 Member States of the Union to consider whether Feta had become a generic name. The results of the survey were that:

- the name Feta was not well-known in the Union;
- most consumers who had heard of Feta, thought that it originated in Greece.

The Commission also asked the Scientific Committee to give its opinion. The Scientific Committee confirmed that it did not believe that the name, 'Feta' had become generic. Feta, was therefore registered as a protected designation of origin in June 1996.[132]

The Danish and French Governments opposed the Registration and brought an action for the registration to be annulled under Article 230 of the Treaty. In March 1996, the Court of Justice found that the Commission had not taken into account the fact that the name, Feta has been produced for a considerable time in Member States other than Greece.[133] It concluded that as there had been an error in law, committed by the Commission when deciding whether or not Feta has become a generic name, then, its registration as a PDO should be annulled. The Commission subsequently amended the Register and deleted the name, Feta.

---

[132] Commission Regulation No. 1107-96 of 12 June 1996.

[133] Judgment of the Court 16 March 1996 trying cases C-298/96, C-293/96 and C-299/96.

In October 1999, the Commission sent to each of the Member States a detailed questionnaire regarding the production and consumption of Feta within their countries. In particular, the Commission took note of the fact that only Greece and Denmark had specific legislation governing the production of Feta cheese. The production of the cheese was found to be substantial in Greece, Denmark, France and Germany. Again, the Commission consulted the Scientific Committee which concluded 'unanimously that the designation Feta is non-generic'. The Scientific Committee explained that the reasons for believing the designation Feta is non-generic are because the production and consumption of Feta is heavily concentrated in Greece. Feta produced in the other Member States is primarily produced from cow's milk using different technology and is exported in large quantities to non-Member countries. In October 2002, the designation Feta was again entered in the Register of protected designations of origin.

Recent Amendments

On 15 March 2003, the Commission adopted a proposal to amend Regulation 2081/92 for the protection of geographical indications and designations of origin for agricultural product or foodstuffs.[134] This proposal was considered under the consultation procedure. On 8 April 2003, the Council adopted a Regulation to amend Regulation 2081/92 which included:

- extending the scope of the Regulation to include mustard and pasta;
- removing mineral and spring waters from the scope of the legislation after a transitional period of 10 years with a progressive phasing out.

The US and Australia, concerned by the extension to the scope of the Regulation, have taken action through the WTO. Arbitration proceedings have begun.

Traditional Speciality Guaranteed

Council Regulation No. 2082/92[135] was adopted in July 1992 as part of the package of proposals aimed to ensure the continuation of traditional European food products. In particular, those products made in rural areas by small producers. Unlike the products registered as protected designation of origin or protected geographical indication, products that are registered as 'traditional speciality guaranteed' do not refer to geographical origin, but, highlight instead a traditional character either of the composition of the product or the way it is produced.

---

134 COM(2002) 0139 OJ C181E, 30/07/2002 P. 0275–0276.

135 OJ L 208, 24/07/1992 P. 9–14.

Adopting a Regulation to protect traditional products was seen as a way in which consumers demand for greater emphasis on quality could be met. It was also seen as a way in which the diversification of agriculture could be encouraged and to assist rural economies particularly in remote or less favoured areas.

It is the responsibility of the Member States to ensure that names registered under the scheme are protected against any misuse. Member States are also obliged to ensure that there is national legislation to protect these products from being imitated and to stop practices that could lead to the public being misled or confused.

Only products that have 'specific character' can be entered in the Register. Specific character is defined in the Regulation as: 'the feature or set of features which distinguishes an agricultural product or a foodstuff clearly from other similar products or foodstuffs belonging to the same category'.

The presentation of a product is not considered to be a 'specific characteristic' which would be sufficient to distinguish the product from other similar products.

The Commission established a register of certificates of specific character which sets out the names of the agricultural products and foodstuffs which have been recognised as having specific character according to Regulation 2082/92. For a product to be entered in the Register, it must be either:

- produced by using traditional raw materials; or
- be characterised by a traditional composition or mode of production and/or processing which reflects a traditional production and/or processing method.

For a name to be entered in the Register it must be either specific in itself or it must 'express the specific character' of the product. The name must be traditional and comply with national provisions or be established by custom. Unfortunately the Regulation does not provide a definition of traditional. However a product cannot be registered if its specific character is due:

- to its provenance or geographical origin; or
- solely to the application of a technological innovation.

Only products that are contained in the agricultural products listed in Annex II to the Treaty intended for human consumption and foodstuffs in the Annex to the Regulation can be entered in the Register. These products include:

- fresh meat and (offal);
- beer;
- chocolate and other food preparations containing cocoa;
- pasta;
- soups and stocks.

As with Regulation 2081/92, only an association of producers and/or processors working with the product or foodstuff to be registered can apply for registration of the product.

When applying for the registration of a product, a product specification must be contained within the application and published in the Register. Set out in the Regulation are a minimum five criteria relating to the products specific character that must be included in the product specification including:

- the name in one or more languages;
- a description of the method of production including the nature and characteristics of the raw material and/or ingredients used and/or the method of preparation of the agricultural product or the foodstuff, referring to its specific character;
- aspects allowing appraisal of traditional character;
- a description of the characteristics of the agricultural product or the foodstuff giving its main physical, chemical, and microbiological and/ or organoleptic characteristics which relate to the specific character;
- the minimum requirements and inspection procedures to which the specific character is subject.

The application for the registration of a product is similar to that described previously in this chapter for PGIs and PDOs.

The Regulation provided a procedure for the Commission to define a Community symbol which could be used in the labelling, presentation and advertising of products set out in the register. The symbol, set out at the beginning of this chapter, was finally adopted in September 1994 in Commission Regulation 2515/94.[136]

Organic Products

In response to a growing demand from consumers for organic products a Council Regulation was adopted in June 1991 setting out a framework of Community rules on the production, labelling and inspection of organic products. This Regulation was also adopted in response to a shift in policy at EU level that agricultural policy should not just focus on productivity gains but should also concentrate on quality and the integration of environmental conservation.

The objectives of organic farming have been identified as comprising of:

> the application of production methods that do not damage the environment, more respectful use of the countryside, concern for animal welfare and the achievement of high quality agricultural products.

The Framework Regulation 2092/91[137] has been amended on more than 20 occasions by Commission and Council Regulations. The Regulation which originally

[136] OJ L 275, 26/10/1994 P. 01–02.

[137] OJ L 198, 22 July 1991, p. 1. Regulation last amended by Commission Regulation 223/2003.

covered agricultural crops was, in July 1999, amended to cover organic livestock products. The Regulation has more recently been amended to include feedingstuffs which fall outside the scope of this book.

Regulation 2092/91 on organic production and indication of agricultural products and foodstuffs

The Regulation as amended sets out the rules governing organic production on farms, labelling requirements, rules on advertising, organic logos and inspection systems. It also sets out requirements for organic products imported from third countries.

Scope of regulation. The Regulation applies to organic products if the products carry, or intend to carry, indications that refer to an organic production method. In particular the Regulation applies to the following products:

- unprocessed agricultural and crop products; and in certain circumstances, livestock and unprocessed livestock products;
- processed agricultural crop and livestock products intended for human consumption that are prepared essentially from one or more ingredient of plant and/or animal origin.

A product is considered to be bearing an indication to an organic production method if in its labelling, advertising material or commercial documents it is suggested to the purchaser that the product or its ingredients have been obtained in accordance with the rules set out in the Regulation. In particular if the following terms or their derivatives or diminutives (e.g. bio) are used:

- in Spanish: ecológico;
- in Danish: økologisk;
- in German: ökologisch, biologisch;
- in Greek: *βιολογικό*;
- in English: organic;
- in French: biologique;
- in Italian: Biologico;
- in Dutch: biologisch;
- in Protuguese: biológico;
- in Finnish: luonnonmukainen;
- in Swedish: ekologisk.

The Regulation also provides that organic products complying with this Regulation must in addition comply with other Community law in respect of foodstuffs and animal nutrition.

Labelling. The labelling and advertising of organic products can only refer to organic production methods where it is clear that they refer to a method of agricultural production, and the product has complied with the rules set out in the Regulation. The name and/or code number of the inspection authority must also be stated. It is for Member States to decide whether they require a reference to the name and/or to the code number.

References to organic production methods can only be made in the sales description where:

- at least 95 per cent of the ingredients of agricultural origin are organic;
- any additional ingredients of agricultural origin used are included in Annex VI of the Regulation; these ingredients are products that are either not available or in very short supply on the Community organic market, (e.g. fructose);
- the product has been produced without involving the use of ionizing radiation;
- the product has not been produced using GMOs and/or any products derived from GMOs.

An indication referring to organic production methods may appear in the list of ingredients where at least 70 per cent of the ingredients of agricultural origin are organic or are derived from organic products. Again, any additional ingredients of agricultural origin used in the product must be included in Annex VI of the Regulation. A separate statement must also appear in the following form:

> 'X per cent of the agricultural ingredients were produced in accordance with the rules of organic production.'

This statement must not appear in a colour, size and style of lettering which is more prominent than the sales description of the product.

In other words, the labelling and advertising of a product must not refer to organic production methods if the ingredients of organic origin constitute less than 70 per cent of the product.

Products that comply with the requirements stated above, but do not comply with the conversion period required for organic production, may state that 'product under conversion to organic farming'. This is only permitted where a conversion period of at least 12 months has been complied with before the harvest.

Rule of production. Set out in Annex 1 of the Regulation are the rules for the production of crops and livestock. Detailed rules are provided including conversion periods. For crop production, the rules include use of livestock manure from organic livestock production, and an appropriate multi-annual rotation programme. Pests, disease and weeds are controlled by a combination of choosing appropriate species and varieties, an appropriate rotation programme and protection of natural enemies of pests through providing a favourable habitat for them, such as hedges and nesting sites.

The general principles for livestock production is stated as being:

> 'a land related activity. Except where authorised by way of exception in this Annex, livestock must have access to a free-range area and the number of animals per unit of area must be limited to ensure integrated management of livestock and crop production on the production unit, so minimizing any form of pollution, in particular of the soil and of surface and ground water. The number of livestock must be closely related to the area available.'

Non-organic ingredients. Annex VI of the Regulation sets out the ingredients of non-agricultural origin, processing aids, and other products used for processing of ingredients of agricultural origin which are not organic, that may be used in a product that can still be referred to as organic. These ingredients and processing aids include food additives, flavourings and micro-organism preparations that can be used in organic products. Water, salt and certain minerals and vitamins can also be used.

It is also important to note that a product may not contain an ingredient that has been produced organically with the same ingredient that has been obtained through conventional methods.

Inspection system. In order to ensure that the rules set down in the Regulation are complied with all operators who produce, prepare, import or market products that are referred to as organic are subject to regular inspections carried out by designated inspection authorities. The Regulation establishes rules for how these inspections should be carried out.

Any operator who produces, prepares or imports organic products for the purpose of marketing them must notify these activities to the competent authority of the Member State in which the activity is carried out.

Member States must set up an inspection system operated by one or more inspection authorities. Where Member States allow private bodies to carry out inspections then an authority must be designated to approve and supervise these private bodies.

Member States must issue a code number, to each inspection body or authority, which must be submitted to the other Member States and the Commission. The Commission then publishes the code numbers. The inspection authority and the approved inspection bodies must ensure that the inspection measures and precautions set out in Annex III are applied to all operators which produce, prepare or import agricultural products or foodstuffs obtained by organic production methods. The operator pays a contribution to the inspection expenses.

Contained in Annex III to the Regulation are detailed requirements for the inspections including general provisions for documentary accounts and the storage of products. It also contains specific provisions for different types of products. The provisions are intended to ensure the traceability of organic products during the entire production chain and to ensure that the provisions of the Regulation are satisfied.

Logo. In 1995 the Regulation was amended to enable the Commission to establish a logo for organic products. In March 2000 the Regulation was again amended to include in Annex V the logo to be used to indicate that a product has been subject to the inspection arrangements referred to above throughout the production and preparation process. Producers are not obliged to use the logo, however, they may use it on a voluntary basis if the product complies with certain prescribed criteria, including:

- at least 95 per cent of the ingredients have been produced by organic methods;
- the product is sold directly by the producer or preparer to the ultimate consumer in sealed packaging or placed on the market as pre-packaged foodstuffs;
- indicating on the label the name and/or business name of the producer, preparer or vendor together with the name or code number of the inspection authority or body.

Set out in Annex V are detailed requirements for the reproduction of the logo.

Imports from third countries. The Commission has established a list of third countries that are allowed to export organic products to the EU.[138] The list is set out in Commission Regulation 94/92 which was most recently, at the time of writing, amended by Regulation 545/2003. The countries contained in the list include Argentina, Australia, Hungary, and Israel.

Until 31 December 2005 importers in a Member State can also be authorised by a competent authority to market products imported from a third country not included in the list. The importer would only be permitted to do so where sufficient information is provided for the competent authority of the importing Member State that the organic products were manufactured according to equivalent production and inspection rules to those set out in the Regulation.

Administrative provisions. Each year by 31 March, Member States must forward to the Commission a list of the inspection bodies that they approved on 31 December of the previous year. The information supplied must include the legal and operational

---

138 Commission Regulation 94/92 laying down detailed rules for implementing the arrangements for imports from third countries provided for in Regulation 2092/91 on organic production of agricultural products and indications referring thereto on agricultural products and foodstuffs (OJ L 11, 17 January 1992, pp. 14–15).

structure of the inspection body, their standard inspection procedure, penalty arrangements, and where appropriate their mark. The Commission publishes every year, in the Official Journal of the European Communities, the lists of approved bodies that it has received from the Member States.

In addition, Member States must inform the Commission by 1 July every year, the measures that the Member State took in the preceding year for the implementation of the Regulation.

Chapter 14

Food Contact Materials

The regulation of food contact materials and articles at EU level are found in:

- the Framework Directive 89/109/EEC which sets out requirements for all food contact materials;
- specific directives which cover groups of materials and articles that have been listed in the Framework Directive.

The Framework Directive 89/109/EEC Relating to Materials and Articles Intended to Come into Contact with Foodstuff

The harmonisation at EU level of legislation on food contact materials aims to both protect the health of the consumer and also to remove technical barriers to trade within the European Union. Differences that existed between the national laws at the time of adoption of the EC legislation impeded free movement. The Framework Directive 89/109 applies to materials and articles, which in their finished state, are intended to be brought into contact with foodstuffs or which are brought into contact with foodstuffs. They include packaging materials but also cutlery, dishes, processing machines, containers etc. Materials and articles which are in contact with water intended for human consumption are also within the scope of the definition, except for fixed public or private water supply equipment. Coverings or coating substances such as substances covering cheese rind, prepared meat products or fruit, which form part of the foodstuff and may be consumed together with the foodstuff are not within the scope of the Framework Directive. In contrast cheese wax that cannot be consumed is a food contact material.

Food contact materials and articles must be manufactured in compliance with good manufacturing practice under the Directive so that under normal foreseeable conditions of use they do not migrate their constituents to foodstuffs in quantities which could either endanger human health or bring about an unacceptable change in the composition of foodstuffs or a degeneration in the organoleptic characteristics of the food.

The Directive makes provision for the following groups of materials and articles to be covered by specific directives;

- plastics, including varnish and coatings;
- regenerated cellulose;
- elastomers and rubber;

- paper and board;
- ceramics;
- glass;
- metals and alloys;
- wood, including cork;
- textile products;
- paraffin waxes and micro-crystalline waxes.

The Framework Directive provides that specific directives adopted under it may include:

(a) a list of substances the use of which is authorised to the exclusion of others, in other words a positive list;
(b) purity standards for such substances;
(c) special conditions of use for these substances and/or the materials and articles in which they are used;
(d) specific limits on the migration of certain constituents or certain groups of constituents into or onto foodstuffs;
(e) an overall limit on the migration of constituents into or onto foodstuffs;
(f) if necessary, provisions aimed at protecting human health against any hazards which might arise through all contact with materials and articles;
(g) any other rules to ensure compliance with the requirement that migration does not endanger human health or change the composition of foodstuffs to an unacceptable level;
(h) basic rules necessary for control and enforcement of the requirements;
(i) detailed rules concerning the taking of samples and methods of analysis required to check compliance with the above requirements.

Even where a positive list referred to above has been drawn up at EU level, a Member State may authorise the use within its territory of a substance not included in the positive list, provided that:

- there is no contradiction with the EU positive list;
- the authorisation is limited to a 2-year period;
- official checks on materials and articles manufactured from the authorised substance must be carried out by the Member States;
- materials and articles manufactured containing the authorised substance must bear a distinctive indication which should be defined under the Member States authorisation.

If a Member States grants such an authorisation, it must forward the text of that authorisation to the other Member States and the Commission. If the Member State wish this substance to be added to the positive list before the expiry of the 2-year authorisation period the Member States may submit to the Commission a request for inclusion of the substance. At the same time it should supply supporting documents and justification. It should also give details of the uses for which the substance is intended. Within an 18 month period a decision will then be taken on the basis of information relating to public health after consultation with the Scientific Committee on Food. The procedure for this decision is a simplified procedure as set down in the Directive. The result of that procedure can be that either the substance is included in the positive list or that the national authorisation should be revoked. If a decision is made to revoke the particular national authorisation it shall also apply to any other national authorisations in respect of the particular substance.

Provision is made for safeguard measures where a Member State, as a result of new information or of a reassessment of existing information made since one of the specific directives was adopted, has detailed grounds for establishing that the use of a material and article endangers human health despite it complying with the relevant requirements under the specific directive. In such circumstances the Member State may temporarily suspend or restrict the application of the EU measures permitting the substance to be placed on the market. Upon making such restriction or suspension the Member State must immediately inform the other Member States and the Commission of its decision and give reasons. The Commission is then under an obligation to, as soon as possible, examine the grounds given by the Member State and deliver an opinion on the substance. If the Commission considers that amendments to the specific directives in question are necessary in order to ensure the protection of human health it can initiate a procedure set down under this framework directive. A Member State which has adopted safeguard measures may, in those circumstances, retain them until the relevant EU amendments have been adopted.

Labelling

There are three distinct types of food contact materials in respect of labelling requirements:

(i) materials and articles already in contact with foodstuffs (e.g. packaged foodstuffs) which do not require specific labelling;
(ii) materials and articles which by their nature are clearly intended to come into contact with foodstuffs for which no labelling is required;
(iii) materials and articles intended to come into, but not already in contact with foodstuffs (e.g. packaging materials for sale such as plastic films) which must, when placed on the market for use as food contact materials and articles, be accompanied by:

- the words 'for food use'; or
- a specific indication as to their use; such as coffee machine, wine bottle, soup spoon; or
- a symbol determined to indicate such, in accordance with a simplified procedure laid down under the directive; and
- where appropriate any special conditions to be observed when they are in use; and
- either the name or trade name and address or registered office or the registered trade mark of the manufacturer or processor or of a seller established within the Community.

The particulars listed above must be clearly legible and indelible. At the retail stage they must be:

- on the materials and articles or on the packaging; or
- on the labels air-fixed to the materials and articles or to their packaging; or
- on a notice in the immediate vicinity of the materials and articles and clearly visible to purchasers.

At the marketing stage other than the retail stage the information can be given on accompanying documents, on the labels, on the packaging or on the materials and articles themselves. Only materials and articles which comply with the articles set down under this Framework Directive and, where relevant, the specific directive will be allowed to carry the indication 'for food use'.

Some Specific Directives

Plastics

In order to protect the health of consumers and to avoid adulteration of foods two types migration limits have been established in the area of plastic materials:

- an Overall Migration Limit (OML) of 60 mg (of substances)/kg (of foodstuffs or food stimulants) that applies to all substances that can migrate from food contact materials to the foodstuff;
- a Specific Migration Limits (SML) which apply to individual authorised substances and are fixed on the basis of toxicological evaluation of the particular substance.

  The SML is generally set according to the acceptable daily intake or the tolerable daily intake set by the Scientific Committee on Food. In order to set the acceptable and tolerable daily intakes, it is assumed that everyday throughout a person's lifetime, a person, weighing approximately 60 kg, eats 1 kg of food packed in plastic containers containing the relevant substances at the maximum permitted quantity.

Directive 90/128/EEC relating to plastic materials and articles intended to come into contact with foodstuffs, as amended.[139] This directive applies to plastic materials and articles and parts thereof consisting either exclusively of plastics or composed of two or more layers of materials each consisting exclusively of plastic which are bound together by means of adhesives or by other means and which in the

---

[139] Council Directive 92/39; Commission Directive 93/9/EEC; Commission Directive 95/3; Commission Directive 96/11/EEC; Commission Directive 1999/91/EC; Commission Directive 2001/62/EEC; Commission Directive 2002/17/EEC.

finished product stage are intended to come into contact with or come into contact with foodstuffs and are intended for that purpose. Plastics are defined as the organic macromolecular compounds obtained by polymerization, polycondensation, polyaddition or any other similar process from molecules with a lower macromolecular weight or by chemical alteration of natural macromolecular molecules. Silicones and other similar macromolecular compounds are also included in the definition of plastics.

The following are not plastics:

- varnished or unvarnished regenerated cellulose;
- elastomers and natural synthetic rubber;
- paper and paper board modified or not by the addition of plastics;
- surface coating obtained from perfume waxes, including synthetic perfume waxes and/or microcrystalline waxes, and mixtures of the waxes listed in the first indent with each other and/or with plastics;
- ion-exchange resins and silicones.

Under Directive 90/128 plastic materials and articles are not permitted to transfer their constituents to foodstuffs in quantities exceeding 10 mg/dm^2 of surface area of material or article. This is known as the overall migration limit. However, this limit is 60 mg of the constituents released per kilogramme of foodstuff in the following cases:

- articles which are containers or are comparable to containers or which can be filled with the capacity of not less than 500 ml and not more than 10 l;
- articles which can be filled and for which issues impractical to estimate the surface area in contact with the food services;
- caps, gaskets, stoppers or similar devices for sealing.

The Directive sets down a positive list of monomers and other starting substances that may be deliberately used in the manufacture of plastic materials and articles for food contact. These substances require an authorisation to be included in the positive list. The list does not include impurities of starting materials, reaction intermediates or decomposition products. However they are taken into account in the evaluation of the technical dossier before a substance is included in the positive list. The list does not include monomers and other starting substances used only in the manufacture of service coatings obtained from resinous or polymerized polics in liquid, power or dispersion form, such as varnishes, lacquers and paints; silicones; epoxy resins; adhesives and adhesion promoters; and printing inks.

The Directive also includes an incomplete list of additives which may be used for the manufacture of plastic materials and articles together with restrictions for use. This list is not a positive list because additives not in the list can be used if they comply with national lists. The Commission services intend to transform it into a positive list by 1 January 2005.

Directive 82/711/EEC laying down the basic rules necessary for the testing migration of the constituents of plastic materials and articles intended to come into contact with foodstuffs, as amended[140] *– the Implementing Legislation.* This directive applies to plastic materials and articles which either consist exclusively of plastics or are composed of two or more layers of materials each consisting exclusively of plastics, which are bound together by means of adhesives or by any other means, which, in the finished product state, are intended to come into contact or are bought into contact with foodstuffs and are intended for that purpose. Annexes to this directive set out the migration tests that are to be used to verify compliance with the overall specific migration levels laid down in the Framework Directive 90/128/EEC. Three different types of migration testing are permitted under the Directive: migration tests, substitute tests, and alternative tests. Migration tests are used for the determination of specific and overall migration and are carried out using the 'food stimulants' listed in the directive. Food stimulants are introduced as it is not always possible to use foodstuffs for testing food contact materials. Substitute tests are carried out if migration testing using fatty food stimulants is not used feasible for technical reasons connected with the method of analysis. Alternative tests are permissible instead of migration tests with fatty food stimulants when specific conditions are fulfilled. Detailed rules are laid down in the annexes of the Directive in respect of all these different tests and stimulants. In particular, specific conditions relating to times and temperature are specified.

The tests must be carried out under the most extreme conditions of time and temperature for actual use. The overall and specific migration levels of constituents of the materials and articles must not exceed limits laid down in Commission Directive 90/128 or any other relevant specific Directives.

Directive 85/572/EEC laying down the list of stimulants to be used for testing migration of constituents of plastic materials and articles intended to come into contact with foodstuffs. This directive was adopted in accordance with Directive 82/71 lays down the stimulants that are permitted to be used for testing the migration of constituents of plastic materials and articles intended to come into contact with a single foodstuff or specific group of foodstuffs. The list of substances and materials set down under this directive are to the exclusion of all others.

Directive relating to vinyl chloride.[141] Directive 78/142 establishes restrictions expressed as SML = 0.01 mg/kg and QM = 1 mg/kg is the finished product to be applied the vinyl chloride monomer, which is the basic substance for the

---

[140] Directive 9318; Directive 97/48.

[141] Directive 78/142/EC limits for vinyl chlorides. Directive 80/766/EC methods of analysis of vinyl chloride in products; and Directive 81/432 on methods of analysis of vinyl chloride migration.

manufacture of PVC. Directive 80/766 and 81/432 establish methods for analysis and enforcement of the SML and QM.

Surface coatings. Coatings are not regulated at EU level yet. The general provision of the framework Directive 89/109 apply. At the time of writing the Commission was undecided whether to extend Directive 90/128/EC to cover coatings. Such an extension would complicate the Directive because of the different technologies involved. The Commission gives the examples of:

- Coated metal surfaces, such as cans;
- Polymer coatings on paper or paperboard substrate such as plastic coated cartons;
- Non-stick kitchenware such as frying pans;
- Laminated aluminium foil.

Pending a decision on the drafting of a directive and in the absence of national legislation the Commission has issued guidance for testing.

Directive 2001/61 on the use of certain epoxy derivatives (BADGE, BFDGE, NOGE), as amended. This Directive applies to:

- materials and articles made of any type of plastic;
- materials and articles covered by surface coatings;
- adhesives;

which are manufactured with or containing one or more of the following substances:

- 2,2-BIS (4-hydroxyphenyl) propane bis (2,3-expoxy propyl) ether (BADGE) and some of its derivaties;
- BIS (-hydroxyphenyl) methane bis (2,3-expoxy propyl) ethers (BFDGE) and some of their derivatives;
- other Novolac glycidy ethers (NOGES) and some of their derivatives.

The use of BADGE, BFDGE, NOGE and derivatives having at least one expoxy or cholorohydrin group is restricted. SMLS are established for BADGE and BFDGE and corresponding derivatives. A maximum quantity (QM) is expressed for NOGE, because of the many compounds involved. The use of these three substances will be forbidden after 1 January 2005.

Multi-layer articles. In relation to materials and articles composed of two or more layers (e.g. plastic/paper/food or paper/aluminium/plastic/food) it is unclear if Directive 89/109/EC and the specific Directives apply to the layers or not in direct contact with foodstuffs or only to the layer in direct contact with the foodstuffs. The European Commission, in its guidance notes has expressed the view that they apply to all layers. In particular, indirect contact may be relevant because of possible migration into food through the layer in direct contact. The directives will only not apply, in the Commission's view, to layers only in indirect contact with foodstuffs, if migration of substances through the direct food contact layer can be ruled out. In other words, if it acts as a 'functional barrier'.

Cellulose

Directive 93/10/EEC relating to materials and articles made of regenerated cellulose film intended to come into contact with foodstuffs.[142,143] Regenerated cellulose film is a thin sheet material obtained from refined cellulose derived from unrecycled wood or cotton. Regenerated cellulose film may be coated on one or both sides. The Directive applies to the generated cellulose film which either constitutes a finished product in itself or forms part of finished product containing other materials and which is intended to come into contact with foodstuffs or which, by virtue of its purpose does come into contact with foodstuffs. However the Directive does not apply to regenerated cellulose film which has a coating exceeding 50 mg/dm^2 or to synthetic casing of regenerated cellulose. Directive 93/10 lists a positive list of substances and groups of substances that can be used in manufacture of regenerated cellulose film covered by this Directive and the conditions which must be applicable to their use. Substances other than those listed may be used when these other substances designed to colour (i.e. dyes and pigments) or as adhesives, provided that there is no trace of migration of the substances into or onto foodstuffs, detectable by a validated method. Printed surfaces of regenerated cellulose film are not permitted to come into contact with foodstuffs.

Ceramics

Directive 84/500/EEC relating to ceramic articles intended to come into contact with foodstuffs. This Directive concerns the possible migration of lead and cadmium from ceramic articles which in their finished state come into contact with foodstuffs. Ceramic articles are articles manufactured from a mixture of inorganic materials with a generally high argillaceous or silicate content which small quantities of organic materials may have been added. The articles are first shaped and then this shape is permanently fixed by firing. The ceramic articles may then be glazed, enamelled and/or decorated. The annexes to this Directive lay down maximum levels of lead and or cadmium that can be permitted to migrate from ceramic articles. The annexes also lay down basic rules for the determination of migration levels of lead and cadmium for example the taking of samples and the various conditions.

---

[142] This consolidates Directive 83/229, 86/388 and 92/15.

[143] Directive 93/111.

Others

The substances that are not generally regulated at EU level at the time of writing include:

- elastomers and rubber (Elastomers and rubber are not regulated at EU level yet, with the exception of the Directive 93/11/EEC concerning the nitrosamines and N-nitrosatable substances released by rubber teats and soothers.);
- silicones;
- paper and board;
- glass;
- metals and alloys;
- cork;
- textile products;
- paraffin, water and microcrystalline;
- waxes;
- ion exchange resins;
- adhesives;
- printing inks.

Reform

At the time of writing, the Commission had recently issued a proposal that would amend and replace the EC Framework Directive on food contact materials. Among other things the draft would establish the general requirement of traceability for all food contact materials and cover 'active' and 'intelligent' packaging. The Commission was also preparing a draft proposal for a 'Super-Directive' on food contact plastics materials.

Chapter 15

Contaminants and Residues

Control of contaminants and residues in foodstuffs is crucial to ensure a high level of consumer protection in the European Union. Legislation has been passed at EU level on four different types of substances:

- *Contaminants*: These are substances which unintentionally enter food during the various stages of production, distribution and marketing of foodstuffs.
- *Residues of substances used in veterinary medicinal products*: These are substances used in the prevention and treatment of disease in food producing animals.
- *Residues of substances used as additives in feed*: These are substances used in feed intended for food producing animals.
- *Residues of substances used in plant protection products*: These are substances used in the prevention and treatment of diseases in plants grown for food and feed production, in other words pesticides.

Contaminants

Contaminants are substances that have entered a foodstuff at a stage of its production, distribution or marketing. They have not been intentionally added to food. The contamination generally impacts negatively on the quality of food and may give rise to risks to human health. Therefore the European Union has legislated to minimise the contaminants in foodstuffs.

Framework regulation 315/93 laying down community procedures for contaminants in food

Regulation 315/93/EEC[144] sets down the basic principles controlling contaminants in foodstuffs at EU level. Generally, food containing a contaminant which is above an acceptable amount from a public health point of view and in particular a toxicological level, is prohibited from being placed on the market. There is the requirement that the contaminant level should be as low as can reasonable be achieved following recommended good working practices. Maximum levels are set in relation to certain contaminants in order to protect human health.

[144] OJ L 037, 13/02/1993 P. 01–03.

Under Regulation 315/93, a contaminant is defined as:

> 'any substance not intentionally added to food which is present in such food as a result of the production (including operations carried out in crop husbandry, animal husbandry and veterinary medicine), manufacture, processing, preparation, treatment, packing, packaging, transport or holding of such food, or as a result of environmental contamination. Extraneous matter, such as, for example, insect fragments, animal hair, etc, is not covered by this definition.'

There is provision for safeguard measures to be taken by Member States where, as a result of new information or of reassessment of existing information a Member State has reason to suspect that a contaminant in food, or their complying with Regulation 315/93 or specific regulations adopted under Regulation 315/93, constitutes a health risk. In this situation a Member State may temporarily suspend or restrict the application of the EU provisions in question in its territory. On doing so the Member State must immediately inform the other Member States and the Commission of this action and give reasons for its decision. The Commission is under obligation to examine the reasons given by the Member States as quickly as possible and deliver its opinion immediately as well as taking any necessary measures.

Regulation 466/2001 setting maximum levels for certain contaminants in foodstuffs

Regulation 466/2001, as amended, sets maximum levels for certain contaminants in foodstuffs.[145] The contaminants for which maximum levels are set include nitrates, mycotoxins and heavy metals (lead, cadmium, mercury and 3-mcpd). In addition, provisions for the sampling and analysis of the official control of such contaminants have been laid down at EU level.[146]

Future maximum levels of other contaminants

Proposals for maximum levels of other contaminants exist such as patulin and fusarium toxins (dioxynivalenol and other trichothecenes, zeaalenone, fumonisins) are being considered. Work is also ongoing within the Commission to reduce levels in food and to clarify possible risks from other substances such as polycyclic aromatic hydrocarbons (PAHS), organotins and acrylamide.

---

[145] Amendments include Commission Regulation 563/2002 (nitrates in lettuce and spinach); Regulation 257/2002 and Regulation 472/2002 (aflatoxins in nuts, dried fruit, cereals, spices and milk); Regulation 221/2002 (lead, cadmium, and mercury in a range of foods); Regulation 375/2001 (dioxins in a range of foods); Regulation 272/2002 (ochratoxin A in cereals and cereal products and dried vine fruit).

[146] Commission Directive 1998/53/EEC as amended by Commission Directive 2002/27/EC for aflatoxin levels; Commission Directive 2001/22 EC for heavy metal and 3-mcpd; Commission Directive 2002/69/EC for dioxin levels; Commission Directive 2002/26/EC for ochratoxin A levels.

Acrylamide, an undesirable substance in food which had received much attention from the press at the time of writing, is a chemical which is present in food as a result of cooking practices. Many of these cooking practices have been used over years and in some cases, centuries. However, certain foods, in particular starchy foods such as potatoes and cereal products, have been shown to be affected when deep fried, roasted or baked at high temperatures. The potential risk to public health is not yet clear. Therefore the Commission in close collaboration with the EFSA is collating all the research that has been done on acrylamide as well as carrying out their own. The Joint Research Centre, part of the Commission, is coordinating work on analytical methods and is collecting data on levels detected in different foods.

The presence of acrylamide in food was highlighted by Swedish authorities in April 2002. However, it was communicated to the public without a full review of the scientific information available. Now the issue has been highlighted, the Commission and other scientific bodies are undertaking work on the issue. The Scientific Committee on Food delivered its opinion on acrylamide in July 2002. It concluded that levels should be reduced to as low as reasonably achievable, although further data is needed in several areas to help to reduce levels and to clarify the safety implications.

Residues of Veterinary Medicinal Products

Animals are treated with medicines to prevent or cure diseases during their lifetime. If such animals are food producing animals (e.g. cattle, pigs, poultry, fish) there may be residues of the medicinal products used for treatment in the food products derived from these animals (e.g. meat, milk, eggs). It is important to ensure that these residues are not harmful to the consumer. In order to protect the consumer and public health, Community legislation requires that the toxicity of potential residues is evaluated before the medicinal substance is used in food producing animals. As required, maximum residue limits (MRLs) are established and in some cases zero tolerance is permitted, in other words, the substance is prohibited. Regulation 2377/90[147] lays out the evaluation process. Separate legislation is in place to regulate the use of hormones in food producing animals (see below under feed additives).

Regulation 2377/90 defines residues of veterinary medicinal products as:

> 'all pharmacological products used as active substances, with active principals, excipients or degradation products, and their metabolites which may be in foodstuffs obtained from animals to which the veterinary medicinal product in question has been administered.'

---

[147] 2377/90EEC: OJ L 224, 18/08/1990 P. 01–08.

Maximum residue limits are defined as:

> 'maximum concentrations of residue resulting from the uses of a veterinary medicinal product which may be accepted by the Community as legally permitted or recognised as acceptable in or on a food.'

The maximum residue level for a particular substance is based on the type and amount of residue considered to be without any toxicological hazard for human health. As expressed by the acceptable daily intake or on the basis of a temporary acceptable daily intake that utilises an additional safety factor. When establishing maximum residue limits consideration must be given to residues that occur in food of plant origin and/or come from the environment. Moreover, a MRL for a particular substance can be reduced to be consistent with good practices in the use of veterinary drugs to the extent that practical, analytical methods are available. Annexes I to IV of the Regulation set out the following:

- Annex I – list of pharmacological active substances for which maximum residue levels have been fixed;
- Annex II – list of substances which do not require maximum residue levels;
- Annex III – list of pharmacological active substances used in veterinary medicinal products for which maximum residue levels have been fixed on a temporary basis;
- Annex IV – list of substances, the administration of which to food producing animals shall prohibited throughout the Community.

The Regulation sets out a simplified procedure for determining into which Annex a particular substance should fall. The EU institutions have not consistently followed this procedure and there have been occasions where companies have had to take the matter through the European Court of Justice[148] to ensure that the correct procedure is followed.

Commission Decision 97/747/EC sets down additional rules for certain animal products in particular milk, eggs, honey, rabbits and game meats.

Directive 96/23/EEC sets out measures Member States should adopt to monitor certain substances and residues in live animals and animal products. It establishes the frequencies and level of sampling and the groups of substances to be controlled for each food commodity. On a yearly basis, Member States should submit reports of the results of their residue monitoring to the Commission. The Commission then compiles summary reports consisting of the results of the implementation of all the national residue monitoring plans in the Member States.

---

[148] *Monsanto* v *Commission Case* C-248/99.

The authorisation, marketing and labelling of feed additives

Directive 70/524/EEC, as amended,[149] lays down the basic rules for authorisation, use and marketing of feed additives. Directive 70/524 applies to feed additives which are defined as substances or preparations used in animal nutrition in order to:

- effect favourably the characteristics of feed materials or of compound feedingstuffs or of animal products; or
- satisfy the nutritional needs of animals or improve animal production, in particular by effecting the gastro-intestinal flora or the digestibility of feedingstuffs; or
- introduce intro-nutrition elements conducive to attaining particular nutritional objectives or to meeting the specific nutritional needs of animals at a particular time; or
- reduce harmful effects caused by animal excretions or improve animal environment.

Additives include preservatives, vitamins, acidity regulators, trace elements, microorganisms, enzymes, growth promoters, coccidiostats, and antibiotics. They do not include processing aids used deliberately as substances in the processing of feed materials or of feedingstuffs in order to achieve a certain technological objective during treatment or processing which can result in the unintentional but technically unavoidable presence of residues of the substance or their derivatives in the final produce, provided that these residues do not present any health risk and do not have any technological effect on the finished product.

---

[149] Directive 73/103; Directive 74/7; Directive 74/38; Directive 74/180; Directive 74/181; Directive 74/182; Directive 74/378; Directive 74/421; Directive 75/50; Directive 75/267; Directive 75/296; Directive 75/696; Directive 76/13; Directive 76/546; Directive 76/603; Directive 76/933; Directive 77/179; Directive 77/471; Directive 77/512; Directive 78/58; Directive 78/117; Directive 78/522; Directive 78/613; Directive 78/743; Directive 78/974; Directive 79/139; Directive 79/553; Directive 79/697; Directive 79/1011; Directive 80/131; Directive 80/440; Directive 80/618; Directive 80/678; Directive 80/884; Directive 80/1139; Directive 80/1156; Directive 81/332; Directive 81/632; Directive 82/91; Directive 82/471; Directive 82/474; Directive 82/822; Directive 83/266; Directive 83/466; Directive 83/615; Directive 84/107;Directive 84/349; Directive 84/542; Directive 84/587; Directive 85/157; Directive 85/312; Directive 85/342; Directive 85/429; Directive 85/520; Regulation 3768/85; Directive 86/29; Directive 86/300; Directive 86/403; Directive 86/525; Directive 87/243; Directive 87/244; Directive 87/316; Directive 87/317; Directive 87/552; Directive 88/228; Directive 88/483; Directive 88/616; Directive 89/23; Directive 89/583; Directive 90/110; Directive 90/206; Directive 90/214; Directive 90/412; Directive 90/643; Directive 90/654; Directive 91/248; Directive 91/249; Directive 91/336; Directive 91/508; Directive 91/620; Directive 92/64; Directive 92/99; Directive 92/113; Directive 93/27; Directive 93/55; Directive 93/107; Directive 93/113; Directive 93/114; Directive 94/17; Directive 94/41; Directive 94/50; Directive 94/77; Directive 95/37; Directive 95/55; Directive 95/69; Directive 96/7; Directive 96/25; Directive 96/51; Directive 96/66; Directive 97/72; Directive 98/19; Directive 98/92; Regulation 2786/98; Regulation 2788/98; Regulation 2821/98; Directive 99/20; Regulation 45/99; Directive 46/01; Regulation 2205/01; Regulation 1756/02.

The authorisation procedure depends upon the type of additive. Additives belonging to the groups of coccidiostats and other medical substances, antibiotics and growth promoters are linked to a legal person or company that has presented a scientific dossier to attain the authorisation at Community level. The initial application for such authorisation is made to a Member States which then acts as rapporteur during the process. The linking of the authorisation of these additives to a particular company is to avoid a similar additive being marketed by others which has been produced in a way that is not in conformity with the authorisation and therefore is potentially unsafe. The period of authorisation for these additives is initially for a maximum of 4 years. After a further evaluation of the additive being used in practice, a 10 year period of authorisation can be granted.

Other types of additives, for example preservatives, vitamins, salinity regulators, trace elements and enzymes are not linked to a single legal person or company. However, any such authorisation is also initially made for a maximum period of 4 years and subsequently, after a further evaluation, for an indefinite period of time.

The Directive sets out detailed rules as to what should be contained in an application and how the Member State acting as rapporteur should ensure that the dossier complies with these requirements. The other Member States and the Commission also receive a copy of the application and dossier.

Included in the dossier must be data on the identity of the additive, characterisation, conditions of use, control methods, the efficacy and the safety of the product. Member States act as rapporteurs between a company and other Member States and the Commission can charge fees to the companies for the examination of the application. The Community system of fees is set up in the animal feed sector under Council Decision 98/728/EEC and Council Directive 98/92/EEC.

The Directive lays down specific rules on labelling. The following compulsory particulars must be clearly readable, legible and indelible for all additives, with the exception of enzymes and micro-organisms:

(a) the specific name given to the additive upon authorisation, the EC Registration number of the additive and in the case of additives antibiotics, coccidiostats or growth promoters, the trade name and the registration number given to the person responsible for putting it into circulation;
(b) the name or business name and address or registered address of business of the person responsible for putting the additive on the market;
(c) the net weight and, in the case of liquid additives, either the net volume or the net weight;
(d) as applicable the approval number of an establishment or intermediary or the registration number assigned to the establishment or intermediary.[150]

Additional labelling requirements are given in relation to specific groups for example antibiotics, growth promoters, coccidiostats and other medicinal substances, vitamins,

[150] Directive 95/69/EEC.

vitamin C, trace elements, enzymes and micro-organisms. However, the scope of this chapter is to concentrate on how feed additives are prevented from becoming contaminants of food rather than the labelling of food additives.

Directive 70/524 makes provision for the withdrawal of authorisations of additives and there are several examples of this in fact taking place with, for example, avoparcin (Commission Directive 97/6/EC), ronidazole (Commission Directive 98/19/EC), and tylosin phosphate (Commission Regulation 2821/98). These additives have all had their authorisation withdrawn because of a substantive reason, for example the authorisation conditions are no longer met because of new scientific evidence or following use of safeguard measures. However, authorisations can be withdrawn for administrative reasons, for example in the case of metichlorpindol, metichlorpindol/methylbenzoquate, amprolium, amprolium/ethopabate, dimetridazole and nicarbazin (Commission Regulation 2205/2001).

A new regulation on feed additives. The Commission presented a proposal for a Regulation for additives used in animal nutrition in March 2002. The proposal aims to consolidate existing rules on additives used in feedingstuffs. This is considered necessary as the basic legislation (Council Directive 70/524/EEC) has undergone five major amendments, with over one hundred modifications to the Annexes. It would also clarify certain procedural aspects related to the evaluation of dossiers and types of authorisation granted. In particular, it would replace the current decentralised authorisation procedure with a centralised Community procedure for the authorisation and supervision of feed additives. In future the EFSA will have the competence and the responsibility to provide a single framework for dossier evaluation for all feed additives in order improve transparency and efficiency. The Regulation would also lay down specific rules concerning the labelling of additives and premixtures. However, the existing EU labelling rules concerning compound feedingstuffs to which additives and premixtures have been incorporated would not be amended by the Regulation. The new legislation will be a Regulation (as opposed to the current Directive) and will therefore be directly applicable in all Member States.

On 18 December 2002, the Commission issued an amended proposal for a new Regulation for additives used in animal nutrition. This incorporates a large number of amendments adopted by the European Parliament (the 'EP') at first reading on 21 November 2002. The Council of Ministers (the 'Council') also accepted many of the EP's amendments in reaching a political agreement on the proposal at the 16–19 December 2002 Agriculture Council.

Additives covered. According to the Commission's amended proposal, the new Regulation shall apply to 'chemically defined or described substances or micro-organisms not normally used as feed materials which are intentionally added to feedingstuffs or drinking water'. It divides feed additives into five broad categories, each of which is then sub-divided into functional categories, as follows:

- *Technological additives* (defined as any substance added to feed for a technological purpose): preservatives, antioxidants, emulsifiers, stabilisers, thickeners, gelling agents, anticaking agents, acidity regulators, binders, coagulants.
- *Sensory additives* (defined as any substance, the addition of which to feed improves or changes the organoleptic properties of the feed, or the visual characteristics of feed derived from animals): colorants, flavouring and appetising compounds.
- *Nutritional additives* (defined as any substance used for nutritional purposes): vitamins, trace elements, amino acids.
- *Zootechnical additives* (defined as any additive used to affect favourably the performance of animals in good health or used to affect favourably the environment): digestibility enhancers, gut flora improvers, growth promoters, substances which have a positive effect on the environmental impact of animal production.
- *Coccidiostats and histomonostats.*

The Regulation would not apply to processing aids (nor to technological but unavoidable residues of processing aids in the final product), or to veterinary medicinal products as defined in Directive 2001/82/EC.

Only additives that have been through the relevant authorisation procedure and are entered in a newly created Community Register of Feed Additives could be put on the market, used or processed. Authorisations for new additives would be for a maximum of 10 years (renewable). Authorisations would be species specific, state maximum dosage allowances, set maximum residue limits (for some additives where this is considered necessary for safety reasons) and set out post-marketing monitoring requirements. Each additive would be allocated to one or more of the technological categories (and functional groups) identified in the Regulation (see above) depending on its principal function and properties.

The EFSA would evaluate applications in the new centralised system, and propose maximum residue limits for some additives, as appropriate, on the basis of residues studies. Specific guidelines for the authorisation of feed additives would be established by the Commission in co-operation with the EFSA within one year of the entry into force of the Regulation for each of the five categories of additives listed in the Regulation. Implementing rules are also expected to be established. Where appropriate these would differentiate between standards for feed additives in respect of animals for food production and standards in respect of other animals, in particular pets.

In order to obtain authorisation a feed additive would have to also meet several key criteria. First, it would not be allowed to: present a risk to animal health, human health or the environment; be presented in a manner which may mislead the user; harm the consumer by impairing the distinctive features of animal products, or mislead the consumer with regard to the distinctive features of animal products. Second, it would have to demonstrate that it has at least one of the following characteristics, that is that it: favourably affects the characteristics of feed; favourably affects the characteristics of animal products; satisfies the nutritional needs of animals; or favourably affects the environmental consequences of animal production.

Transitional measures have been proposed for additives already authorised for use in the European Union to avoid disruptions in the market. Companies marketing feed additives authorised under existing legislation would have to apply for re-authorisation, with specific procedures laid down for notification and authorisation. In addition, a simplified authorisation procedure would apply to those additives which have successfully undergone the authorisation procedure for food use (under Directive 89/107/EEC).

The EU's Scientific Steering Committee has recommended the progressive phasing out of the use of all antibiotics as growth promoters while preserving animal health. The European Union has already banned antibiotics used in human medicine from being added to animal feed. The new Regulation will complete this ban by prohibiting the use of four additional drugs not used in human medicine that are still currently allowed on the EU market. These are: monensin sodium, salinomycin sodium, avilamycin, and flavophospholipol. The European Parliament supported the broad lines of the Commission's proposal on antibiotics. However, it wished to bring the deadline for phasing out forward from 2006 to 1 January 2005. The Commission's amended proposal suggests that they should be prohibited as of 1 January 2006.

Following the political agreement reached in December, the Council has adopted its formal Common Position. It was largely in line with the Commission's amended proposal, although the political agreement made a number of additions and changes to the functional groups listed under some of the feed additive categories and to some of the proposed definitions. Once adopted, the Common Position was forwarded to the European Parliament for its second reading, (which normally has to be completed within 3 months of formal receipt of the Common Position.) The Parliament adopted amendments to the Common Position and the dossier was returned to the Council for completion of its own second reading. The most controversial question was the phasing out date for the use of antibiotics as growth promoters which the European Parliament wants to see happen as early as possible. The final adoption of the Regulation was on 22 September 2003. It was published in the Official Journal on 18 October 2003 and so will enter into force on 18 October 2004.

PESTICIDE RESIDUES

Current pesticide maximum residue level legislation is derived from four Council Directives:

- Council Directive 76/895/EEC[151] establishing MRLs for selected foods and vegetable oils;
- Council Directive 86/362/EEC[152] establishing MRLs for cereals and cereal products;
- Council Directive 86/363/EEC[153] establishing MRLs in products of animal origin;
- Council Directive 90/642/EEC[154] establishing MRLs in products of plant origin, including fruits and vegetables.

The framework directive. In 1991 the Council adopted Directive 91/414/EEC concerning the placing of plant protection products on the market. The Directive provides for the Commission to examine pesticide active substances under all their safety aspects. Generally Member States are prohibited from permitting plant protection products on their market unless they have been authorised in accordance with Directive 91/414/EEC. However, once a product has been authorised it will benefit from free movement. Member States are required to prescribe that plant protection products must be used properly and labelled as required. Plant protection products will not be authorised unless the following conditions are met:

- its active substances are listed in the annex to Directive 91/414/EEC and all conditions laid down in the Directive in relation to that specific substance are fulfilled;
- it is established in light of current scientific and technical knowledge and shown from the appraisal of the dossier that it is sufficiently effective; it has no unac-

---

[151] Directive 80/428; Directive 81/36; Directive 82/528; Directive 85/768; Directive 88/298; Directive 89/186; Directive 93/58; Directive 96/32; Directive 97/41; Directive 00/24; Directive 00/57; Directive 02/66; Directive 02/71; Directive 02/79.

[152] Directive 97/41; Directive 97/71; Directive 98/82; Directive 99/65; Directive 99/71; Directive 00/24; Directive 00/42; Directive 00/48; Directive 00/58; Directive 00/81; Directive 01/39; Directive 01/48; Directive 01/57; Directive 02/23; Directive 02/42; Directive 02/66; Directive 02/71; Directive 02/76; Directive 02/79; Directive 02/97.

[153] Directive 93/59; Directive 94/29; Directive 95/39; Directive 96/33; Directive 97/41; Directive 97/71; Directive 98/82; Directive 99/71; Directive 00/24; Directive 00/42; Directive 00/58; Directive 00/81; Directive 01/39; Directive 01/57; Directive 02/23; Directive 02/42; Directive 02/66; Directive 02/71; Directive 02/79; Directive 02/97.

[154] Directive 93/58; Directive 94/30; Directive 95/38; Directive 95/61; Directive 96/32; Directive 97/41; Directive 97/71; Directive 98/82; Directive 99/65; Directive 99/71; Directive 00/24; Directive 00/42; Directive 00/48; Directive 00/57; Directive 00/58; Directive 00/81; Directive 01/35; Directive 01/39; Directive 01/48; Directive 01/57; Directive 02/05; Directive 02/23; Directive 02/42; Directive 02/66; Directive 02/71; Directive 02/76; Directive 02/79; Directive 02/97; Directive 02/100.

ceptable effect on plant or plant products; it does not cause unnecessary suffering and pain to vertebrates to be controlled; it has no harmful effect on human or animal health, directly or indirectly (e.g. through drinking water, food or feed) or on ground water; it has no unacceptable influence on the environment, having particular regard to its fate and distribution in the environment (especially its contamination of water) and its impact on non-target species;

- the nature and quantity of its active substances and where appropriate any toxicological or ecotoxicological significant impurities and co-formulants can be determined by appropriate methods;
- its residues, resulting from authorised uses, and which are of toxicological or environmental significance, can be determined by appropriate methods in general use;
- its physical and chemical properties have been determined and deemed acceptable for the purpose of the appropriate storage of the product;
- maximum residue levels in the agricultural product referred to in the authorisation have been provisionally established by the Member States and notified to the Commission in accordance with the procedure set down in Directive 91/414/EEC (the Commission then has three months to consider the notification and whether the provisional maximum levels established by the Member State are acceptable).

Authorisations may be reviewed at any time if it appears that any of the requirements are not complied with. The inclusion of active substances in the accepted lists under the Directive shall be for an initial period not exceeding 10 years. For inclusion of an active substance in the said list, account should be taken of, where relevant, the acceptable daily intake for humans and the acceptable operator exposure level, an estimate of its fate and distribution in the environment as well as its impact on non-target species. Inclusion in the active substances list may be subject to requirements such as the minimum degree of purity of the active substance, the nature and maximum content of certain impurities, restrictions arising from evaluation of information referred to taking account of the agricultural, animal health and the environmental conditions in question, type of preparation and manner of use. Directive 91/414/EEC sets out detailed requirements for the application of authorisation, mutual recognition of authorisations when granted, exchange of information between the Member States and the Commission in the event of an authorisation or withdrawal and the packaging and labelling of plant protection products.

On 14 March 2003, the Commission issued a proposal for a Regulation harmonising all maximum residue levels (MRLs) of pesticides permitted in food and agricultural products. It would consolidate into a single legislative act the existing MRL Directives: Directive 76/895/EEC (fruit and vegetables), Directive 86/362/EEC (cereals), Directive 86/363 (food of animal origin), and Directive 90/642/EEC (certain products of plant origin). The proposal also provides for harmonised MRLs for substances not currently covered. Subject to certain conditions, MRLs would be set at 0.01 mg/kg. Member States would no longer set national MRLs. The proposal would clarify the role of the EFSA in risk assessment and of the Commission in risk management. It is expected that the Regulation would apply from 1 January 2005 in respect of fresh products and 1 July 2005 in respect of stored products.

Chapter 16

Hygiene

Introduction

Over the last forty years since the first directive on meat hygiene was adopted in 1964,[155] EU hygiene legislation has been developed piecemeal, reacting to sector specific issues, this has resulted in more than fifteen vertical directives being adopted that cover a wide-range of products including frogs legs, milk and meat. Many directives contain provisions on hygiene, animal health and official controls. The hygiene regime has been based on a prescriptive approach, setting out in detail the measures and processes that industry must comply with.

Over time, and largely due to this piecemeal sector specific approach, hygiene legislation has become a very complex area of law with a large number of directives being amended on numerous occasions, and in some cases creating inconsistencies between directives. More than ten directives have been adopted that cover food of animal origin, often with similar or identical provisions on key issues.

Concerns have been raised by both industry and enforcement agencies as to the difficulties in interpretation and enforcement of EU hygiene legislation. These issues combined with recent food emergencies, such as BSE and the subsequent reduction in consumer confidence, has led to a change in approach to hygiene legislation.

In the 1990s, the recasting of existing hygiene legislation was considered to reduce the detailed rules, inconsistencies and repetition present in the current regime. It was argued by industry that the prescriptive approach was failing to keep up with changes in technology and was not allowing industry to be sufficiently innovative.

In 1993, the general hygiene Directive was adopted which emphasises the importance of consumer confidence in the safety and standards of hygiene of foodstuffs circulated within the EU.[156] The general hygiene Directive applies to foodstuffs that do not fall within the scope of one of the vertical directives. For the first time, a more general approach was taken to hygiene legislation. The general hygiene Directive applies many of the HACCP (Hazard Analysis Critical Control Points) principles. HACCP is a document based system requiring food operators to identify and manage potential food safety hazards. The Directive reflects a move away from detailed prescriptive legislation to a system where more responsibility is placed on food producers.

---

[155] Directive 64/433/EEC on health problems related to Intra-Community trade in fresh meat OJ No P 121, 29/07/1994, P. 2012–2032.

[156] Directive 93/43/EEC lays down the general hygiene rules for foodstuffs OJ L No 175, 19/07/1993, P. 1–11.

In July 2000, the Commission adopted a package of hygiene proposals which would repeal the general hygiene Directive and seventeen sector specific directives. The aim of the proposals is to simplify hygiene rules and to extend these general hygiene rules to food of animal origin and to all stages of production, including primary production. It would place more emphasis on the use of the HACCP system and increase the traceability of foodstuffs. The proposed legislation would include regulations on general hygiene and food of animal origin.

General Directive on the Hygiene of Foodstuffs (Directive 93/43)

Directive 93/43[157] lays down the general hygiene rules for foodstuffs, and sets out the procedures for verifying that these rules have been complied with. The Directive applies only where specific food hygiene rules have not been adopted. A presumption is made in the Directive that the principle of the free movement of foodstuffs implies consumer confidence in the safety and standards of hygiene of foodstuffs circulated within the EU. The general hygiene Directive introduces a more general approach to hygiene legislation though it still contains, in its Annex, many detailed provisions with which food businesses must comply. It places the responsibility for the hygiene conditions of a food business on the food business operator.

Scope

The Directive applies to all stages of the food chain after primary production, during preparation, processing, manufacturing, packaging, storing, transportation, distribution, handling and offering for sale or supply to the consumer. Primary production which includes harvesting, slaughter and milking is expressly excluded from the scope of the Directive. The Directive applies to both public and private food businesses whether profit making or not for profit.

Food hygiene is defined in the Directive as 'all measures necessary to ensure the safety and wholesomeness of foodstuffs'. Wholesomeness is defined as food that is, as far as hygiene is concerned, fit for human consumption.

Article 3 of the Directive sets out the provisions that food business operators must comply with including a general hygiene obligation, compliance with HACCP principles and the provisions set out in the Annex to the Directive.

HACCP (Hazard Analyse and Critical General Points)

Central to the Directive is the obligation placed upon food business operators to ensure that adequate safety procedures are identified, implemented and reviewed.

[157] OJ L 175, 19/07/1993 P. 01–11.

This must be carried out on the basis of the principles that were used to develop the system of HACCP:

- analysing the potential food hazards in a food business operation;
- identifying the points in those operations where food hazards may occur;
- deciding which of the points identified are critical to food safety;
- identifying and implementing effective control and monitoring procedures at those critical points; and
- reviewing the analysis of food hazards, the critical control points and the control. These procedures must be monitored periodically, and whenever there are changes to the food business operations.

The HACCP system is internationally recognised and has been endorsed by the Codex Alimentarius.[158] It is based on seven principles that focus on identifying and controlling potential hazards. The HACCP system has been expanded to include not only microbiological hazards but also chemical and physical hazards.

Common potential hazards in food production can include physical hazards such as fragments of glass or metals, chemical hazards such as toxins, which could include residues of medicinal products, and biological hazards such as bacterial pathogens including salmonella. Critical controls points that could be identified would include cooking, packaging and maintaining appropriate temperatures during storage and transportation.

A procedure is established in the Directive for adopting microbiological criteria and temperature control criteria for certain classes of foodstuffs.

Detailed provisions

Food business operators must also comply with the provisions set out in the Annex to the Directive which consists of ten chapters. Chapter I sets out the general requirements for all food premises except for specific food premises referred to in Chapter III. These general requirements include having sufficient washbasins and flush toilets, and ensuring that the premises are kept clean and in good repair. Chapter II sets out requirements for rooms where food is prepared, treated or processed. Dining rooms and premises specified in Chapter III do not have to comply with Chapter II. Chapter III establishes requirements for: movable and/or temporary premises including market stalls; premises that are primarily a private dwelling house; premises only used occasionally for catering purposes; and vending machines. Chapter IV considers the hygienic transportation of foodstuffs including the possible contamination of foodstuffs. Chapters V to X of the Annex apply throughout all the stages from food preparation, to the offering for sale or supply of

---

[158] The Codex Alimentarius Commission adopted Guidelines for the Application of the HACCP System in 1993 which has subsequently been revised.

foodstuffs to consumers. However, it is important to note that they do not apply to the primary production stage. They cover requirements for: equipment that come into contact with foodstuffs; food waste and other refuse; water supply; personal hygiene; provisions applicable to foodstuffs; and training.

The Directive sets out the minimum provisions applicable to hygiene, but Member States are allowed to introduce more stringent provisions provided that they do not constitute a 'restriction, hindrance or barrier to trade' in foodstuffs.

Guides to good hygiene practice

The Directive provides that Member States should encourage the publication of guides to good hygiene practice. The guides are to be developed by food business sectors, representatives of appropriate authorities and consumer groups in consultation with 'parties that are substantially affected'. When developing these guides, the Recommended International Codes of Practice (RICP), and the General Principles of Food Hygiene (GPFH) of the Codex Alimentarius should be taken into account. The guides may then be developed under the aegis of one of the national standards institutes referred to in List 2 of the Annex to Directive 83/189.[159] After assessing that a guide complies with Article 3 of the Directive, Member States are required to forward the guide to the Commission so that it can be made available to other Member States. Many guides have been prepared at national level.

Where it is considered by Member States or the Commission that there is a need for a European guide to good hygiene practice, a consultation process would be started that includes Member States and other interested parties, such as consumer groups and business representatives. The need for such voluntary guides in the particular sector or activity concerned would be the focus of the consultation process. Where a guide is considered necessary, the consultation will also:

- indicate the scope, subject matter and timetable for the development of the guide;
- refer the guide for development and assessment under the aegis of a European Standards Agency

When developing European guides, the RICP and the GPFH must be taken into account as well as national guides. A guide must also be practicable, for the particular food sector, throughout the whole of the Community.

European guidelines when approved will be published in the Community series of the Official Journal, and Member States must bring them to the attention of relevant food businesses and appropriate authorities within their borders. Member States can recommend to food operators that they apply the European standards of the EN 29,000 series (now EN ISO9000), where appropriate, to assist in the implementation of the general hygiene rules and the guides to good hygiene practice.

---

[159] Directive 83/189/EEC laying down a procedure for the provisions of information in the field of technical standards and regulations OJ No L 109, 26/4/1983, P. 08.

Health Rules for the Production and Placing on the Market of Raw Milk, Heat-Treated Milk and Milk-Based Products (Directive 92/46)

This Directive is one of the many product specific hygiene directives. It is also one of the Directives that would be repealed if the food hygiene package of proposals is adopted as legislation. In this chapter this Directive is given as an example of the specific directives. The stated aims of the Directive are: to ensure high levels of protection of public health; to establish the internal market; and to ensure that checks are uniformly carried out.

The Directive lays down health rules for the production and placing on the market of raw milk, heat-treated milk, milk for the manufacture of milk-based products and milk-based products intended for human consumption ('milk products'). These milk products are detailed in the Directive. Certain milk products sold directly by a producer to the consumer are excluded from the scope of the Directive.

The Directive applies to the production, wrapping, storage and transportation of milk products. The Directive sets out detailed requirements that must be followed by operators from the conditions that milk products must meet, to the procedure for the approval of establishments, and the hygiene conditions that establishments must comply with once they have been approved.

The prime responsibility for compliance with the Directive lies with producers, with Member States being obliged to make sure that the producers are complying with the Directive.

Products with traditional characteristics

The Directive allows Member States to grant derogations from the requirements set out in the Directive for milk-based products with traditional characteristics. This provision is intended to assist small producers who would find implementing all the provisions too onerous. A list of milk-based products that Member States are permitted to grant derogations for was compiled by the Commission and is set out in Decision 96/536[160] (as amended by Decision 97/284[161]).

Checks by the operator/manager

The operator or manager of a treatment and/or processing establishment must carry out checks based on the following principles:

- identification of critical points in the establishment on the basis of the processes used;
- monitoring and checking of such critical points by appropriate methods;

---

160 OJ L 230, 11/09/1996 P. 12–15.

161 OJ L 114, 01/05/1997 P. 45–46.

- taking samples for analysis to a laboratory recognised by the competent authority. The samples are analysed to check the cleaning and disinfection methods in the establishment, and that the standards established by the Directive are being complied with;
- tests must be carried out to detect any residues of antibiotics, pesticides, detergents and other harmful substances;
- keeping a written or registered record of these checks and the results of the tests, with a view to submitting the information to the competent authority. The results of the different checks and tests must be kept by the producer, in most cases, for a period of at least two years.

An obligation is placed on the operator or manager to inform the competent authority of any serious health risk that is revealed by these checks and tests.

Set out in the Directive are microbiological criteria (for example listeria monocytogenes and salmonella) for certain milk products including milk-based products and drinking milk.

Health marks

The Directive provides that milk-based products must carry health marks. These health marks show the competent authority in the place that the product is destined for, that the product complies with the provisions set out in the Directive. The operator or manager of the establishment must guarantee the correct administration of the health mark. The health mark particulars must be contained within an oval surround and include the name (or initials) of the consigning country, the approval number of the establishment and the initials of the EEC.

Responsibilities of Member States

Member States must draw up a list of approved establishments, with certain exceptions, and give each of these establishments an approval number.

It is also the responsibility of the Member States to ensure that operators or managers of a treatment and/or processing establishment are complying with the Directive. Experts from the Commission are, however, permitted to make on-site checks if it proves necessary to ensure that the Directive is being applied in a uniform manner and that the competent authorities are co-operating.

Member States have a discretion as to what 'appropriate' administrative or penal measures they can invoke for non-compliance with the Directive, in particular, for infringements in respect of:

- certificates or documents drawn up, which do not correspond with the actual state of the products;

- health marks on the products which do not comply with the rules;
- products which have not undergone the checks required under the Directive or that the products have not been used for their original intended purpose.

Authorisation of imports

The Directive establishes a procedure for compiling a list of third countries authorised to provide imports of milk and milk-based products to the EU. The most recent list of authorised third countries is contained in the Commission Decision 2001/743.[162]

PROPOSED NEW HYGIENE RULES

The existing hygiene legislation was adopted in response to the internal market and has been developed gradually over forty years. This has led to overlaps, inconsistencies and gaps. In particular primary production, though covered by certain sector specific directives, is specifically excluded from the scope of the general hygiene Directive. Many hygiene rules were also adopted according to whether the food referred to is of animal origin. Due to the lengthy, detailed and prescriptive nature of the rules concerns have been raised that the regime does not allow businesses to take advantage of technological developments.

The proposed new hygiene regime would be based on a comprehensive 'stable to table' approach. The objectives of the proposals are: to simplify hygiene rules; remove inconsistencies; make the regime more transparent; and make the rules easier to interpret and enforce.

It was proposed by the Commission that the existing large number of directives should be repealed and replaced by four regulations. These regulations would have direct effect and would not require implementing provisions in each Member State. The Commission has justified its choice in using regulations on the basis that this will ensure a 'coherent hygiene regime throughout the EU.' Moreover, the Commission believes that adopting regulations will allow the legislation to be more easily updated to take into account new technical and scientific developments.

The White Paper on Food Safety highlighted new hygiene rules as action points for the Commission. On 17 July 2000, the Commission published its package of proposals to recast current hygiene legislation. The proposals consisted of four regulations and a directive including:

- a directive to repeal certain directives on the hygiene of foodstuffs and the health conditions for the production and placing on the market of certain products

[162] OJ L 278, 23/10/2001 P. 32–34.

of animal origin intended for human consumption, and amending Directives 89/662[163] and 91/67;[164]

- a Council regulation laying down the animal health rules governing the production or placing on the market importation of products of animal origin intended for human consumption (subsequently adopted as a Council Directive);
- a regulation on the hygiene of foodstuffs;
- a regulation laying down specific hygiene rules for food of animal origin.

The Commission also proposed a regulation laying down detailed rules for the organisation of official controls for products of animal origin intended for human consumption. However, this last proposal was subsequently withdrawn by the Commission. This proposal was withdrawn because of new information made available to the Commission since the proposal was first developed, in particular, in respect of meat safety. On 11 July 2002, the Commission adopted a new proposal for a regulation on the organisation of official controls on food of animal origin. The proposal focuses on controls of meats, live bivalve molluscs, and milk and dairy products. In addition, the Commission is working on a proposal for a regulation that would lay down general principles which would be the basis for official food controls (See Chapter 18).

Proposed Directive to Repeal Directives on Hygiene of Foodstuffs

This proposed directive would amend Directives 91/67and 89/662 and repeal the general hygiene Directive 93/43 together with sixteen sector specific directives:

1. Council Directive 64/433/EEC[165] of 26 June 1964 on health conditions for the production and marketing of fresh meat,[166] as last amended by Directive 95/23/EC.[167]
2. Council Directive 71/118/EEC of 15 February 1971 on health problems affecting the production and placing on the market of fresh poultry meat[168] as last amended by Directive 97/79/EC.[169]
3. Council Directive 72/461/EEC[170] of 12 December 1972 on health problems affecting intra-Community trade in fresh meat,[171] as last amended by the Act of Accession of Austria, Finland and Sweden.

[163] OJ L 395, 30/12/1989 P. 13–22.
[164] OJ L 046, 19/02/1991 P. 01–18.
[165] OJ P 121, 29/07/1964 P. 2012–2032.
[166] OJ 121, 29/7/1994, P. 2012/64.
[167] OJ L 243, 11/10/1995, P. 7.
[168] OJ L 55, 8/3/1971, P. 23.
[169] OJ L 24, 30/1/1998, P. 31.
[170] OJ L 302, 31/12/1972 P. 24–27.
[171] OJ L 157, 19/7/1993, P.1.

4. Council Directive 77/96/EEC[172] of 21 December 1976 on the examination for trichinae (*Trichinella spiralis*) upon importation from third countries of fresh meat derived from domestic swine,[173] as last amended by the Act of Accession of Austria, Finland and Sweden.
5. Council Directive 77/99/EEC[174] of 21 December 1976 on health problems affecting the production and marketing of meat products and certain other products of animal origin,[175] as last amended by Directive 97/76/EC.[176]
6. Council Directive 80/215/EEC[177] of 22 January 1980 on animal health problems affecting intra-Community trade in meat products,[178] as last amended by the Act of Accession of Austria, Finland and Norway.
7. Council Directive 89/362/EEC[179] of 26 May 1989 on general conditions of hygiene in milk production holdings.[180]
8. Council Directive 89/437/EEC[181] of 20 June 1989 on hygiene and health problems affecting the production and the placing on the market of egg products,[182] as last amended by Directive 96/23/EC.[183]
9. Council Directive 91/492/EEC[184] of 15 July 1991 laying down the health conditions for the production and the placing on the market of live bivalve molluscs,[185] as last amended by Directive 97/79/EC.
10. Council Directive 91/493/EEC[186] of 22 July 1991 laying down the health conditions for the production and the placing on the market of fishery products,[187] as last amended by Directive 97/79/EC.
11. Council Directive 91/494/EEC[188] of 26 June 1991 on animal health conditions governing intra-Community trade in and imports from third countries of fresh poultry meat,[189] as last amended by Directive 93/121/EC.[190]
12. Council Directive 91/495/EEC[191] of 27 November 1990 concerning public health and animal health problems affecting the production and placing on

---

172 OJ L 026, 31/01/1977 P. 67–77.
173 OJ L 395, 30/12/1989, P. 13.
174 OJ L 026, 31/01/1977 P. 85–100.
175 21 OJ L 62, 15/3/1993, P. 49.
176 OJ L 46, 19/2/1991, P. 01.
177 OJ L 047, 21/02/1980 P. 04–07.
178 OJ L 189, 3/7/1998, P. 12.
179 OJ L 156, 08/06/1989 P. 30–32.
180 OJ 121, 29/7/1964, 2012–2064.
181 OJ L 212, 22/07/1989 P. 87–100.
182 OJ L 243, 11/10/1995, P. 7.
183 OJ L 55, 8/3/1971, P. 23.
184 OJ L 268, 24/09/1991 P. 01–14.
185 OJ L 24, 30/1/1998, P. 31.
186 OJ L 268, 24/09/1991 P.15–34.
187 OJ L 268, 24/9/1991, P. 15.
188 OJ L 268, 24/09/1991 P. 35–40.
189 OJ L 268, 24/9/1991, P. 35.
190 OJ L 340, 31/12/1993, P. 39.
191 OJ L 268, 24/09/1991 P. 41–55.

the market of rabbit meat and farmed game meat,[192] as last amended by the Act of Accession of Austria, Finland and Sweden.

13. Council Directive 92/45/EEC[193] of 16 June 1992 on public health and animal health problems relating to the killing of wild-game and the placing on the market of wild-game meat,[194] as last amended by Directive 97/79/EC.
14. Council Directive 92/46/EEC[195] of 16 June 1992 laying down the health rules for the production and placing on the market of raw milk, heat-treated milk and milk-based products,[196] as last amended by Directive 96/23/EC.[197]
15. Council Directive 92/48/EEC[198] of 16 June 1992 laying down the minimum hygiene rules applicable to fishery products caught on board certain vessels in accordance with Article 3(1)(a)(i) of Directive 91/493/EEC.[199]
16. Council Directive 94/65/EC[200] of 14 December 1994 laying down the requirements for the production and placing on the market of minced meat and meat preparations.[201]

These repealed directives would be replaced by regulations covering general hygiene rules, hygiene rules for food of animal origin, animal health rules and official controls of food of animal origin.

Hygiene of Foodstuffs

The proposed regulation on the hygiene of foodstuffs would replace and expand the provisions set out in the general hygiene Directive. The provisions contained in the proposed regulation are generally in line with the general hygiene Directive and would retain many of its key principles:

- a general obligation on food businesses to operate hygienically;
- an emphasis on the development of guides to good hygiene practice;
- developing hygiene systems based on the HACCP; and
- procedures for the adoption of microbiological and temperature control measures.

---

192 OJ L 268, 24/9/1991, P. 41.
193 OJ L 268, 14/09/1992 P. 35–53.
194 OJ L 268, 14/9/1992, P. 35.
195 OJ L 268, 14/09/1992 P. 01–32.
196 OJ L 268, 14/9/1992, P. 01.
197 OJ L 125, 23/05/1996 P. 10–32.
198 OJ L 187, 07/07/1992 P. 41–44.
199 OJ L 268, 24/09/1991 P.15–34.
200 OJ L 368, 31/12/1994 P. 10–31.
201 OJ L 368, 31/12/1994, P. 10.

The Annex to the proposed regulation also contains many of the same detailed provisions set out in the Annex to the general hygiene Directive.

The proposal does, however, introduce significant changes to the scope of the current legislation. It is based on the 'stable to table' approach and would apply to primary producers and food of animal origin, both excluded from the general hygiene Directive. It would also introduce the compulsory registration of all food businesses to ensure that food, and food ingredients, can be traced.

The definition of food hygiene would be amended. The requirement to 'ensure safety' would be replaced by an obligation 'to control hazards'. The intended use of the food would also be taken into account.

Hazard analysis and critical control points

The HACCP system would be extended to include a requirement that food businesses retain documents and records to show that the system is being effectively applied. These documents would have to be kept at least for the shelf-life of the product and to be shown to officials on request. No specific provisions are given for products without a specified shelf-life. Although primary producers would not be obliged to implement the full HACCP system, they would have to monitor possible hazards and eliminate or reduce them to an acceptable level.

Extension of detailed provisions

Set out in Annex II of the proposed regulation are many of the detailed provisions contained in the annex to the existing general hygiene Directive. These provisions would be extended to also include the wrapping and packaging of foodstuffs, and special conditions for processing by heat-treatment, smoking and salting.

Flexibility for SMEs

The Commission has been anxious to emphasis that at the same time as harmonising the hygiene rules, it wants to ensure that the rules are flexible, in particular for food businesses in remote geographical regions. The proposal contains several provisions to allow the Commission and Member States to assist SMEs. The Commission would be able to adopt further measures to assist small businesses in complying with the HACCP system. Many small and medium sized enterprises may not have the specialised staff to implement the full HACCP system. Moreover, Member States would be allowed to adapt the provisions contained in Annex II of the proposed regulation to assist food businesses in remote areas or those using traditional methods. These new rules would, however, be obliged to ensure that the objectives of food hygiene are not comprised. If Member States decide to adopt these provisions, they must inform the Commission and the other Member States.

Hygiene guides

The use of guides on the application of HACCP in conjunction with guides to good practice would be encouraged. Where both national and EU guides are produced, food businesses would be able to choose which guide to use.

Responsibilities of operators and Member States

The regulation would also introduce new responsibilities for food businesses and Member States to improve traceability of foodstuffs. Member States would be obliged to create a register of food businesses covered by the regulation and allocate a registration number to a food business. Food businesses, except retailers, would have to ensure that foodstuffs produced by them could be identified by their registration number. This is aimed at improving consumer protection and making it easier for official controls by Member States. Competent authorities could, if they felt it was necessary, require that a food business obtain prior approval by the competent authority before being allowed to operate. Before approving a food business the competent authority would be obliged to carry out a site visit to confirm that the food business meets the provisions in the regulation. The proposal does not provide the criteria for the registration or authorisation of food businesses.

A food business would be required to put in place procedures for the withdrawal of foodstuffs immediately a serious risk has been identified and to inform the competent authorities. A record of suppliers of ingredients, food, and, where appropriate, the provenance of animals would have to be kept.

Food safety objectives

The Commission refers to food safety objectives (FSOs) in its proposal. A hygiene regime based on FSOs would focus on objectives rather than detailed provisions. This type of system could allow food businesses to devise their own systems for complying with FSOs without the need for highly detailed legislation. The Commission did not set out FSOs in the current proposal as it believes that FSOs should be based on sound scientific advice which take time to formulate. However, the proposed regulation would allow, through the comitology procedure and with the assistance of the Standing Veterinary Committee and the Standing Committee on Foodstuffs, for targets and performance standards to be set in the future. In the meantime, detailed legislation would remain in place.

Hygiene Rules for Food of Animal Origin

The proposed regulation on hygiene rules for food of animal origin would replace sector specific directives that would be repealed by the proposed directive contained in the reform package. The proposed regulation is aimed to simplify, remove inconsistencies and in some cases extend the existing legislation. Food businesses would be obliged to comply with both the provisions set out in the proposed general hygiene regulation, referred to previously, and the proposed regulation specifically referring to food of animal origin.

There are three Annexes to the proposed regulation containing detailed provisions: Annex I provides definitions including those for meat, eggs, milk and frogs' legs; Annex II sets out detailed provisions for specific products; and Annex III lays down the requirement for imports from third countries.

Scope of proposed regulation

Only unprocessed and processed products of animal origin must comply with the detailed rules set out in Annex II. Processed products are defined as:

> 'foodstuffs resulting from the application to unprocessed products of a treatment such as heating, smoking, curing, maturing, drying, marinating, etc., or a combination of these processes and/or products; substances necessary for their manufacture or for giving specific characteristics to the product may be added.'

Composite products are not subject to the provisions set out in Annex II, however, there would be an obligation to identify possible hazards resulting from the use of ingredients of animal origin. These hazards are to be eliminated or reduced where necessary.

Detailed sector specific rules

Annex II contains specific provisions for certain types of food of animal origin as well as common provisions including approval of establishment and health marks. This would allow a degree of simplification to the existing legislation.

Annex II contains fifteen sections containing detailed provisions for particular foods of animal origin including: meat of domestic ungulates; poultry meat; meat of farm game; wild game meat; minced meat, meat preparations and mechanically separate recovered meat; meat products; live bivalve molluscs; fishery products; milk and milk products; eggs and egg products; frog legs; snails; treated stomachs, bladders, and intestines; animal fats and greaves; and gelatine. In addition, set out in Annex II are detailed requirements including: the responsibilities of manufacturers; the obligations of authorities; technical requirements for the structure and organisation of establishments; hygiene requirements; procedures for the approval of establishments; and storage and transport conditions.

Annex II only applies to the retail sector in prescribed circumstances. This has raised concerns as many of the big retailers now carry out much of their meat preparation in-house, including cutting and boning of carcases.

In some case the existing legislation would be tightened for example in view of the problems highlighted by BSE certain parts of animals would no-longer be permitted to be used in the production of mechanically separated meat (MSM).

Requirements for imports

Annex III provides the requirements that third countries would have to comply with before they would be permitted to export food of animal origin to the European Union. It sets out the provisions for drawing up lists of third countries from which imports of products of animal origin would be permitted. The provisions are to ensure that the third countries comply with the general provisions set out in Article 12 of the proposed regulation on hygiene of foodstuffs.

Amending the annexes

A provision has been included in the proposed regulation that the Annexes would be amended through the comitology procedure. Amendments to the existing Directives have to be agreed after following the co-decision procedure. The comitology procedure is often invoked to enable technical aspects of legislation to be amended more quickly. Concerns have been raised, in particular, by the European Parliament, that by allowing these Annexes to be amended through the comitology procedure the European Parliament would be excluded from the process.

Animal Health Rules of Food of Animal Origin

On 16 December 2002 Council Directive 2002/99 was adopted laying down the animal health rules governing the production, processing, distribution and introduction of products of animal origin for human consumption. This Directive was one of the proposals contained in the Hygiene package adopted by the Commission in 2002, originally envisaged as a Regulation. The aim of the Directive is to prevent animal diseases, that are not believed to transmissible to humans such as foot-and-mouth disease, spreading as a result of products of animal origin being placed on the market. The proposal is aimed at removing possible inconsistencies between existing animal health legislation.

The Directive contains provisions on: animal health requirements for the production, processing, and distribution of products of animal origin within the Community; and imports from third countries. It would allow experts from the Commission to carry out audits and inspections in cooperation with the competent authorities of the Member State to ensure that the regulation is being uniformly applied.

Member States should transpose the provisions in the Directive by 1 January 2005. At the time of writing, the remainder of the Hygiene package was about to enter its second reading at the Parliament and Council, under the co-decision procedure.

Chapter 17

Zoonoses/Microbiological Criteria

Introduction

Zoonoses have been defined as 'any disease and/or infection which is likely to be naturally transmitted from animals to man' and a zoonotic agent as 'any bacterium, virus or parasite which is likely to cause a zoonoses'. Examples of zoonoses include brucellosis, salmonellas, listeria, rabies and tuberculosis.

Generally speaking there are in practice four ways in which zoonoses can be transmitted from animals to humans: person to person; food borne (in particular raw meat, pasteurized milk and drinking water); environmental; and direct contact with animals.

Salmonellas, campylobacter and VTEC (a group of *E. coli* that produce verotoxin) are some of the most commonly found zoonotic food borne pathogens. They are present in the intestines of animals used in food products. Zoonotic agents often reach the consumer through contaminated meat, raw milk, infected eggs, vegetables and water. Meat can be contaminated at the slaughter house through faecal contamination. Vegetables are more often contaminated through irrigation water or animal manure.

Other parasitic pathogens such as trichinella can be passed on to the consumer through rodents being present in animal pens or food stores; and the introduction of raw or improperly heated meat as feed.

According to a report by the Commission on 'the trends and sources of zoonotic agents in animals feedingstuffs, food and man in the European Union and Norway in 1999' published in August 2001, there were more than 300,000 reported cases of human illness caused by zoonoses in the European Union in 1999 including:

- salmonellas which is generally associated with the consumption of poultry or eggs. Salmonellas is the most reported zoonotic disease in the European Union;
- campylobacter is the second most commonly reported zoonotic disease and can in some cases lead to a nerve disorder and in severe cases paralyses; the campylobacter infection is more often found in chicken meat;
- listeria which can cause abortions, stillbirth, and in infants and people with weakened immune systems it may lead to blood poisoning and meningitis. Listeria is generally associated with the consumption of soft cheese and processed meat products.

The incidence of zoonotic diseases in the European Union is high and for some zoonotic agents the figures are increasing. It has been difficult for the European

Union institutions to assess the extent of the problems relating to the zoonotic food borne agents because it seems likely that many infections are not recorded and it would not be unreasonable to assume that the cases reported only represent the more severe cases of the diseases. However, it is accepted by the Commission that zoonotic diseases represent a significant food safety issue.

Commissioner David Byrne stated that 'we should not forget that the VTEC and other food-born pathogens are a major health concern'.

Existing Community Legislation

Community legislation controlling zoonotic diseases is contained in Directive 92/117[202] commonly referred to as the 'Zoonoses Directive'. In addition, Community legislation on animal health and hygiene also contains provisions relating to zoonotic diseases and microbiological criteria:

- Council Directive 64/432[203] on animal health problems affecting intra-Community trade in bovine animals;
- Council Directive 92/46[204] which sets out the provisions for brucellosis and tuberculosis status of holdings for milk production;
- Directive 64/433[205] which establishes measures for the inspection of meat for the presence of parasites such as trichinella.

Decision 2119/98[206] established a Community network for the epidemiological surveillance and control of communicable diseases including zoonoses.

Zoonoses Directive (Directive 92/117)

The Zoonoses Directive established a two stage approach to the control of zoonoses. First, the Directive requires Member States to collect information on certain zoonotic agents and the presence of certain zoonoses such as salmonellas and brucellosis. Member States are obliged to report to the Commission by the 31 March every year with an evaluation of the information collected including the trends and the sources of zoonotic infections recorded during the previous year. Secondly, the Commission evaluates this information and compiles a report based on the information received from the Member States for the Standing Veterinary Committee by 1 October each year. The information provided, allows proposals for appropriate control measures to be developed.

---

[202] OJ L 268, 14/09/1992 P. 33–34.
[203] OJ P 121, 29/07/1964 P. 1977–2012.
[204] OJ L 268, 14/09/1992 P. 01–32.
[205] OJ P 121, 29/07/1964 P. 2012–2032.
[206] OJ L 268, 03/10/1998 P. 01–07.

Currently the control measures set out in the Directive focus on salmonellas in poultry breeding flocks. However, the Directive contains provisions allowing for the extension of the types of zoonoses to be considered in the future to include, listeria and campylobacter. In Annexes II and III of the Directive provisions are given for: the criteria for drawing up plans for monitoring salmonellas in foul flocks; the monitoring and control of the presence of salmonellas in breeding flocks; and the inspection for salmonellas at the final production stage of compound feedingstuffs for poultry.

According to the Scientific Committee on Veterinary measures relating to Public Health (SCVPH) the collection of data has improved but not too such an extent that it is possible to carry out comparative studies of the instances and prevalence of zoonoses. Despite the fact that the Member States are submitting annual reports as required under the Directive, the monitoring and surveillance systems used throughout the Member States is not harmonised. It has been argued that to ensure an integrated approach to food safety the scope of the Zoonoses Directive would need to be extended to cover other animals and other zoonoses.

The Directive sets out the requirements for third countries who are authorised, in health terms, to export products to the European Union, and a list of these countries established. To be admitted or retained on this list, a third country is obliged to put forward a plan setting out the guarantees that it can give regarding the checks it can make for zoonoses. At the very least, these guarantees must result in an equivalent level of protection as that provided for in the Directive.

The Zoonoses Directive has been amended by Council Directive 97/22[207] and a Directive of the European Parliament and the Council 1999/72. These Directives were adopted to assist in the implementation of the Zoonoses Directive. Member States were required under Directive 97/22 to implement the measures set out in the Zoonoses Directive in respect of salmonellas controls in poultry breeding flocks from 1 January 1998. The Zoonoses Directive also requires the Commission to submit a report to the Council on the control and prevention of zoonoses. Directive 1999/72 extended the time for presenting the report to 30 March 2000. In fact the Commission adopted a report and proposals for change to the existing zoonoses legislation in August 2001 (see below).

Network for the epidemiological surveillance in control of communicable diseases in the community

Council Decision 2119/98 established a Community network for the epidemiological surveillance in control of communicable diseases including zoonoses. The objective of the surveillance system is to assist in identifying, monitoring and controlling the outbreaks of communicable diseases.

---

[207] OJ L 113, 30/04/1997 P. 09–10.

The Commission, under Decision 2119/98 is responsible for developing the network and co-ordinating its activities. The network assists in the prevention and control of the communicable diseases in the Community through Member States consulting each other and liaising with the Commission. The Community network is aimed to promote 'co-operation and co-ordination' between the Member States.

Decision 2000/57[208] and Decision 2000/96[209] were adopted to implement an 'early warning' and 'response system'. Decision 2000/57 sets out the types of issues that should be reported, the information to be exchanged and reporting procedures to be followed. Decision 2000/96 sets out the communicable diseases which over a period of time would come under Community surveillance. In addition, it establishes the criteria for the selection of the communicable diseases. The communicable diseases include zoonoses but also include other communicable diseases such as legionnaire's disease.

Disease specific networks at Community level have been set up, though Decision 2000/57 provides that, even where such a network has not been established, events that could lead to an outbreak of community significance should be reported. Annex I of the Decision sets out the events that should be reported within the early warning and response system. Annex II of the Directive gives three 'activation' levels:

- *Level one*: 'Information exchange' occurs where information collected by one or more Member State or other recognised source suggest that an event is likely.
- *Level two*: A 'potential threat' occurs when information on an event points to a potential public health threat.
- *Level three*: A 'definite threat' occurs where an event results in a public health threat.

The procedures for exchange of information, consultation and co-operation under the early warning and response system are set out for each of the different activation levels. Member States are required under Decision 2000/57 to submit annual analytical reports, no later than the 31 March, of the events and procedures that have been applied within the early warning and response system. The Commission on the basis of the information supplied by the Member States is required to prepare an annual report on the operation of the early warning and response system and where necessary propose changes to the system.

Food Scares

Bovine spongiform encephalopathy

Bovine spongiform encephalopathy (BSE) was first identified in UK cattle in 1985. It is a fatal neurodegenerative disease of cattle which has been traced to an agent

[208] OJ L 021, 26/01/2000 P. 32–35.
[209] OJ L 028, 03/02/2000 p. 50–53.

related to scrapie in sheep. Meat-and-bone meal additives used in cattle feed were contaminated by recycled bovine carcases which has led to an epidemic of more than 180000 diseased animals in the UK alone.

In 1996 a new spongiform encephalopathy which is transmissible to humans called variant Creutzfeldt–Jakob disease (vCJD) was described. vCJD has been linked to the exposure of the human population to BSE in foodstuffs.

The first legislation at EU level to deal with BSE was introduced in 1989. A number of pieces of Community legislation have subsequently been adopted. The BSE crisis has had an enormous impact on the proposals that are being developed by the Commission on hygiene, controls and zoonotic measures. It is largely also as a result of the BSE crisis that the Commission has adopted its 'farm to fork' or 'stable to table' approach to food safety.

E. coli

The Food and Veterinary Office carried out visits to six Member States between January 2001 and June 2001 to review the monitoring and control systems in the Member States for VTEC infection in relation to bovine meat, meat products, mince preparations, minced meat and milk production. The Food and Veterinary Office decided to carry out these visits because of a number of 'high profile outbreaks of food poisoning' which had resulted in some fatalities. *E.coli* is considered to be a particularly serious food safety problem due to the low dose level of *E.coli* necessary to become infected. This makes it particularly difficult to control through the use of microbiological sampling (see below). The Commission published a staff paper on the results of the Food and Veterinary Office inspection programme in 2001.

Proposals for Change

EU food scares such as BSE have provided the impetus for change to the existing Community legislation in respect of zoonoses. In 1997 Dr Franz Fischler (now Commissioner Fischler) acknowledged that:

> 'although the Zoonoses Directive is an essential element in consumer protection, it is not a sufficient one … the Zoonoses Directive must help to ensure that a proper food borne disease reporting system is established, so as to allow food legislation to be adapted quickly to the hazard occurring at a given time.'

The White Paper on Food Safety adopted by the Commission in January 2000 also considered the need for Community monitoring of food borne diseases and an introduction of harmonised reporting requirements. It was suggested that this information would assist the Commission in reducing the prevalence of zoonotic diseases and also assist in the creation of a better defined programme at Community level. It was recognised in the White Paper that:

> 'animal welfare questions need to be integrated more fully with regards to food policy. In particular the impact on the quality and safety of products of animal origin intended for human consumption needs to be reflected in the legislation.'

In the White Paper it was proposed that the Zoonoses Directive be amended to improve the monitoring and reporting systems and also to reduce the prevalence of specific zoonoses such as salmonellas. It was also proposed that a decision should be adopted in respect of Member States and third country programmes for the control of zoonoses agents in animal products exported to the Community. The decision would require Member States to implement measures to control zoonotic agents and for third country products to be controlled to the same level as Community products.

Commission report on the measures to be put in force for the control and prevention of zoonoses

On 1 August 2001 the Commission presented a report on measures for the control and prevention of zoonoses. The report is in response to the requirement under the Zoonoses Directive for the Commission to submit a report to the Council regarding the control and prevention of zoonoses. The report suggests that a review of the current legislation should lead to an intensification of the monitoring and controlling of zoonoses. The report refers to:

- new rules for the reporting systems for zoonoses;
- methods for collecting samples and for examinations in approved national laboratories;
- the control of salmonellas in poultry laying flocks;
- the control of salmonellas in poultry breeding flocks and in compound feedingstuffs for poultry;
- any measures to combat zoonoses other than salmonellas.

The Commission is concerned to ensure that there is coherency between specific zoonoses legislation, the general food hygiene and food control legislation, in particular, with the reforms currently being proposed in respect of food hygiene legislation. The Commission suggests that the control measures provided under the Zoonoses Directive for certain types of salmonellas should be extended to other food borne pathogens.

According to the report, the Commission realises that not all Member States would be able to fully implement the systems for monitoring and control of zoonoses set out in the Zoonoses Directive. Moreover only six Member States have fully implemented the salmonellas control of breeding flocks provisions. The Commission favours a policy based on risk analysis which would include risk assessment, risk management and risk communication. The Commission suggested putting forward two proposals:

- a proposal for a directive of the European Parliament and of the Council on the monitoring of zoonoses and zoonotic agents. This proposal would cover the data collection of instances and prevalence of risks and also the transparency of the data collected;
- a proposal for a regulation of the European Parliament and of the Council on the control of salmonellas and other food borne zoonotic agents. This second proposal would cover the risk management issues.

The Commission envisages a role for the European Food Safety Authority in the collection of data and the communication of the data collected. The proposed regulation and directive follow on from the action plan set out in the White Paper on food safety and also the opinion by the Scientific Committee on Veterinary Measures relating to Public Health on zoonoses published in April 2000.

On 1 August 2001, the Commission adopted a proposal which incorporated:

- a draft regulation on the control of salmonella and other food borne zoonotic agents, which would amend Directives 64/432,[210] 72/462[211] and 90/539[212];
- a draft directive on the monitoring of zoonoses and zoonotic agents, which would amend the Zoonoses Directive and Decision 90/424[213] on expenditure in the veterinary field.

Proposal for a regulation on the control of salmonellas and other food borne zoonotic agents. The stated aim of the proposed regulation is:

> 'to ensure that proper and effective measures are taken to control salmonellas and other zoonotic agents in order to reduce their prevalence and the risk they pose to public health.'

The proposed regulation would cover:

- the adoption of targets for the reduction of prevalence of specified zoonoses in animal populations, in particular the primary stage of production of animals, but also, where necessary, at other stages in the food chain;
- the approval of specific control programmes established by Member States and food business operators;
- the adoption of specific rules concerning certain control methods applied in the reduction of prevalence of zoonoses and zoonotic agents;
- the adoption of rules concerning intra-Community trade and imports from third countries of certain animals and products thereof.

---

210 OJ P 121, 29/07/1964 P. 1977–2012.
211 OJ L 302, 31/12/1972 P. 28–54.
212 OJ L 303, 31/10/1990 P. 06–28.
213 OJ L 224, 18/08/1990 P. 19–28.

The proposed regulation sets out definitions for zoonoses and zoonotic agents. The current definition for zoonoses would be: 'any disease and/or infection which is naturally transmissible directly or indirectly from animals to humans'. 'Naturally' would therefore replace 'likely to be' in the definition contained in the Zoonoses Directive. The definition for zoonotic agents has also been amended to include fungus and 'other biological entity'.

The regulation would, in principle, cover all zoonoses, however currently only requirements in respect of salmonellas have been set out in Annex I of the regulation. Annex I of the draft regulation sets out the specified zoonoses and zoonotic agents for which Community targets for the reduction of prevalence would be established through the regulation. The Commission suggest that before targets can be set, further scientific evidence and knowledge is required. The targets for the reduction of salmonellas are to be established by a range of dates between 2003 and 2006 depending on the type of animal such as laying hens (2004) and turkeys (2006).

Member States would be required to encourage food business operators to establish their own control programmes which would cover at least feedstuff production and primary production of animals. Food business operators would be obliged to submit their control programmes for the approval of the competent authority of the Member State.

The regulation would establish procedures for designating Community and national reference laboratories. In addition, the regulation sets out quality requirements for laboratories participating in control programmes.

The regulation sets out requirements concerning intra-Community trade and imports from third countries to ensure that the purchaser knows the status of the holding of origin of the animals. The Commission proposes that in due course information concerning zoonoses control should be added to health certificates. The results of testing for salmonellas in the flock or herds of origin would also be set out in health certificates. Third countries would be required to implement equivalent measures.

It is proposed that the regulation would amend: Directive 64/432 on animal health problems effecting intra-community trade in bovine animals in swine; Directive 72/462 on health and veterinary inspection problems upon importation of bovine, ovine, caprene animals and swine, fresh meat or meat products from third countries; and Directive 90/539 on animal health conditions governing intra-community trade and imports from third countries of poultry and hatching eggs.

Proposed directive on the monitoring of zoonoses and zoonotic agents. The proposed directive would repeal the Zoonoses Directive (Directive 92/117). Set out in Annex I of the draft directive are the zoonoses and zoonotic agents to be monitored including salmonellas, VTEC and campylobacteriosis. The draft directive specifically excludes transmissible spongi form encephalopathy. The Commission has indicated that they propose to present, in due course, a specific set of rules in respect of transmissible spongi from encephalopathy.

The stated purpose of the proposed directive is:

> 'to ensure that zoonoses and zoonotic agents are properly monitored so that the necessary information may be collected in the Community to evaluate trends and sources of zoonoses and zoonotic agents. That evaluation shall provide a basis for the action to be taken to prevent and control zoonoses and zoonotic agents relevant to the community.'

The directive would require Member States to monitor zoonotic organisms. It would also allow the establishment of co-ordinated Community monitoring programmes and the monitoring of antibiotic resistance in zoonotic organisms.

The draft directive would require Member States to ensure that food business operators inform the competent authorities as soon as an operator became aware that a foodstuff produced or processed by him has caused or is likely to cause a food borne outbreak. The competent authority would then be obliged to investigate the outbreak and transmit a report to the Commission and the European Food Safety Authority (EFSA) on the results of its investigations.

Food business operators would be obliged to keep a record of the results of the zoonoses testing that they carry out and to pass this information onto the competent authority if requested to do so. Member States would be required to prepare annual reports on the trends and sources of zoonoses for the Commission and the European Food Safety Authority. The EFSA would then prepare a report based on the information received from the Member States and including any other relevant information from other Community sources.

Political agreement was reached in respect of these two proposals in September 2003. They are expected to be formally adopted in the near future.

Microbiological Criteria

Microbiological criterion for foodstuffs has been defined as:

> 'the acceptability of a process, product or food lot based on the absence or presence, or number of micro-organisms and/or quantity of their toxins/metabolites, per unit of mass, volume or area.[214]'

Microbiological criteria is used to assess the amount of a pathogen within a foodstuff. However, due to the uneven distribution of micro-organisms, microbiological testing is only one of several methods to ensure the safety and quality of foods including the use of good hygiene practices and the hazard analysis critical control point principles. Microbiological criteria levels are set for specific foodstuffs in the following directives and decisions:

- Council Directive 89/437 on hygiene and health problems effecting the production and the placing on the market of egg products.

---

214 Opinion of the SVPH on the evaluation of microbiological criteria for food products of animal origin for human consumption 23 September 1999.

- Council Directive 91/492[215] laying down the health conditions for the production on the placing on the market of live bivalve molluscs.
- Council Directive 92/46 laying down the health rules for the production and placing on the market of raw milk, heat treated milk and milk based products.
- Commission Decision 93/51[216] on the microbiological criteria applicable to the production of cooked crustaceans and molluscon shell fish.
- Council Directive 94/65[217] laying down the requirements for the production and placing on the market of minced meat and meat preparations.
- Commission Decision 2001/471[218] laying down rules for the regular checks on the general hygiene carried out by the operators of establishments according to Directive 64/433 on health conditions for the production and marketing of fresh meat and Directive 71/118[219] on health problems affecting the production and placing on the market of fresh poultry meat.

Microbiological criteria can also be used to monitor whether the prevalence of a pathogen in specific foods is increasing or decreasing. However, concerns have been raised regarding the reliability of sampling of foodstuffs due to the uneven distribution of micro-organisms. It has been said that if five samples are randomly taken and it is found that none of them are positive it would give a 95 per cent confidence level that the food lot is less than 50 per cent contaminated.[220] Therefore the number of samples needed to be certain that a food lot is not contaminated is very high, and according to the Scientific Committee on Veterinary measures relating to Public Health (SVPH) 'it is important to emphasise that no sampling plan can assure the absence of a pathogen from a foodstuff'. The SVPH has emphasised the fact that microbiological criteria should only be one of several measures to ensure that foodstuff is safe, and stressed, in particular, the promotion of the use of hazard analysis at critical control points and the use of general good hygiene practice (see Chapter 16).

Certain problems have been identified with current EU microbiological criteria partly due to the fact that many criteria were developed between five and ten years ago. There has also been criticism that the microbiological criteria generally apply only to the food producer and not the food retailer.

It is understood that the Commission is developing a draft regulation on microbiological criteria for foodstuffs. The draft regulation is expected to set out the microbiological criteria for certain micro-organisms such as salmonellas and listeria in specific food categories such as processed dairy products. The food business operator would be responsible for ensuring that the foodstuffs meet the criteria throughout the entire shell life of the product.

---

[215] OJ L 268, 24/09/1991 P. 01–14.

[216] OJ L 013, 21/01/1993 p. 11–13.

[217] OJ L 031, 04/02/1994 P. 29–46.

[218] OJ L 165, 21/06/2001 P. 48–53.

[219] OJ L 055, 08/03/1971 P. 23–39.

[220] Opinion of the SVPH on the evaluation of microbiological criteria for food products of animal origin for human consumption 23 September 1999.

Chapter 18

Food Controls and Official Inspection of Foodstuffs

Introduction

Legislative requirements for official controls have been adopted to ensure the safe production of food within the EU and for foodstuffs that are imported into the EU from third countries. It is primarily the responsibility of the national authorities of Member States to maintain control systems to ensure that food safety standards are adhered to by food operators. This includes ensuring the compliance of foodstuffs, food additives and food contact materials with the relevant legislation.

Regulation 178/2002[221] lays down the general principles of food law. The Regulation sets out basic principles in particular that:

> 'Member States shall enforce food law and monitor and verify that the relevant requirements of food law are fulfilled by feed and food business operators at all stages of production, processing and distribution. For that purpose, they shall maintain a system of official controls and other activities as appropriate to the circumstances, including public communication on feed and food safety and risk, feed and food safety surveillance and other monitoring activities covering all stages of production, processing and distribution. Member States shall also lay down the rules on measures and penalties applicable to infringements of feed and food law. The measures and penalties provided for shall be effective, proportionate and dissuasive.'

The rules on official controls provide in more detail how Member States must comply with and implement these principles.

The Commission, through the Food and Veterinary Office (FVO), carries out on the spot inspections and audits to ensure that the Member States are providing effective control systems.

Directive 89/397[222] on the official controls of foodstuffs sets out the general principles governing the official inspections of foodstuffs. It provides a useful definition of official control of foodstuffs hereafter referred to as 'controls'. Controls mean, for the purposes of the Directive:

> inspections by the competent authorities of the compliance, for example, of foodstuffs, with provisions aimed at preventing risks to public health, guaranteeing fair

[221] OJ L 031, 01/02/2002 P. 1–24.

[222] OJ L 186, 30/06/1989 P. 23–26.

commercial transactions or protecting consumers' interests, including provisions on consumer information.

Rules for products of animal origin, such as meat, milk and eggs are also contained in many sector specific pieces of legislation.

The inadequacies of national systems of control have been highlighted by the recent food crises such as BSE. In the White Paper on Food Safety, the Commission claimed that 'there is a need to clarify and update existing food control legislation and ensure that it covers all steps in the production'.

In response to this, the Commission has adopted proposals to cover controls of food of animal origin and secondly controls of food and feed. The Commission's aim is to create a more comprehensive official controls system covering feed as well as foodstuffs and all stages of production. The proposal will follow the 'farm-to-fork' approach.

Official Controls

Directive 89/397 – Official controls of foodstuffs

Directive 89/397 establishes the general principles governing official inspections with the objective of preventing risks to public health and protecting the interests of consumers. To meet this objective, 'competent authorities' in Member States are authorised to carry out inspections of foodstuffs, materials intended to come into contact with foodstuffs, trace elements, food additives and mineral salts.

Competent authorities must carry out controls in accordance with the general principles set out in the Directive to ensure that food business operators are identifying steps in their activities which are critical to ensure food safety, and implementing and reviewing adequate safety procedures based on the HACCP system (see Chapter 16). The Directive lays down rules for the organisation of national official controls including the right of appeal against measures taken by a competent authority and the organisation of controls in accordance with plans that must be established in advance. The controls must comprise one or more of the following procedures:

- inspections;
- sampling and analysis;
- inspection of staff hygiene;
- examination of written and documentary material;
- examination of any verification systems set up by the undertaking and of the results obtained.

Directive 89/397 sets out the procedures by which inspectors must carry out their inspections. The inspections must be carried out regularly and generally without prior warning. In each case, inspectors must select the stage or stages which are most appropriate for the inspection including the production, manufacturing, storage, distribution and trade stages.

If inspectors find that a food business operator has failed to comply with the provisions contained in Article 3 of the general hygiene Directive 93/43[223] (see Chapter 16), Member States can, if necessary, withdraw or destroy the foodstuffs in question or close the undertaking for a period of time. If a hygiene problem which is likely to pose a serious risk to human health, arises from the territory of a third country, the Commission can, either on its own initiative or, at the request of a Member State:

- lay down special conditions for the foodstuffs from all or part of the third country concerned; and/or
- suspend imports from the third country concerned and, where necessary, from any transit third countries.

If such a hygiene problem does arise, the Commission may also take interim protective measures regarding the foodstuffs concerned. However, the Commission is obliged to consult the Member States before taking such measures, except in an emergency. The Council can confirm, amend or revoke any decision adopted by the Commission.

If a Member State officially informs the Commission of its concerns about a hygiene problem, the Member State can take interim protective measures with regard to imports of the foodstuffs if the Commission fails to take the protective measures referred to above. If a Member State decides to take interim protective measures, it must inform the other Member States and the Commission.

Member States are obliged to draw up a programme for the frequency and nature of inspections. In addition, Member States must, on an annual basis, forward information to the Commission as to how these programmes have been implemented. An EU-wide coordinated inspection programme is adopted annually by the Commission. This programme is based on the information the Commission receives from the Member States. In 1994 the Commission published a Report on the national and coordinated programmes,[224] as provided for in the Directive. The Commission found that the national programmes and the EU programme were not comparable. The Commission has therefore decided:

- to monitor national programmes to control foodstuffs;
- to evaluate their equivalence and effectiveness;
- to monitor the implementation of legislation.

Directive 89/397 was supplemented by Directive 93/99.[225] One of the main objectives of Directive 93/99 is to create a quality standard system for laboratories used

---

[223] OJ L 175, 19/07/1993 P. 01–11.

[224] (COM (94) 567) Commission Report to the Council and the European Parliament on the application of Article 14 of Directive 89/397 not published in the Official Journal.

[225] OJ L 290, 24/11/1993 P. 14–17.

by the Member States for testing data. Member States are obliged to ensure that the laboratories comply with the general criteria laid down in European standard EN45001.

Official controls for food of animal origin

There are a number of product specific Directives that contain rules for controls by competent authorities relating to food of animal origin. These include Directives relating to meat, meat products, egg products and milk products (see Chapter 16). There are, however, two Directives that apply to all food of animal origin:

- Directive 89/662/EEC concerning veterinary checks in intra-Community trade with a view to the completion of the internal market;
- Directive 97/78/EC laying down the principles governing the organisation of veterinary checks on products entering the Community from third countries.

Directive 89/662[226] provides measures for the establishment of control plans, actions to be taken where a food emergency arises, and provisions for the organisations of controls in Member States. One of the key objectives of the Directive is to ensure that checks of products are carried out at the place of dispatch and not at the borders between Member States.

Directive 97/78[227] sets out the checks that must be carried out on products that are exported to the European Union from third countries. The Commission has approved a list of border inspection posts and products must be cleared at an approved inspection post. It must also be checked physically, as well as submitted to a documentary and identity check.

Directive 85/73[229] as amended by Directive 96/43[228] sets out provisions to ensure that veterinary inspections and controls of products of animal origin are properly financed.

Member States are obliged to cooperate with the Commission and between themselves to ensure that legislation on veterinary and zootechnical matter is correctly applied. Directive 89/608[230] sets out detailed rules for this cooperation.

THE FOOD AND VETERINARY OFFICE

In April 1997, the Food and Veterinary Office (FVO) was established as part of DG Health and Consumer Protection. The mission statement of the FVO at the time of

---

[226] OJ L 395, 30/12/1989 P. 13–22.
[227] OJ L 024, 30/01/1998 P. 09–30.
[228] OJ L 162, 01/07/1996 P. 01–13.
[229] OJ L 032, 05/02/1985 P. 14–15.
[230] OJ L 351, 02/12/1989 P. 34–37.

its establishment was:

> 'to monitor the observers of food hygiene, veterinary and plant health legislation within the European Union and elsewhere, and to contribute towards the maintenance of confidence in the safety of food offered to the European consumers.'

The FVO on behalf of the Commission carries out inspections in Member States and third countries to check that the competent authorities are implementing and enforcing EU legislation correctly. The FVO publishes annual reports outlining its main activities undertaken during the previous year. The reports contain the results from the inspections that have been carried out, together with conclusions and recommendations.

If after an inspection has taken place, the FVO considers that the competent authority of a Member State has not implemented or enforced EU legislation correctly, it will make a recommendation to the authority to change its current systems in order to address the problems which have been identified. The authority is requested to prepare a plan as to how it intends to improve its control systems. The FVO evaluates the plan and monitors its implementation.

The FVO also makes recommendations to the Commission for the amendment or clarification of existing legislation, and the need for new legislation where appropriate.

The FVO states that it will follow three main principles when carrying out its duties:

- independence, so that consumers can be sure that their interests are properly protected;
- transparency, so that its findings are available and understandable to everyone, thereby helping consumers to make informed choices;
- excellence, so that its consumer health protection responsibilities are carried out to the highest standards, in a way that would build consumer's confidence.

The FVO also follows the principle that the whole of the food protection chain must be controlled and that the FVO should monitor the authorities responsible for ensuring these standards at national level. In the 2001 annual report published by the FVO, it states that the FVO's mission is:

- to promote effective control systems in the food safety and quality, veterinary and plant health sectors;
- to check on compliance with the requirements of EU food safety and quality, veterinary and plant health legislation within the European Union and in third countries exporting to the European Union;
- to contribute to the development of EU policy in the food safety and quality, veterinary and plant health sectors;
- to inform stakeholders of the outcome of the evaluations.

The FVO conducted 209 inspections within the Member States and third countries throughout 2001. The FVO's inspection programme concentrated on four main issues:

- inspections of hygiene control systems in the production of food of animal origin in the Member States such as poultry, eggs and milk;

- inspections on TSE in all the Member States and some candidate countries;
- the outbreaks of Foot-and-Mouth Disease in four Member States;
- inspections in candidate countries.

Proposals for Change

Commissioner David Byrne recently stated that he sees that:

> 'development of a new approach to official controls as being the 'third pillar' in the Community's food safety policy. The first pillar is an effective range of food safety legislation. The second pillar being the European Food Safety Authority. It is only when we have all three pillars in place, can we be reasonably assured that we can have a safe supply of food from farm-to-table.'

Set out in the White Paper on Food Safety is a proposal for a regulation on food and feed safety controls. The Commission stated that there is a need to establish a Community framework for official controls on all food and feed safety aspects along the feed and food chain. The White Paper also identified differences between the national systems in relation to the fees charged to cover the costs of controls.

The Commission is in favour of Member States playing a more active role in policing the implementation of food safety legislation. Commissioner Byrne would like to see effective and dissuasive sanctions at all levels of the food safety system. In particular, he would like to see more effective measures regarding the current infringement proceedings at community level and that the Commission should have powers to withhold or suspend Community finance under CAP or under the Veterinary Fund.

Currently the Commission has three ways to ensure that EU legislation has been properly implemented and effectively enforced throughout the 15 Member States:

- it can verify that the relevant EU legislation has been properly implemented by the Member States and if not it can take measures against the Member State(s), ultimately resulting in an action before the European Courts;
- it analyses reports of Member States and third importing countries on how they apply EU legislation;
- on-the-spot inspections in Member States and third countries by the FVO.

The Commission is concerned that the current system lacks teeth and is fragmented. It therefore considers there is a need to streamline and strengthen the system of official controls of food and feed at EU level.

Proposed Legislation on Food and Feed Controls

On 5 February 2003, the European Commission adopted a proposal for a Regulation on official controls of food and feed. It aims to streamline and reinforce existing control systems as well as strengthening enforcement measures. The proposal aims to develop a harmonised EU approach to official controls that would cover all food and feed throughout the different stages of the production chain, from 'farm to fork'. Whilst enforcement would remain primarily the responsibility of the Member States, a Community framework would be developed for the design and development of national control systems.

The proposed Regulation, if adopted, would reinforce the verification of compliance with EU rules at all levels of the food chain by introducing performance criteria for competent authorities. The Commission would, in consultation with Member States, draw up guidelines on the structure and organisation of national control systems as well as national control plans. Member States would be required to produce an integrated multi-annual national control plan specifying operational criteria including: impartiality, efficiency, effectiveness, training of staff and documented control procedures. Member States would also be required to establish contingency plans for the management of crises in the food or feed sector.

On the basis of the national plans produced by the Member States, the FVO would carry out a general audit of each Member State by evaluating their performance against the national control plan. The FVO would move away from inspecting individual sites and concentrate more on evaluating the operation of the national control systems. However, where necessary the general audits would be supplemented by inspections of specific areas of production or legislation.

Where the results of official controls require action by more than one Member State the proposal makes provision for administrative assistance and co-operation between the relevant competent authorities.

The proposal puts forward new general rules applicable to all food and feed controls, both produced in the European Union and imports. However, controls that have already been established to deal with specific problems e.g. residues, pesticides, BSE and zoonoses would remain in place. The Commission does not rule out the possibility of developing in the future, specific rules to deal with particular problems.

Under the proposal third countries would have to guarantee that exported products meet EU standards. These guarantees would take the form of control plans covering the particular sector, and records of the implementation of the control plan. These plans would be the basis for the audits and inspections carried out by the FVO. The FVO would also be allowed to carry out more specific inspections and audits of the food and plant health sectors, in addition to the current veterinary and feed inspections.

The regulation, if adopted as drafted, would require Member States to impose criminal sanctions for serious offences that have been committed 'intentionally or through gross negligence'. A list of offences is included for example, the illegal handling and placing on the market of specified risk materials. Criminal sanctions would apply if food or feed that did not comply with certain provisions in the Regulation were introduced into the European Union from a third country. Administrative sanctions would also be used including the withdrawal or suspension of an approval or the withdrawal of a product from the market.

The proposal makes provision for enforcement measures at EU level where the Commission has proof that a Member State's control system is inadequate. In this situation the proposal would permit the Commission to take interim measures to ensure the protection of human health, animal health, animal welfare and the environment. The measures would usually be taken in co-operation with the Member States through the Standing Committee, however provision is made for the Commission to act on its own initiative in serious cases. Possible measures, as outlined in the proposal, could include the suspension of the placing of food or feed on the market.

Member States would be obliged to ensure that the official controls system is adequately financed. However, it would be for the individual Member State to decide how it will finance its official controls. Where inspection fees are imposed there would be common principles for the level of such fees.

The proposal includes activities that will require financing at EU level including designation of reference laboratories, the organisation of workshops, the participation of national experts in FVO missions and the standardisation of the methods of analysis. Currently food and feed safety controls amount to about €3 million out of the annual EU budget. It is estimated that implementing all the measures set out in the proposal would increase this figure to about €16 million.

The proposal is subject to the co-decision procedure. If the regulation is adopted it would have direct effect without the necessity of implementing measures in each Member State. However, the Commission stresses that the proposed regulation should be seen as a framework containing the essential requirements with further detailed rules being implemented in the future if necessary.

Proposal for a Regulation for the Organisation of Official Controls on Products of Animal Origin Intended for Human Consumption

A proposal on official controls was originally adopted in July 2000 as part of the food hygiene package (see Chapter 16) but, was subsequently withdrawn. This was because the Commission received new scientific advice on issues that relate to meat safety, it also wanted to coordinate the work being carried out on the proposed horizontal regulation on official food and feed controls within the proposal on controls for products of animal origin.

The Commission submitted a revised proposal on 11 July 2002 for a regulation laying down specific rules for the organisation of official controls on products of animal origin intended for human consumption. The proposed regulation mainly concerns official controls for fresh meat and risk management measures for live bivalve molluscs, and milk and milk products. The proposed regulation would bring the 'farm to fork' approach to the meat inspection system providing for information to be passed between primary producers and slaughterhouses. The proposal would ensure that meat inspection legislation is compatible with the recently adopted proposals in respect of hygiene, zoonoses and official feed and food controls. The frequency and intensity of official controls would be based on the level of the health risk presented by the type of animal and process. Some flexibility would be given for small enterprises. The proposal also contains procedures for controls of relevant microbiological and chemical food safety hazards.

Live bivalve molluscs are filter-feeders that can present certain risks to human health due to their capacity to concentrate in their tissue toxins, micro-organisms and other contaminants. The proposal would establish monitoring programmes to check for the presence of these contaminants. If Community levels are exceeded the production area would have to be closed until it was shown to meet the Community standards.

The proposal also provides that farmers are required to take corrective action to ensure that raw milk which does not meet the Community health standards would not be delivered for human consumption.

The proposal is subject to the co-decision procedure. At the time of writing the proposal was about to enter second reading.

Chapter 19

The International Context

The European Union is an example of regional co-operation within the context of which a comprehensive system of food law has been constructed in a very short time. There is much interaction between European food policy and law, and international food policy and law. The principles of both systems strongly influence the other. The continuing globalisation of the market place has led to many changes in EU food law and policy. Additionally other regions, are occasionally influenced by aspects of the EU food law system, therefore the impact and influence of EU food law and policy reaches far beyond the EU borders. This chapter will briefly explain the state of play of international food law which is an important backdrop to food law and policy within the European Union.

International Organisations Active in the Application of International Food Law

International bodies operate to draft international harmonised rules to address consumer concerns and facilitate international trade. CODEX Alimentarius develops food standards and the World Trade Organization[231] (WTO) tries to remove national regulations which act as barriers to free trade.

Commission on CODEX Alimentarius

In 1963 the Food and Agricultural Organisation (FAO) and the World Health Organisation (WHO) set up a joint FAO/WHO Commission on CODEX Alimentarius to prepare standards, recommendations and guidelines with a view to protecting consumer health, ensuring fair trade practices and facilitating international trade. In 1998 the joint FAO/WHO CODEX Alimentarius Commission comprised of 163 member countries, representing 97 per cent of the world's population. It continues to formulate international standards on codes of practice on a wide range of food commodities as well as putting forward recommendations on issues relating to food safety. These standards are generally adopted and incorporated into national legislation.

---

[231] The WTO is the only global international organisation dealing with the rules of trade between nations. At the centre of the WTO are the agreements that have been negotiated, signed and ratified by a large proportion of the worlds trading nations.

EU measures frequently refer to the CODEX Alimentarius as the basis for their requirements and vice versa.

The statutes of CODEX Alimentarius makes it responsible for the implementation of the joint FAO/WHO food standards programme. The objectives of this include:

- protecting the health of consumers and insuring fair practices in the food trade;
- promoting co-ordination of all food standards work undertaken by international governmental and non-governmental organisations;
- determining priorities and initiating and guiding the preparation of draft standards through, and with the aid of, appropriate organisations;
- finalising standards elaborated (under the bullet above), and after acceptance by governments, publishing them in CODEX Alimentarius either as regional or world-wide standards, together with international standards already finalised by other bodies (under the second bullet point above), wherever this is practical;
- amending published standards, after an appropriate survey, in light of developments.

The CODEX Alimentarius Commission has been criticised due to the lengthy decision process which can take years of deliberations to adopt an international standard. Further the CODEX Commission bases all its decisions exclusively on the principles of science. For example, the CODEX Commission began examining in 1993 on the labelling of GMOs and food and feed derived from GM. So far no international standards have been set in relation to GMOs. By the time the CODEX actually comes up with an international standard it is probably going to be out of date.

The World Trade Organisation

Many WTO agreements recognise CODEX standards as bench marks for quality and safety requirements for food products in international trade. Two WTO agreements in particular encourage the international harmonisation of food standards: The Agreement on Technical Barriers to Trade (TBT) and the Agreement on the Application of Sanitary and Phytosanitary measures (SPS).

The agreement on the application of sanitary and phytosanitary measures

The SPS agreement is a product of the Uruguay Round of multi-national trade negotiations. The SPS agreement cites CODEX standards, guidelines and recommendations as the preferred international measure for facilitating international trade in food. Therefore CODEX standards have become ‘bench marks’ against which national food measures and regulations are evaluated within the legal parameters of the Uruguay Round Agreements.

The SPS Agreement acknowledges that governments have the right to take sanitary and phytosanitary measures necessary to protect human health. However under the SPS Agreement, governments may apply them only to the extent that they are required to protect human health. It does not permit discrimination in respect of different countries.

A sanitary or phytosanitary measure is defined as a measure:

- to protect animal or plant life or health within the territory of a member country from risks arising from the entry, establishment or spread of pest, diseases, disease-carrying organisms, or disease-causing organisms;
- to protect human or animal life or health within the territory of the member country from risks arising from additives, contaminants, toxins or disease-causing organisms in food, beverages or animal food;
- to protect human life or health within the territory of the a member country from the risks arising from diseases carried by animals, plants or products there are, or from entry or establishment of spread of pest;
- to prevent or limit other damage within the territory of the a member country from the entry, establishment or spread of pest.

This agreement applies to all such measures which may affect international trade. For example any measures affecting GMOs would fall under this agreement. Any measure taken must be necessary to achieve its aim and be based upon scientific principles. There should be no discrimination between members. In no circumstances are such measures to be applied in a way which would act as a disguised restriction on international trade. A member is permitted to adopt or implement a stricter level of protection than the international standards if they believe that standard is not sufficient to achieve the appropriate level of protection provided that the member can prove that it has scientific justification for the stricter standard and that the new standard is based on a level of risk assessment appropriate to the particular situation. For example, a risk assessment level may be greater if the risk of establishment or spread of a pest or disease within a territory of a member is high. If no international standard exists, members are to observe the same procedure concerning risk assessment and ensuring that no distortions of trade are caused by the implementation of a particular measure. This system does not allow for mutual recognition of measures taken by Member States. All measures must be published and transparent.

The agreement on the technical barriers to trade (TBT)

The TBT Agreement was also a product of the Uruguay Round. It seeks to ensure that technical regulations and standards, including packaging, marking and labelling requirements, as well as analytical procedures for assessing conformity with technical regulations and standards do not create unnecessary obstacles to trade. All Members of the WTO have the right to implement regulations and/or standards that they consider necessary to protect health and safety and the environment. However the WTO recognises that it is important that these technical regulations and standards do not create unnecessary barriers to trade. The scope of this agreement comprises of all products whether they are industrial or agricultural. If a member is preparing, adopting or implementing a technical regulation which may significantly affect trade with other members, that member can be required to justify the regulation upon the request of the affected members.

If a proposed technical agreement does not meet with international standards the notification of the proposed regulation should be done well in advance and other members should be notified of the products covered by the proposed regulation. If requested, the member is to provide copies of the proposed regulation to other members and they are to give time to other members to make written comments. All adopted regulations should be made available to any interested parties and members. The technical barriers to trade agreements are particularly important in the food market, especially in relation to justifications for any measure taken which must be based upon scientific and technical reasons.

WTO settlement procedure

Effective enforcement is key to any successful system of rules. If a WTO member fails to comply with relevant international standards, including those in the TBT and SPS agreements, they may be challenged in several ways. First, the WTO members who consider the national measure, notified to them under the notification procedures, to be in conflict with either of the above agreements can ask for justification. National measures may be brought before the two committees responsible for managing the above agreements. A WTO member who fails to apply the appropriate international standard will have to explain its reasons to the appropriate committee. Finally, a special panel within the framework of the WTO may settle disputes that have failed to be settled by either of the committees in charge of managing the above agreements. However, a new dispute settlement mechanism has been established. The General Council of the WTO convenes a Dispute Settlement Body (DSB) to deal with dispute arising from any WTO agreement, including the SPS and TBT agreements. The DSB has sole authority to establish dispute settlement panels, adopt panels and appellate reports, maintain surveillance of the implementation of rulings and the recommendations, and authorise suspension of concessions in the case of non-implementation of recommendations.

Several of the panels that have been formed have concerned matters that ultimately affect food law:

- European Communities: measures affecting importation of certain poultry products;
- European Union: trade description of scallops;
- Japan: taxes on alcoholic beverages;
- European Union: duties on imports of cereals;
- European Union: regime for the importation, sale and distribution of bananas;

- Brazil: measures affecting designated coconut;
- European Union: measures concerning meat and meat product (hormones).

If a panel or appellate report is not implemented or compensation is not agreed upon an aggrieved country will be permitted to take retaliatory measures. Ultimately decisions on appeals from any of the panels (which are possible on points of law) are made by the WTO's full membership. No single country can block these.

Chapter 20

Conclusion

In a famous speech in 1962 John F Kennedy referred to the right to safety and health as one of the fundamental rights of a consumer. Consumers must be able to buy food without risking disease. However, as we have discussed, in Europe there are food safety issues. Recently there has been various food scares including dioxin, BSE, and the outbreak of *E. coli* and foot-and-mouth disease. In recent years the whole question of food safety has become increasingly elevated in the mind of European consumers. These food scares have once again highlighted the vulnerability of consumers in the very normal activity of purchasing food. Consequently consumer confidence in the EU food industry has suffered a gigantic blow. The advent of biotechnology processes has heightened consumer fears in relation to the food products they purchase. The debate continues to rage as to whether products produced from biotechnology core processes are either good or wholesome to eat or if there are reasons to fear for the long-term health effects from eating such foods.

The EU agro-food sector plays a significant role in European economy as a whole. As noted at the very outset of this book, the food and drink industry is a leading industrial sector and has an annual production worth almost €600 billion. The European Union is the world's largest producer of food and drink products. In the European Union 2.6 million people are employed in the food and drink industry. In addition, the agriculture section has an annual production of about €220 billion and provides about 7.5 million fulltime jobs. A lack of consumer or trade confidence has a direct impact on these sectors and people's livelihoods. In light of this, it is absolutely crucial to ensure consumer confidence, as well as trading partner confidence throughout the world.

Additionally, now more than ever before, European consumers are concerned with other aspects of food other than safety. They are interested in the quality, the taste, the nutritional value and ethical values relating to their food. They want to know the processes that have been used to produce the foods and how they have impacted upon the environment and animal welfare. Consumers increasingly want to receive more and clearer information about the food they buy. They want this to be delivered to them in a comprehensive and meaningful way to allow them to make informed choices about the food that they buy.

This book began by setting the historical and social context in which food law and policy has emerged. Initially it was against the backdrop of the European Economic Community, free movement being the focus of many of the developments in food law. However, more recent developments have lead the European Commission to re-evaluate its approach to EU food law and policy. In 2000 it issued a White Paper on food safety. The Commission in this paper underlined its commitment to restoring consumer and trading partner confidence by putting into place the most effective, up-to-date food safety regime in the world. A new comprehensive and integrated approach has been adopted from 'farm-to-fork' or from 'stable-to-table'. About two-thirds of the reforms set out in the White Paper had been undertaken at the time of writing. The cornerstone Regulation, setting down the general principles of food law and establishing a European Food Safety Authority, had already come into force. The European Food Safety Authority had been established in order to provide an independent authority with a high level of accountability. The institutions have already simplified, codified and modernised certain areas of food legislation. They are currently looking at how to take this forward to other areas. Labelling will be the focus of the Commission's work in the short term. A proposal on health claims was brought out in the summer of 2003. At the end of 2003 a proposal on nutrition labelling is expected to be brought forward. Also by the end of 2003 a consultant's report on labelling throughout the European Union is expected to have been completed. This will form the basis for a fundamental review of the labelling, presentation and advertising of foodstuffs. The review will look at mandatory labelling, voluntary labelling information, and presentation and advertising. DG Sanco is then expected to turn its attention to post-White Paper issues such as nutrition and diet.

Food law and policy is a dynamic branch of EU policy and legislation which is developing with some momentum. Significant steps have been taken to establish an effective and up-to-date food safety system. The Commission is now moving forward to look at other elements, such as quality and information. The momentum created by this groundbreaking reform seems to be gaining speed. The EU institutions are determined to rebuild consumer confidence in the EU agricultural and food sectors by establishing an effective and comprehensive system of food law and policy.

Annex I

Action Plan on Food Safety

No	Action	Objective
I. Priority Measures		
1	Proposal for setting up a European Food Authority	To set up an independent European Food Authority.
2	Proposal for laying down procedures in matters of food safety	To introduce a comprehensive safeguard measure covering the whole food chain, including feed. To establish a comprehensive Rapid Alert System covering all feed and food emergencies with harmonised requirements and procedures, including third countries on the basis of reciprocity.
3	Proposal for a General Food Law Directive	To establish food safety as the primary objective of EU food law. To lay down the common principles underlying food legislation (in particular; scientific basis, responsibility of producers and suppliers, traceability along the food chain, efficient controls and effective enforcement). To increase transparency, consistency and legal security.
4	Proposal for a Regulation on official food and feed safety controls	To establish a Community framework for official controls on all food and feed safety aspects along the feed and food chain by • merging and completing existing rules for national controls and Community controls and inspections within the European Union, at the borders and in third countries. • integrating existing monitoring and surveillance systems so as to establish a comprehensive and effective food safety monitoring and surveillance system from farm to table.

(*Continued*)

Annex 1 (*Continued*)

No	Action	Objective
		• establishing a framework for organising consolidated annual programs for controls of foodstuffs. • merging existing Community rules on mutual assistance and administrative co-operation. • creating a Community approach towards a financial support for official controls.
5	Proposal for a Regulation on feed	To establish animal and public health as the primary objective of EU feed legislation. To lay down common principles underlying feed legislation (in particular; scientific basis, responsibility of producers and suppliers, systematic implementation of hazard analysis and critical control points (HACCP), traceability, efficient controls and enforcement). To recast all existing measures on feedingstuffs so as to create a comprehensive legislative tool increasing transparency, consistency and legal security.
6	Proposal for a Regulation on novel feed	To put into plan a centralised system for the authorisation of use in animal nutrition of non conventional products, in particular of GMOs and GMO derived feedstuffs.
7	Amendment to the Annex of Directive 96/25/EC on the circulation of feed materials	To amend the definitions of feed materials listed in the Annex to Decision 96/25/EC, particularly with regard to oils and fats and animal products.
8	Proposal for a Regulation on hygiene	To recast horizontal and vertical Directives on hygiene of food of plant and animal origin. To clarify responsibility of food operators and to introduce the systematic implementation of HACCP. To apply hygiene rules at all levels of the food chain, including primary production.
9	Amendment to Decision 98/272/EC on epidemio-surveillance of transmissible spongiform encephalopathies (TSEs)	To reinforce TSE surveillance including a study on mandatory testing (rapid post-mortem test) on targeted groups of cattle. To reinforce TSE surveillance in small ruminants.
10	Decision on Member State and third country residue programmes	To ensure efficacy of residue testing in Member States and third countries.
11	Proposal for amending Directive 89/107/EEC of food additives	To confer implementing powers for maintaining the lists of permitted food additives and to lay down specific provisions in respect of enzymes.

12	Proposal for amending Directive 95/2/EC on food additives other than colours and sweeteners	To update and revise the list of food additives other than colours and sweeteners.
13	Proposal for amending Directive 88/388/EEC on flavourings for use in foodstuffs	To clarify the scope and update definitions, to set maximum limits for toxic substances and to confer implementing powers to the Commission.
14	Proposal for amending Regulation 258/97 on novel foods and novel food ingredients	To make the necessary adaptations in the light of the conclusions of the report on the implementation of the Regulation and in accordance with the new regulatory framework of Directive 90/220/EEC.
15	Regulation on the labelling of GMO-free foodstuffs	To give operators the possibility to use labelling claims referring to the absence of use of genetic engineering techniques for the production of foodstuffs.
16	Proposal for amending Directive 79/112/EEC on the labelling, presentation and advertising of foodstuffs	To remove the possibility not to indicate the components of compound ingredients forming less than 25 per cent of the final product and lay down a list of allergenic substances.
17	Proposals for Commission Directives to fix maximum residue levels (MRLs) of pesticides in food and agricultural commodities	To fix MRLs for pesticides residues for, inter alia: 36 pesticides with existing open positions in the residues directives that will automatically go to zero in July 2000 unless the Commission adopts other values. To set MRLs at zero for eight pesticides that were excluded from Annex 1 to Directive 91/414/EEC. To set MRLs for new active substances included in Annex 1 to Directive 91/414/EEC.
18	Communication on an action plan on nutrition policy	To develop a comprehensive and coherent nutrition policy
II. Feedingstuffs		
19	Proposal for amending Directive 70/524/EEC concerning additives in feedingstuffs	To consolidate the Directive. To fix maximum residue limits for additives. To clarify certain aspects of the procedure (evaluation reports) and the authorisation (generic versus specific).
20	Amendment to Decision 91/516/EEC on the list of ingredients the use of which is forbidden in compound feedingstuffs	To introduce the changes deemed necessary to the list of feed materials the use of which must be prohibited in compound feedingstuffs, with particular reference to certain by-products from fat processing.
21	Amendment to the Annex of Directive 1999/29/EC on the undesirable substances and products in animal nutrition	To fix the maximum limits of dioxins for oils and fats, and for other or all feed materials. To collect information on background contamination of PCB and dioxin-like PCB, MRLs for other potential contaminants of feedingstuffs will also be fixed.

(*Continued*)

Annex 1 (*Continued*)

No	Action	Objective
22	Proposal for amending Directive 96/25EEC on the circulation of feed materials	Following reflection to decide whether an exclusive positive list of authorised feed materials should be established.
23	Proposal for amending Directive 95/53/EEC fixing the principles governing the organisation of official inspections in the field of animal nutrition	To foresee a legal basis for a safeguard clause in case of appearing or spreading hazards related to feedingstuffs likely to pose a risk to human health. To introduce an obligation for Member States to carry out a monitoring programme for contaminants in feedingstuffs. To introduce a Rapid Alert System for feed to be integrated in the Rapid Alert System for food (to be integrated in action 2).
24	Proposal for amending Directive 79/373/EEC on the marketing of compound feedingstuffs	To review current provisions for the labelling of compound feedingstuffs.
25	Proposal for amending Directive 95/69/EEC laying down the conditions and arrangements for approving and registration of certain establishments and intermediaries operating in the feedingstuffs sector	To introduce provisions for: • Approval or registration of manufacturers of compound feedingstuffs • Approval of manufacturers of certain feed materials • Improving traceability of feed materials and identification of critical points • Establishing a code for good manufacturing practice for animal feeding.
III. Zoonoses		
26	Proposal for amending Directive 92/117/EEC on zoonoses	To improve monitoring and reporting system for diseases transmissible from animals to man and to reduce prevalence of specified zoonoses (e.g. salmonella).
27	Decision on Member State and third country programmes for the control of zoonotic agents on animal products exported to the Community	To ensure that Member States implement adequate measures to control zoonotic agents. To ensure that third country products are controlled to the same level as Community products.
IV. Animal Health		
28	Proposal for a Regulation on animal health requirements for products of animal origin	To recast existing animal health rules for products of animal origin.
29	Increase budgetary allocation for actions provided for in Council Decision 90/424/EEC on expenditure in the veterinary field	To enable actions to improve animal disease eradication (brucellosis, turberculosis, etc.). To create a task force for monitoring disease eradication in the Member States.

No.	Measure	Objective
V. Animal by-products		
30	Proposal for amending Directives 90/667/EEC and 92/118/EEC on animal waste and derived products	To recast existing measures of animal by-products not destined for human consumption (meat and bone meal, rendered fats, manure, etc.). To ensure that only animal by-products derived from animals declared fit for human consumption can enter the animal feed chain. To clarify responsibility of animal by-products operators. To tighten up official control and to improve traceability.
VI. BSE/TSE		
31	Decision on classification according to BSE status	Classification of individual countries in view of changes in BSE status (post-mortem tests).
32	Amendment to Decision 94/381 (feed ban)	To amend the Decision in the light of recent scientific opinions.
	Decision on the removal of specified risk materials (SRMs) replacing Decision 97/534/EC	To replace Decision 97/534/EC laying down the rules on the prohibition of the use of materials that present risks as regards TSEs. Amendment of the TSE framework proposal accordingly.
33	Decision on the harmonisation of BSE rules for imports of live animals and products from third countries	To harmonise the BSE import rules for other third countries.
VII. Hygiene		
34	Report on the testing of residues in Member States and third countries	To evaluate the performance of national and third country residue programmes.
35	Modification of the Annex to Council Directive 96/23/EC on residue monitoring	To re-enforce the monitoring and detection of PCBs and dioxins in food of animal origin.
36	Proposal for a Decision to review the ante- and post-mortem procedures for animals and meat	To make ante- and post-mortem inspections risk based, and to review inspection methods applied at present.
37	Decision on microbiological standards on certain foods	To fix the maximum limits of undesirable micro-organisms in foodstuffs, after risk assessment.
VIII. Contaminants		
38	Amendment to Regulation No 194/97 setting maximum limits for certain contaminants	To set up limits for several contaminants: ochratoxin A, cadmium, lead, 3-MCPD, dioxin and possible, PCBs.

(*Continued*)

Annex 1 (*Continued*)

No	Action	Objective
IX. Food additives and flavourings		
39	Report on the intake of food additives	To provide an overview of the intake of food additives in the European Union.
40	Proposal for amending Directive 94/35/EC on sweeteners	To update and revise the list of sweeteners for use in foodstuffs.
41	Amendment to Directives 95/31/EC, 95/45/EC and 96/77/EC on purity criteria for food additives (including sweeteners and colours)	To update and complete existing provisions. To introduce a general requirement for a new safety evaluation for permitted additives made from new sources or with new methods.
42	Amendment to Directive 81/712/EEC laying down Community methods of analysis for the respect of purity criteria	To replace existing provisions with a set of general principles and a reference to other similar provisions.
43	Decision amending the Community register of flavouring substances used in or on foodstuffs	To update the register.
44	Regulation establishing a programme for the evaluation of flavouring substances	To set priorities and time limits for evaluation.
45	Proposal for a Regulation on additives used in flavourings	To lay down a list of additives authorised for use in flavourings.
46	Proposal for a Regulation on smoke flavourings	To lay down the conditions for the production of smoke flavourings.
X. Materials in contact with food		
47	Proposal for amending Directive 89/109/EEC on food contact materials	To allow the update of specific Directives through regulatory procedure and to change or add provisions on the labelling of contact materials.
48	Amendment to Directive 90/128/EEC on food contact plastics	To update the list of authorised food contact plastics.
49	Practical guide on food contact materials	To provide guidance on the application of Community provisions relating to contact materials.
XI. Novel foods/Genetically modified organisms		
50	Regulation clarifying the authorisation procedure for novel foods and novel food ingredients	To clarify and make more transparent the procedure laid down in Regulation 258/97 for the authorisation of novel foods and novel food ingredients.

51	Report on the implementation of Regulation 258/97 on novel foods and novel foods ingredients	To examine the application of the 'novel food' legislation and assess its impact on public health, consumer protection and information, and the functioning of the internal market.
52	Regulation on the labelling of food containing or derived from genetically modified organisms	To further harmonise the provisions governing the labelling of food, additives and flavourings containing or derived from GMO material.
XII. Irradiation of food		
53	Proposal for amending Directive 1999/3/EC on foods and food ingredients treated by irradiation	To complete the Community list of foods and food ingredients which may be treated with ionising radiation.
54	Decision establishing the list of irradiation facilities	Publication of the list of irradiation facilities authorised in the Member States and those in third countries which have been approved by the European Union.
XIII. Dietetic foods/food supplements/fortified foods		
55	Directive on foods intended for intense muscular effort	To lay down specific provisions for foods intended to meet the expenditure of intense muscular effort, especially by sportsmen.
56	Report on foods intended for persons suffering from diabetes	To assess the need for specific provisions for food for people with carbohydrate-metabolism disorders.
57	Proposal for amending Directive 89/398/EEC on dietetic foods	To define the conditions for making the claims 'low-sodium' or 'sodium-free', and 'gluten-free'.
58	Directive on purity criteria for nutritional substances in food for particular nutritional use	To lay down purity criteria for nutritional substances which are added to food for particular nutritional use or which are present in food supplements and foods to which nutrients are added.
59	Directive on substances added for nutritional purposes in food for particular nutritional uses	To establish a positive list of the various substances which may be added for nutritional purposes in foods for particular nutritional uses.
60	Proposal for a Directive on food supplements	To lay down common criteria for marketing concentrated source of nutrients (vitamins and minerals).
61	Proposal for a Directive on fortified foods	To lay down provisions for marketing foods to which nutrients such as vitamins and minerals have been added.
62	Amendment to Directive 91/321/EEC on infant formulae and follow-on formulae	To set up a list of pesticides not to be used in agricultural products intended for use in these formulae

(*Continued*)

Annex 1 (*Continued*)

No	Action	Objective
63	Amendment to Directive 96/5/EEC on processed baby foods	To set up a list of pesticides not to be used in agricultural products intended for infants and young children.
64	Amendment to Directive 80/777/EEC on mineral waters	To lay down a list of constituents of mineral waters and the conditions of use for the treatment of certain mineral waters with ozone enriched air.
XIV. Labelling of food		
65	Proposal for amending Directive 79/112/EEC on the labelling, presentation and advertising of foodstuffs	To specify the conditions under which 'functional claims; and 'nutritional claims' may be made.
66	Proposal for amending Directive on nutrition labelling	To bring the provisions on nutrition labelling into line with consumer needs and expectations.
67	Proposal for amending Directive on misleading advertising	To clarify the scope of the Directive with regard to claims concerning in particular food, health and the environment.
XV. Pesticides		
68	Regulation on monitoring of pesticide residues in food	To improve co-ordination and quality of monitoring of pesticides in foods.
69	Recommendation for a co-ordinated Community Monitoring Programme for pesticides residues in Foods for the year 2001	Recommendation for a co-ordinated Community Monitoring Programme for pesticides residues in Foods for the year 2001.
70	Commission Decisions for pesticide active substances including in or excluding from Annex 1 to Directive 91/414/EEC	Pesticides active substances evaluated in the framework of Directive 91/414/EEC need, after the evaluation to be either included in Annex 1 or withdrawn from the market.
71	Regulation on the evaluation of existing pesticides active substances	To fix a priority list of substances for evaluation at Community level; to introduce a notification procedure for all remaining substances. To lay out the ground rules for the final stage of the Community evaluation of active substances.
72	Proposal for amending Directive 91/414/EEC	*Inter alia, to* • extend competence to include genetically modifies organisms; • allow a harmonised Community regime to charge fees for the evaluation of new pesticides active substances;

		• develop a fast-track procedure for low-risk substances; • clarity problems relating to data protection, working-sharing, parallel imports, classification and labelling, borderlines with biocides legislation etc.
73	Directive to develop and adopt the Annexes to Directive 91/414/EEC	To develop Community data requirements for non-GMO microbial plant protection products.
	;	To develop a harmonised set of risk and safety phrases.
		To establish uniform principles for assessment of safety of micro-organisms as plant protection products.
XVI. Nutrition		
74	Proposal for Council Recommendations on European dietary guidelines	To support the Member States in their development of nutrition policy at the national level.
		To streamline the flow of information to enable consumer to make informed choices.
XVII. Seeds		
75	Proposal for a Regulation concerning environmental risk assessment in respect of genetically modified plant varities	To lay down the specific conditions for the conduct of the risk assessment applicable to genetically modified varieties of agricultural and vegetable plant species, as required under Council Directive 98/95/EC, as required under Council Directive 98/95/EC.
76	Directives on environmental risk assessment principles laid down in Regulation 258/97, in respect of genetically modified plant varieties	To provide for technical and scientific guidance for the conduct of the assessment applicable to genetically modified varieties of agricultural and vegetable plant species.
77	Directives amending the Annexes of the Directives on the marketing of seeds	To lay down the details of the labelling requirement as established by Council Directive 98/95/EC for seeds of genetically modified plant varieties of agricultural and vegetable plant species.
		To lay down the growing conditions and other requirements for purity concerning the adventitious presence of genetically modified seeds in seed lots of traditional plant varieties.
78	Proposal for a Directive amending Directive 68/193/EEC on the marketing of material for the vegetative propagation of the vine	To lay down assessment procedures and labelling requirements for propagating material of genetically modified varieties of the vine.

(*Continued*)

Annex 1 (*Continued*)

No	Action	Objective
XVIII. Supporting measures		
79	Proposal for a Regulation on the financial support for food safety actions at Community level	To provide for a uniform legal basis to ensure adequate Community financial support of actions necessary to enhance food safety (liaison and reference laboratories, exchange of officials, training of officials etc.).
80	Proposal for a Decision establishing a data base of dietary intakes across the whole EU population	To create a basis of exposure data used in risk assessments and nutrition.
81	Decision on an Advisory Committee on Food Safety	To improve involvement of all stakeholders in the Community food safety policy by streamlining the existing Advisory Committees.
XIX. Third country policy/international relations		
82	Proposals for agreements with third countries	To establish further agreements with third countries on veterinary and/or phyto-sanitary issues.
83	Proposal for accession of the European Community to Codex Alimentarius	To reinforce the participation of the European Union in the elaboration of international food standards.
84	Proposal for accession of the European Community to OIE	To reinforce the participation of the European Union in the elaboration of international animal health standards.

List of Permitted Food Colours (Directive 94/36)

EC number	Common name
E100	Curcumin
E101	(i) Riboflavin
	(ii) Riboflavin-5′-phosphate
E102	Tartrazine
E104	Quinoline Yellow
E110	Sunset Yellow FCF
	Orange Yellow S
E120	Cochineal, Carminic acid, Carmines
E122	Azorubine, Carmoisine
E123	Amaranth
E124	Ponceau 4R, Cochineal Red A
E127	Erythrosine
E128	Red 2G
E129	Allura Red AC
E131	Patent Blue V
E132	Indigotine, Indigo carmine
E133	Brilliant Blue FCF
E140	Chlorophylls and
	Chlorophyllins:
	(i) Chlorophylls
	(ii) Chlorophyllins
E141	Copper complexes of chlorophylls and chlorophyllins
	(i) Copper complexes of chlorophylls
	(ii) Copper complexes of chlorophyllins
E142	Greens S
E150a	Plain caramel
E150b	Caustic sulphite caramel
E150c	Ammonia caramel
E150d	Sulphite ammonia caramel
E151	Brilliant Black BN, Black PN
E153	Vegetable carbon
E154	Brown FK
E155	Brown HT
E160a	Carotenes:
	(i) Mixed carotenes
	(ii) Beta-carotene
E160b	Annatto, bixin, norbixin
E160c	Paprika extract, capsanthin, capsorubin
E160d	Lycopene
E160e	Beta-apo-8′-carotenal (C 30)
E160f	Ethyl ester of beta-apo-8′-carotenic acid (C 30)

(Continued)

Annex II (*Continued*)

EC number	Common name
E161b	Lutein
E161g	Canthaxanthin
E162	Beetroot Red, betanin
E163	Anthocyanins
E170	Calcium carbonate
E171	Titanium dioxide
E172	Iron oxides and hydroxides
E173	Aluminium
E174	Silver
E175	Gold
E180	Litholrubine BK

Annex III

Fortification

VITAMIN FORMULATIONS AND MINERAL SUBSTANCES WHICH MAY BE ADDED TO FOODS

Vitamin formulations

Vitamin A
retinol
retinyl acetate
retinyl palmitate
beta-carotene

Vitamin D
cholecalciferol
ergocalciferol

Vitamin E
D-alpha-tocopherol
DL-alpha-tocopherol
D-alpha-tocopheryl acetate
DL-alpha-tocopheryl acetate
D-alpha-tocopheryl acid succinate

Vitamin K
phylloquinone (phytomenadione)

Vitamin B1
thiamin hydrochloride
thiamin mononitrate

Vitamin B2
riboflavin
riboflavin 5′-phosphate, sodium

Niacin
nicotinic acid
nicotinamide

Pantothenic acid
D-pantothenate, calcium
D-pantothenate, sodium
dexpanthenol

Vitamin B6
pyridoxine hydrochloride
pyridoxine 5′-phosphate
pyridoxine dipalmitate

Folic Acid
pteroylmonoglutamic acid

Vitamin B12
cyanocobalamin
hydroxocobalamin

Biotin
D-biotin

Vitamin C
L-ascorbic acid
sodium-L-ascorbate
calcium-L-ascorbate
potassium-L-ascorbate
L-ascorbyl 6-palmitate

Mineral substances

calcium carbonate
calcium chloride
calcium salts of citric acid
calcium gluconate
calcium glycerophosphate
calcium lactate
calcium salts of orthophosphoric acid
calcium hydroxide
calcium oxide
magnesium acetate
magnesium carbonate
magnesium chloride
magnesium salts of citric acid
magnesium gluconate
magnesium glycerophosphate

magnesium salts of orthophosphoric acid
magnesium lactate
magnesium hydroxide
magnesium oxide
magnesium sulphate
ferrous carbonate
ferrous citrate
ferric ammonium citrate
ferrous gluconate
ferrous fumarate
ferric sodium diphosphate
ferrous lactate
ferrous sulphate
ferric diphosphate (ferric pyrophosphate)
ferric saccharate
elemental iron (carbonyl + electrolytic + hydrogen reduced)
cupric carbonate
cupric citrate
cupric gluconate
cupric sulphate
copper lysine complex
sodium iodide
sodium iodate
potassium iodide
potassium iodate
zinc acetate
zinc chloride
zinc citrate
zinc gluconate
zinc lactate
zinc oxide
zinc carbonate
zinc sulphate
manganese carbonate
manganese chloride
manganese citrate
manganese gluconate
manganese glycerophosphate
manganese sulphate
sodium bicarbonate
sodium carbonate
sodium chloride
sodium citrate
sodium gluconate
sodium lactate

sodium hydroxide
sodium salts of orthophosphoric acid
potassium bicarbonate
potassium carbonate
potassium chloride
potassium citrate
potassium gluconate
potassium glycerophosphate
potassium lactate
potassium hydroxide
potassium salts of orthophosphoric acid
sodium selenate
sodium hydrogen selenite
sodium selenite
chromium (III) chloride and its hexahydrate
chromium (III) sulphate and its hexahydrate
ammonium molybdate (molybdenum (VI))
sodium molybdate (molybdenum (VI))
potassium fluoride
sodium fluoride

Food Supplements

Vitamin and Mineral Substances which may be Used in the Manufacture of Food Supplements

A. Vitamins

5. *Vitamin A*
   (a) retinol
   (b) retinyl acetate
   (c) retinyl palmitate
   (d) beta-carotene

6. *Vitamin D*
   (a) cholecalciferol
   (b) ergocalciferol

7. *Vitamin E*
   (a) D-alpha-tocopherol
   (b) DL-alpha-tocopherol
   (c) D-alpha-tocopheryl acetate
   (d) DL-alpha-tocopheryl acetate
   (e) D-alpha-tocopheryl acid succinate

8. *Vitamin K*
   (a) phylloquinone (phytomenadione)

9. *Vitamin B1*
   (a) thiamin hydrochloride
   (b) thiamin mononitrate

10. *Vitamin B2*
   (a) riboflavin
   (b) riboflavin 5′-phosphate, sodium

11. *Niacin*
   (a) nicotinic acid
   (b) nicotinamide

12. *Pantothenic acid*
    (a) D-pantothenate, calcium
    (b) D-pantothenate, sodium
    (c) dexpanthenol

13. *Vitamin B6*
    (a) pyridoxine hydrochloride
    (b) pyridoxine 5′-phosphate
    (c) pyridoxine dipalmitate

14. *Folic acid*
    (a) pteroylmonoglutamic acid

15. *Vitamin B12*
    (a) cyanocobalamin
    (b) hydroxocobalamin

16. *Biotin*
    (a) D-biotin

17. *Vitamin C*
    (a) L-ascorbic acid
    (b) sodium-L-ascorbate
    (c) calcium-L-ascorbate
    (d) potassium-L-ascorbate
    (e) L-ascorbyl 6-palmitate

B. Minerals

calcium carbonate
calcium chloride
calcium salts of citric acid
calcium gluconate
calcium glycerophosphate
calcium lactate
calcium salts of orthophosphoric acid
calcium hydroxide
calcium oxide
magnesium acetate
magnesium carbonate
magnesium chloride
magnesium salts of citric acid
magnesium gluconate
magnesium glycerophosphate

magnesium salts of orthophosphoric acid
magnesium lactate
magnesium hydroxide
magnesium oxide
magnesium sulphate
ferrous carbonate
ferrous citrate
ferric ammonium citrate
ferrous gluconate
ferrous fumarate
ferric sodium diphosphate
ferrous lactate
ferrous sulphate
ferric diphosphate (ferric pyrophosphate)
ferric saccharate
elemental iron (carbonyl + electrolytic + hydrogen reduced)
cupric carbonate
cupric citrate
cupric gluconate
cupric sulphate
copper lysine complex
sodium iodide
sodium iodate
potassium iodide
potassium iodate
zinc acetate
zinc chloride
zinc citrate
zinc gluconate
zinc lactate
zinc oxide
zinc carbonate
zinc sulphate
manganese carbonate
manganese chloride
manganese citrate
manganese gluconate
manganese glycerophosphate
manganese sulphate
sodium bicarbonate
sodium carbonate
sodium chloride
sodium citrate
sodium gluconate
sodium lactate

sodium hydroxide
sodium salts of orthophosphoric acid
potassium bicarbonate
potassium carbonate
potassium chloride
potassium citrate
potassium gluconate
potassium glycerophosphate
potassium lactate
potassium hydroxide
potassium salts of orthophosphoric acid
sodium selenate
sodium hydrogen selenite
sodium selenite
chromium (III) chloride and its hexahydrate
chromium (III) sulphate and its hexahydrate
ammonium molybdate (molybdenum (VI))
sodium molybdate (molybdenum (VI))
potassium fluoride
sodium fluoride

Glossary

Additives

Directive 89/107 provides a definition of food additives, a substance that is not normally consumed as a food and not normally used as an ingredient of food whether or not it has a nutritive value and it is deliberately added to food for a technological purpose in the manufacture, processing, preparation, treatment, packaging, transport or storage of such food. The food additive or its by-products may become directly or, could reasonably be expected to become, indirectly a component of the food.

Animal Welfare

The European institutions are required to take animal welfare into account when drafting and implementing Community legislation in the fields of the common agricultural policy, transport, the internal market and research.

Co-decision Procedure

The co-decision procedure is a legislative process that involves the Commission as initiator, and the Council, and European Parliament as co-decision makers. The procedure consists of three stages. At each stage of the process it is decided whether the proposal for legislation should be abandoned, adopted as legislation or, during stages one or two, whether the proposal should proceed to the next stage for further consideration.

There are no given time limits during the first stage of the co-decision procedure. However, there are specified time limits throughout the second and third stages which can be extended within prescribed limits if both the Council and the European Parliament agree.

Codex Alimentarius Commission

The Codex Alimentarius Commission was set up in 1963. It is a joint Commission of the United Nations Food and Agriculture Organisation (FAO) and the World Health Organisation (WHO). It produces guidelines and standards for foodstuffs.

Comitology Procedure

The Commission implements legislation at Community level. The Commission is assisted by a committee in accordance with the comitology procedure. The committees consist of representatives from Member States and are chaired by a Commission representative.

Set out in Council Decision 1999/468 are the types of committees, such as regulatory committees and the procedures that govern them.

Committee of the Regions

The Committee of the Regions consists of 222 representatives of local and regional authorities. These representatives are proposed by Member States and then appointed by the Council for 4 years. It is consulted by the Council or the Commission in areas affecting local and regional interests. The Committee can produce opinions on its own initiative and may be consulted by the European Parliament.

Common Agricultural Policy (CAP)

The aims of the common agricultural policy are to ensure reasonable prices for Europe's consumers and fair incomes for farmers, agricultural expenditure amounts to approximately 45 per cent of the Community budget. The European Parliament is consulted on CAP, but policy is decided by qualified majority vote in the Council.

Consultation Procedure

Under this procedure the Council is obliged to consult the European Parliament. However, the Council is not bound by Parliament's position. The procedure applies to the common agricultural policy, and the legislation regarding agricultural products.

Consumer Protection

Consumer protection is dealt with in Article 153 of the EC Treaty. It is intended to promote consumers' health, safety, economic and legal interests, and their right to information.

Coreper

Coreper is the acronym by which the Permanent Representatives Committee is known. It consists of the Member States' Permanent Representatives (Ambassadors) and is responsible, for assisting the Council. It is divided in two: Coreper I, consisting of the

Deputy Permanent Representatives; and Coreper II, consisting of the Permanent Representatives themselves.

Council of the European Union

The Council of the European Union is the European Union's main decision-making institution. It consists of the ministers of the fifteen Member States responsible for the particular matters to be discussed such as the Agriculture Council will consist of the Agriculture Minister of each of the fifteen Member States. Each country in the Union in turn holds the chair for 6 months.

Court of Justice

The Court of Justice of the European Communities consists of 15 judges who are assisted by nine advocates-general appointed for 6 years by agreement among the Member States. It has two principal functions: to check whether instruments of the European institutions and governments are compatible with the Treaties; and, at the request of a national court, to pronounce on the interpretation or the validity of provisions contained in Community law.

European Commission

The European Commission is a body with powers of initiative, implementation, management and control. It is the guardian of the Treaties. It is composed of twenty independent members (two each from France, Germany, Italy, Spain and the United Kingdom and one each from all the other countries), including a President and two Vice Presidents. It is appointed for a five-year term, by agreement among the Member States. It is subject to a vote of appointment by the European Parliament, before it can be sworn in. The Commissioners are assisted by an administration made up of directorates-general and specialised departments whose staffs are divided mainly between Brussels and Luxembourg.

European Council

The European Council is the regular meetings of the Heads of State or Government of the European Union Member States.

European Parliament

The European Parliament is the assembly of the representatives of the 370 million Union citizens. Since 1979 they have been elected by direct universal suffrage and today total 626 distributed between Member States by reference to their population.

Food

Food is defined in Regulation 2002/178 as any substance or product, whether processed, partially processed, or unprocessed, intended to be, or reasonably expected to be, ingested by humans. It includes drink, and any substance intentionally incorporated into the food during its manufacture.

Food Supplements

Food supplements are defined in Directive 2002/46 as 'foodstuffs for the purpose of which is to supplement the normal diet and which are concentrated sources of nutrients or other substances with a nutritional or physiological effect, alone or in combination, marketed in dose form, namely forms such as capsules, pastilles, tablets, pills and other similar forms, sachets of powder, ampoules of liquids, drop dispensing bottles and other similar forms of liquids and powders designed to be taken in measured small unit quantities.

The Food and Veterinary Office

The FVO on behalf of the Commission carries out inspections in Member States and third countries to check that the competent authorities are implementing and enforcing EU legislation correctly. The FVO publishes annual reports outlining its main activities undertaken during the previous year. The reports contain the results from the inspections that have been carried out, together with conclusions and recommendations.

Green Paper

Commission Green Papers are documents intended to stimulate debate and launch a process of consultation at European level on a particular topic (such as social policy, the single currency, telecommunications). These consultations may then lead to the publication of a White Paper, translating the conclusions of the debate into practical proposals for Community action.

Hazard Analyse and Critical General Points (HACCP)

The HACCP system is internationally recognised and has been endorsed by the Codex Alimentarius. It is based on seven principles that focus on identifying and controlling potential hazards. The HACCP system has been expanded to include not only microbiological hazards but also chemical and physical hazards.

Mutual Recognition

Member States can not prohibit the sale within their own territory as their product lawfully produced marketed in another Member State. This principle applies even if the product was produced according to different standards to those required under the national legislation of the Member State. Member States are only permitted to prevent sale of such products under very strict conditions to protect public health, consumers or the environment. If a Member State just prohibits the sale of a product under one of these headings, then, the Member State would also have to prove that the prohibition was proportionate and can not be achieved by other methods.

Official Controls

Controls mean, for the purposes of Directive 89/397, 'inspections by the competent authorities of the compliance, for example, of foodstuffs, with provisions aimed at preventing risks to public health, guaranteeing fair commercial transactions or protecting consumers' interests, including provisions on consumer information'.

Parliamentary Committees

The European Parliament is based on a committee system. Seventeen committees, including legal Affairs and Internal market, and Agriculture and Rural Developments Committees, have been set up within the European Parliament. The members of each committee are elected at the beginning of and half-way through each parliamentary term, according to their political affiliation and their expertise. Proposals are first considered by one or more committees before it is voted on by the Parliament as a whole in Plenary.

Presidency of the Union

The Presidency of the Union is held in turn on a 6-monthly basis by each Member State. A stint in the Presidency is a duty and a contribution that each Member State makes to the proper functioning of the Community institutions. At present, a Member State holds the Presidency every seven and a half years upon enlargement.

Processing Aids

In Directive 89/107, a processing aid is defined as any substance not consumed as a food ingredient by itself and intentionally used in the processing of raw materials, foods or their ingredients, to fulfil a technological purpose during treatment or processing, which may result in the unintentional but technically unavoidable presence of residues of the substance or its derivatives in the final product. Residues that remain in the final product must not present any health risk and must not have any technological effect on the finished product.

Public Health

Public health is covered by Article 152 of the EC Treaty. Community action focuses on the prevention of illnesses, by promoting research into their causes and their transmission, as well as health information and education. The Treaty requires that the definition and implementation of all Community policies and activities ensure a high level of human health protection.

Community measures may be adopted to complement action by the Member States. But generally the subsidiarity principle should be followed and cooperation between the Member States, encouraged.

Qualified Majority

A qualified majority is the number of votes required in the Council for a decision to be adopted under Article 205(2) of the EC Treaty. The number of votes required for a qualified majority is set at 62 votes out of 87 (71 per cent). Member States' votes are weighted on the basis of their population as follows: France, Germany, Italy and United Kingdom 10 votes each; Spain 8 votes; Belgium, Greece, the Netherlands and Portugal 5 votes each; Austria and Sweden 4 votes each; Denmark, Ireland and Finland 3 votes each; Luxembourg 2 votes.

Quid Labelling

Where the presence of a particular ingredient or category of ingredients is emphasised in the labelling of a foodstuff generally speaking, the quantity of that ingredient or category of ingredients must be indicated on-pack.

Unanimity

The term 'unanimity' refers to the requirement for all the Member States meeting in the Council to be in agreement before a proposal can be adopted.

White Paper

Commission White Papers are documents containing proposals for Community action in a specific area. They usually follow on from discussion papers in the form of Green Papers or communications.

Zoonoses

Zoonoses have been defined as 'any disease and/or infection which is likely to be naturally transmitted from animals to man' and a zoonotic agent as 'any bacterium, virus or parasite which is likely to cause a zoonoses'. Examples of zoonoses include brucellosis, salmonellas, listeria, rabies and tuberculosis.

Index

www.ingramcontent.com/pod-product-compliance
Lightning Source LLC
LaVergne TN
LVHW020642300926
849161LV00004B/770